FORGOTTEN AMERICANS

15 Footnote Figures Who Changed American History

FORGOTTEN AMERICANS

15 Footnote Figures Who Changed American History

WILLARD STERNE RANDALL & NANCY NAHRA

BARNES & NOBLE

NEW YORK

To
Our Fathers

ISBN-13: 978-0-7607-8871-4
ISBN-10: 0-7607-8871-5

Printed and bound in the United States of America

1 3 5 7 9 10 8 6 4 2

CONTENTS

INTRODUCTION

Sometimes known as the American century, the twentieth century has made awareness of the United States unavoidable in the global culture. In many countries knowledge of American English has become a requirement for the class in ascendancy. But Americans in America have not necessarily deepened their awareness of their own culture as the evolved product of the peculiarly American past.

Each of the people profiled in this book was celebrated, or notorious, in his or her time. Today even the educated public has largely forgotten them. Only our Virginian in the Lake Country, Thomas Jefferson, is viewed as a major historical figure, but the contribution he made by taking his supposed "summer vacation" in 1791—and the impact it had on our politics—is little known. Sitting Bull remains a household name, but few Americans distinguish him from other Indian leaders, defiant or assimilationist. The rest of these celebrities faded from view, preserved mainly as names on roadside markers or in book footnotes.

The reasons America forgot these Americans are as varied as their lives. Some were on the losing side of a war (Teedyuscung, Franklin), rarely a good way to be remembered. Others won those wars, but their activities came to be seen as distasteful (Quick) or of minor importance (Wittenmyer). In one or two cases their contributions were deliberately kept out of official histories (Arnold, Bradwell). And it should come as no surprise that so many of these people are female, or from the ethnic minorities who suffered discrimination not only through history but in history books. Nonetheless, each of their stories illuminates the forces that pulled at the nation during their lives.

The first eight Americans we profile struggled not only over what sort of America should be built but also whether there should be an America at all. Today the United States bestrides its continent and dominates the world economically and militarily. We must recall that in the seventeenth century, when Anne Hutchinson came to the New World, only two of the many settlements along the Atlantic coast were English. The French and the Spanish had been on the continent for decades, and the Dutch and Swedes were also building outposts in the New World.

Such fragility lingered long after the United States declared its independence. People from Tom Quick to James Forten were caught up in the struggle in its first armed stage, the American Revolution. The new nation had vast lands, but was surrounded by the even larger territories of Britain, France, and Spain (and indigenous nations lived on all these lands). The United States' founders proposed a monumental task: to practice republican ideals that had never been projected on such a vast scale, much less reconciled with race-based slavery and the displacement of other peoples. The survival of an independent America remained in doubt until the War of 1812.

Even afterwards, the nineteenth century, the ground beneath most of the lives recounted in this book, did not yet belong to America. In its outlook and values, it was dominated by Great Britain, the world of Charles Darwin but also of Charles Dickens. An awareness of great vitality and also great brutality informed the mindset of Americans who, unlike their European cousins, experienced the beginning of the nineteenth century on the edge of an immense continent that, like Nature, needed to be tamed. So different from our habits of thought, their beliefs about the world held exploitation to be a constructive notion and growth an aspiration that constituted proof of wise management. Restraint had to be counted as timorous.

But not all Americans came from Great Britain, especially as the century grew older. And as the frontier, the wild edge of America, crept farther inland, reaching the Mississippi, not all its settlers came from the nation's eastern seaboard. Many, arriving directly from Europe, brought with them a fully developed culture. Along with their cooking pots they packed violins and volumes of Goethe. But the rough frontier life that they found made them wait before building opera houses. The huge effort of starting up demanded so much strength that every able body had to help: women could not stay indoors. Even men and women working together could not do enough in an era before chemical fertilizers and heavy farm equipment.

The undeniable fact of American life in the early decades of the nineteenth century was a country growing at two different speeds. On one hand was a rural economy based on agriculture so primitive that bodies served as machines, making the best bodies ones that were reliable and cheap. The solution to an unquenchable demand for strong, cheap bodies was slavery. At the other speed, America boasted a mercantile economy that invited and created capital.

If each side had tended its own way of life, maybe an uneven coexistence could have continued. But the government of the United States, set up by the best minds of the eighteenth century, provided for and insisted on a coming together of the regions to articulate the national aim of producing a coherent vision that might direct the rampant growth, the vigorous fact of expansion. What kind of a country would the new part of the continent resemble? Which speed? The great national trauma of America's nineteenth century, the Civil War, announced the violent answer, that in the era of Darwin it would have to be one or the other. Only one speed could win. The country that had conflicting sets of rules inevitably encouraged both rebels and creators on both sides.

Each biographical sketch in this book tells one story, humanizing at least one part of how that collision course became inevitable, and how that national trauma changed not only America but every single American, every family. Within families men and women could no longer rely on old patterns of regarding each other. Long absences from home had made men less sober in every sense. Women learned, because they had to, how to be self-reliant when they could not be only helpmates.

After the Civil War, white Americans had to deal with freed blacks, a bewildering new population, and a social challenge created by the outcome of a military conflict. Grown men and women suddenly found themselves declared to be no longer children or property but responsible adults. Homeless people, most illiterate, who had not been allowed into white society now had to define and claim their place. Some blacks wanted to turn their backs on America and return to their Old Country, to Africa, while others saw themselves as having earned a stake in the republic, especially compared with the thousands of white newcomers whose ancestors had done nothing to build America.

The mess left by the Civil War could not be swept away by using prewar America as a model of right order. Maybe wiser, surely sadder, the young country of less than a hundred years old had to work hard at forgetting and at remembering. It had to forget the explosion of regional differences in order to function as one polity; it had to remember the ideals of its leaders; and it had to calm down and grow. The West, so vast and empty of white or black Americans, begged to be exploited. After the small matter of exterminating an indigenous population was taken care of, a problem already solved in the East in earlier centuries, half a continent was left wide open, full of places already legendary for mineral riches. The Far West was becoming a new world for the New World; the East was its Europe.

In its protracted and tormented period of transition from preindustrial backwater to rich industrial giant, America made extraordinary demands of extraordinary people. Their stories could not be more American, the lucky fruit of the chance to begin again.

ACKNOWLEDGMENTS

The collective subject of this book helped inspire a constructive spirit of cooperation that left many people encouraged and hopeful. Various kinds of assistance made a crucial difference at moments when we needed help. Here are some of the people who have our gratitude. At Addison Wesley Longman, we owe thanks to Bruce Borland, executive editor, who first encouraged the idea of *American Lives,* the biographical textbook from which this volume is adapted. In furthering that project, Betty Slack, director of development, extended many courtesies and James Strandberg, development editor, did many jobs meticulously and cheerfully to transform the idea into bound pages. John Bell, general editor at Addison-Wesley, enthusiastically adopted the project and made a selection of subjects that brought our earlier ideas into sharper focus. Ray Lincoln, agent and friend, gave exactly the suggestions and opinions that we would have asked for. Ruth Gminski helped a great deal with the early library searches. Dr. Vincent Naramore, emeritus professor of mathematics at Saint Michael's College, helped us with many useful observations. Diann Varricchione helped us, as usual, in her competent and unflappable way as she prepared the many drafts of the manuscript.

The manuscript got better as it passed through the hands of a team of careful historians whose expertise sharpened points and refined factual distinctions at different stages. They include Anne B. Harris, Old Dominion University; Philip H. Vaughan, Rose State College; Theresa Kaminski, University of Wisconsin–Stevens Point; Hilliard J. Goldman, Meramec Community College; Jerry Thompson, Texas A&M International University; Timothy Koerner, Oakland Community College–Royal Oak Campus; B. B. McCool, Arkansas Tech University; David Dixon, Slippery Rock University; Michael Weiss, Linn-Benton Community College; Mark C. Herman, Edison Community College; David A. Walker, University of Northern Iowa; Deborah M. Jones, Bristol Community College; Tommy Stringer, Navarro College; Kenneth H. Williams, Alcorn State University; Ellen Shockrow, Pasadena City College; Valeen T. Avery, Northern Arizona University; and David Godshalk, Shippensburg University. Errors that may remain, of course, should be attributed not to them but to us.

We also wish to thank many people who helped us with our primary research. We are indebted to J. Robert Maguire of Shoreham, Vermont, for permission to draw upon James Madison's journal of his 1791 trip to Vermont. We are grateful to the staff of the manuscript division of the New York Public Library; the Henry E. Huntington Library in San Marino, California; the Alderman Library of the University of Virginia; the William L. Clements Library of the University of Michigan; the Loyalist Museum of Saint John, New Brunswick; the Princeton University Library; the New Jersey State Archives; the Historical Society of Pennsylvania; the Yale University Library for permission to quote from *The Papers of Benjamin Franklin*, 28 volumes, edited by Leonard W. Labaree et al.; and from the *Papers of Thomas Jefferson*, 28 volumes, edited by Julian Boyd, Charles T. Cullen, John Catanzariti, et al., published by Princeton University Press. Once again, we are indebted to the generosity of reference librarians, including Patricia Mardeusz and Jake Barickman at the Bailey/Howe Libraries of the University of

Vermont and Kristin Hindes at Saint Michael's College in Colchester, Vermont.

Many other people have provided help and support. We owe special thanks to the staff of the Vermont Council on the Humanities; to Michael Bouman, executive director of the Missouri Council on the Humanities; and to Linda Gilbertson of the Vermont Preservation Division. Frederick Allen, managing editor of *American Heritage,* and Governor Thomas P. Salmon, in his role of president of the University of Vermont, asked very good questions. Our thanks to Robert Dean, a vigilant bibliographer who ambushed pertinent books for us. Michel Roy of Saint-Malo, France, made it possible for us to keep working at a difficult time. Finally, Douglas Denby, president of John Cabot University in Rome, was generous and understanding, as were so many of our colleagues on the Via della Lungara, including Francesca Gleason, Franco Pavoncello, Ann Besser, Christopher Neenan, James Bowditch, Larry Gray, Giosy Cesarini, Jasmine Kavanos, Kathleen Quinn, Paulyne Day, Evelyn Hockey, Fabiana Moriconi, and Catherine Denby.

ANNE MARBURY HUTCHINSON: THIS GREAT AND SORE AFFLICTION

*T*HE LAST EUROPEAN POWER TO ENTER THE race for New World territories and riches was England. While Portugal and Spain expanded their imperial possessions rapidly at the close of the fifteenth century, not until Elizabeth I came to the throne in 1558 did an English monarch think at all of competing with her mainland rivals—and then she was satisfied with commissioning marauders to poach the wealth of the New World from treasure ports and fleets. James I, who came to the throne in 1603, launched the first for-profit English settlement at Jamestown and also chartered the Plymouth Plantation (half the passengers on the *Mayflower* were merchants). By the time continued religious persecution in Europe sent a large English contingent toward Massachusetts Bay in 1629, prospective English colonists had their choice of colonial destinations —and the managers of colonies had to compete with each other for settlers.

⊰⊱

FOR NEARLY A DECADE in the early years of New England's history, women enjoyed more rights and respect, less abuse, and the promise of a progressively better way of life than in Old England, their homeland. They emigrated willingly to Boston with their husbands, brothers, and fathers, as relieved as the men to escape the tightening noose of religious persecution, until by 1637 there were two women in Massachusetts Bay colony for every three men, the highest ratio in the American colonies. Then, suddenly, as democracy, led by a woman, began to call into question many of the church-state conventions, including the differences between the rights of men and of women, a harsh crackdown put an end to this brief outbreak of sexual equality.

The Puritan fathers at first outdid themselves pampering, as they would have seen it, female colonists, probably not seeing where it could lead. In tracts such as William Wood's *New England's Prospect,* written to promote immigration to the edge of the wild American continent, women were told that members of their sex had already taken several upward steps in the New World. In England, wife beating was commonly used to keep women in their place; in New England, it was forbidden. Furthermore, men were forbidden to treat their wives as servants. Heavy fines punished infractions of either offense. In the early years after Boston's founding in 1630, New England authorities took pains to make women happy so that they would write glowing letters back to England to lure more of their sisters.

One of the more eager recipients of this good news from America was Anne Marbury Hutchinson, the cheerful, middle-aged wife of a prosperous silk manufacturer and, with all the hard work and risk it implied, already the mother of fourteen children. Married to a man who believed in equality of the sexes, Anne Hutchinson was also a devoted follower of a charismatic Puritan divine, a religious leader who also saw women and men as equals. As it became apparent that Puritans would have to flee intensifying persecution by the English government, Anne, her husband, and their seven younger children left behind the comfortable life of English gentry to become pioneers on the edge of the American wilderness.

Greater equality for women did not seem a distant prospect

or a hypothetical philosophical concept when Anne Hutchinson was born in England in 1591. A woman was on the throne of England. Elizabeth I was not just a stand-in marking time between male rulers; she was the second queen in a row to rule England, and she spent much of her forty-five-year reign contending not only with less successful male European kings but with other powerful and ambitious women, including the cousin she would put to death, Mary Queen of Scots. It was, in fact, an age of queens in Europe, from Isabella of Spain to Margaret of Austria. The specter of enduring female power alarmed many Protestant rulers, including John Knox, Scottish founder of the Presbyterian Church and spiritual father of Puritanism, who denounced government by women in his treatise, *The First Trumpet Blast Against the Monstrous Regiment of Women* (1557). Elizabeth established herself as the unchallenged power of Europe by defeating the Spanish Armada three years before Anne Hutchinson's birth and remained, all through Anne's childhood, the figure of a brilliant woman towering over England.

Queen Elizabeth repeatedly jailed Anne's uncle, Sir Anthony Cope, for opposing her middle-of-the-road church policies. Cope once spent a month in the Tower of London on Elizabeth's instructions after he proposed a change known as Cope's Bill and Book; if passed, it would have allowed the Puritans to revise the official *Book of Common Prayer,* the defining religious document of the Church of England. When Elizabeth came to the throne, it was widely assumed that she would push ahead the radical Reformation agenda of the Puritans, who wanted to "purify" the Church of England of all remaining traces of the Church of Rome, including vestments, incense, and bishops. But her Act of Settlement suppressed zealous reformers: she preferred to downplay religious contention and made it clear from time to time by exemplary execution that on the subject of religion she would tolerate neither criticism nor open opposition, whether from Puritan reformers or Catholics.

The daughter of a Church of England preacher and a Puritan mother who was descended from a noble Lincolnshire family, Anne Marbury grew up in the small market town of Alford,

114 miles northeast of London, in a house full of books, daughters, and religious disputation. Her father, Francis Marbury, was master of Alford Grammar School and preacher at 250-year-old Saint Wilfrid's Church, hub of Alford's religious, social, and political life. Francis Marbury was frequently in trouble with the bishops for loudly denouncing the lazy, uneducated clergy of the Church of England. Twice he was tried by church courts and stripped of his living for his outspoken views. His pet targets were the "self-seeking soul-murdering" bishops and the low preaching standards of the country priests. In virtual house arrest throughout much of Anne's childhood, he had plenty of time to instruct his eager daughter, often his only appreciative audience, and treated her as a son.

A born bookworm with a retentive memory, Anne, a kinswoman of playwright John Dryden on her mother's side, spent more time reading than sewing. But she learned midwifery by helping at several of her mother's deliveries and also became a skilled nurse and herbalist. All these skills made her a respected figure among other women. Inspired no doubt by a queen who had not only mastered Latin but read Plato in the original Greek and could argue in French, Spanish, Portuguese, Italian, and Welsh, Anne grew up at a time when female literacy in England was higher than it had ever been or would be again until the late nineteenth century. One widely read London educator, Richard Mulcaster, argued "that young maidens can learn, nature doth give them, and that they have learned, our experience doth teach us. What can more assure the world of this truth," asked Mulcaster, headmaster of Saint Paul's School, "than our diamond [Queen Elizabeth] at home?"

At times, Francis Marbury was the sole voice advocating Puritan reforms to the Church of England. On trial, he argued bravely and uncompromisingly in the face of grillings by powerful bishops. Anne could not but mark the lesson. She also must have been aware that, after Elizabeth I died and the misogynist King James I ascended the throne, more Puritan women were beginning to lecture publicly across England—and that they, too, were persecuted. When Anne was thirteen, her father was knighted and made pastor of the vast parish of Saint Martin in the Vintry, London, in the shadow of Saint Paul's.

It was in London that Anne first imbibed the ideas of Familism, a radical sect that preached direct communication between each individual, male or female, and God. Its teachings rejected the Calvinist doctrines of predestination, which precluded individual free will, and original sin, which denounced Eve and blamed women for all sin. Young Anne began to listen closely to women's voices in the nonconformist sects sprouting in London—she was attracted at various times by Familism, Separatism, and Puritanism, to which her mother subscribed. London women took active roles in the Puritan movement. Some two hundred of them were hauled before the bishop of London in Star Chamber ecclesiastical courts. A majority of these women were tried. They suffered heavy fines and imprisonment for, among other offenses, keeping secret the locations of clandestine Puritan printing presses. London women not only supported the Puritan underground but held the equivalent of salons in their parlors to preach and lead religious discussions.

At James I's accession in 1603, he, too, was expected to unleash a Puritan reform movement, but at the Hampton Court conference of church leaders, he proclaimed that Puritanism "agrees as well with a monarchy as God and the Devil." He attacked not only Puritans but women, several times digressing from his prepared speech to disparage them. His bishops took his cue and imposed, among other strictures, a ban on infant baptism by midwives, even when no priest was available and the baby was dying. As James took every opportunity to reverse Elizabeth's policies toward women, he introduced a stiff new antiwitchcraft law and, in his best-selling book, *Demonology,* declared that of every twenty-one witches, twenty were women. James argued that all women were weak and lustful and easy prey to "the snares of the Devil as was ever well proved to be true by the Serpent's deceiving of Eve at the beginning." In his first speech to Parliament, James lashed out at women, paraphrasing Scripture: "The head of every man is Christ and the head of the woman is man." In a widely printed letter to his son, the king instructed his son, "Teach your wife that it is your office to command, hers to obey. Women must never be allowed to meddle in the government."

By the time Anne was seventeen, separatists who had given up on reforming the Church of England were trying to escape, first to Holland. Anne had her first glimpse of persecuted Englishwomen driven from their homeland as she witnessed the fleeing Pilgrims.

When Anne was twenty, her father, her soul mate and intellectual companion, died. He left his wife as the sole executrix of his will, an uncommonly liberal gesture for the time, and left each of his twelve children 200 marks, a tidy sum. One year later, Anne married William Hutchinson, aged twenty-six, a wealthy textile merchant. The first of their fifteen children was born soon after they moved back to their childhood home, Alford. Along the North Sea, in the shadow of Dutch windmills, new religious winds were blowing. Women were appearing in pulpits as preachers, a practice that had originated across the sea in Holland. Soon there were women ministers all over England, many of them preaching the reform doctrines of Familism. This sect held that the spirit was superior to the Bible, believed that women and men could return to the innocence that preceded the Fall, advocated the election of the clergy by the people, and put reason above ritual.

The rapid spread of this radical agenda by women preachers brought intensifying persecution by the established church. In January 1620, the bishop of London told all his clergy to preach vehemently against the insolence of women and to condemn their "wearing of broad-brimmed hats, pointed doublets, hair cut short or shorn" and their carrying of daggers and swords. One Londoner recorded, "Our pulpits ring continually of the insolence and impudence of women."

In rural Alford, Anne had little contact for many years with persecution until the mid-1620s, when Charles I succeeded James and stepped up persecution of dissenters even further. Anne flirted at first with separatism but then seems to have rejected the idea of leaving her father's church after she heard the preaching of a charismatic Puritan preacher, John Cotton, at Boston, on the east coast. Frequently, she and her husband journeyed to Boston, twenty-four miles away, to hear him preach his gentle version of Puritanism. Cotton had won a reputation all over England as a biblical scholar and, as the leading nonconforming minister in the Church of England, for his evangelical preaching of the "covenant of grace," which he described as a covenant between God and man whereby God drew the soul to salvation. He preached that there was nothing a man—or woman—could do to acquire this covenant. If Anne Hutchinson was predestined to salvation, God would endow her with faith and fulfill the covenant. This doctrine differed somewhat from the version that the founders of Massachusetts Bay Colony declared as orthodox when they sailed to Boston in 1630. The faithful were expected to "prepare" themselves for God's saving grace by good works, especially following the laws of the New England church state. Anne espoused John Cotton's evangelical preaching of divine omnipotence and human helplessness. She believed with him that to draw comfort from doing good works was presumptuous, that God acted alone, and that humans had no way of preparing for divine grace.

In the winter of 1629, as the persecution of Puritans worsened, John Winthrop, a Cambridge-educated London barrister, was elected governor of a company of a thousand Puritans preparing to establish a permanent settlement in New England. The company made strong overtures to women, clearly implying that the New World would have no use for Old World, women-trammeling traditions, one leader writing of "the kind usage of the English [in Massachusetts Bay] to their wives" and of households where "equals gather with equals." The 1620s had been years of severe restrictions and heavy taxes on English businessmen and of drought and famine in the English cities and towns. Reports from the New World, on the other hand, emphasized abundant game, seafood, fruit, berries, pumpkins for the taking. In the sermon John Cotton preached to the Puritans departing on the four ships commanded by Governor Winthrop, he emphasized the economic opportunities for merchants like Anne's husband:

> Nature teaches bees [that] when the hive is too full, they seek abroad for new dwellings . . . [so it is] when the hive of [England] is so full that the tradesmen cannot live one by another, but eat up one another. . . .

What may have pushed the Hutchinsons off the fence in favor of emigrating was the latest policy of King Charles I, who combined unparalleled taxation and religious persecution by exacting forced loans from Puritans. Anne's uncle, seventy-year-old Erasmus Dryden, owner of Canons Ashby, one of England's great houses, was jailed when he refused to lend the king money. William Hutchinson believed it was only a matter of time before his turn came. Anne's brother-in-law, the Puritan preacher John Wheelwright, was arrested even as she learned that John Cotton was on the run from Archbishop Laud's agents. In disguise and using an assumed name, he was living in hiding in a series of Puritan hideaways. In July 1633, the Reverend Cotton boarded the *Griffin* and escaped to New England. Two members of the Hutchinson family sailed with him to begin transferring the family business to Boston. Then, shortly after their twelfth child was born, Anne and William gave away their belongings, sold their home of twenty years, and prepared to emigrate.

Almost from the moment she stepped on board the *Griffin*, bound for Boston on Massachusetts Bay, Anne Hutchinson spoke her mind, perhaps feeling she was safely away from the inhibiting atmosphere of England's church spies. And almost immediately, she incurred the wrath of two Puritan ministers who, along with a hundred head of cattle, were crowded in among the voyagers to the New World. The Reverends Zechariah Symmes and William Bartholomew reported to Boston authorities that Anne had confided to Bartholomew "that she had never had any great thing done about her but it was revealed to her beforehand." To claim that she communicated directly with

God through revelations was heretical enough for the two ministers: that a *woman* claimed direct contact with God smacked of witchcraft.

To make matters worse, Anne had quickly grown tired of the Reverend Symmes's five-hour, nonstop shipboard sermons, especially his constant belittling of women. After announcing that, as soon as she reached Boston, she would expose his claims as a tissue of errors, Hutchinson began holding women's meetings, as she had done for years unmolested in Alford, on board ship. She was surprised that some of the men aboard objected, confronting her with the verse, "And if they [women] will learn anything, let them ask their husbands at home" (1 Corinthians 14:35). Anne was next shocked on her arrival at the mean, uncouth look of Boston, a flat, swampy backwater town of crowded, unpaved streets with pigs rooting in the filth, its hundred-odd houses dominated by the square, barnlike Puritan meetinghouse. Inside, she received another shock: instead of automatic admission to membership, she was subjected to an all-day hearing conducted by Governor Thomas Dudley. Her other interrogators included her old pastor, the Reverend Cotton; the pastor of her new Boston church, the Reverend John Wilson; and the Reverend Symmes, one of the shipboard clergymen she had openly criticized. Finally "satisfied that she held nothing different from us," Governor Dudley urged her admission to the church. But if Anne Hutchinson had expected freedom of expression or the right to dissent in Massachusetts, she must have been sadly disappointed.

For the next two years, Anne and William Hutchinson were busy building and furnishing a spacious, thatch-roofed wattle-and-daub house in Boston's Cornhill section. They lived right across the street from John Winthrop, who had recently been displaced as governor because many country clergy thought he had been too lenient with dissenters and had closed an eye to sharp business practices. Demoted to the colony's council, he was waiting for the next election to prove his toughness: he had received a copy of Anne's hearing record and had already put her down as someone to watch. Oblivious and hard at work, Anne was busy building her practice as one of only four midwives in all Boston, while she cared for her large family. She still found a way to organize weekly meetings in her home to discuss with other women the finer points of Mr. Cotton's sermons, a joy for her to be able to hear every week.

In these meetings, soon so popular that sixty or seventy people packed in and stood for an hour or two as Anne elaborated Cotton's teachings, she began to take Cotton's principles of divine omnipotence and human helplessness in a new direction. Her first principle was "that the person of the Holy Ghost dwells in a justified person [predestined for salvation]." This view threatened the fundamental doctrine on which the Puritans had built their church state, namely, that God's will could be fathomed only in the pages of the Bible. She further claimed that a good life—"sanctification"—offered no guarantee of being saved—"justification." This dictum undermined the whole Puritan belief that good works were necessary to "prepare" for salvation. Anne's emphasis on personal revelation minimized the role of the clergy. She also maintained that "justified" people knew by revelation from the Holy Spirit that they were already "justified" and could tell on the basis of this mystical insight whether other people were "under a covenant of grace" (saved) or "under a covenant of works" (damned because they were depending on good works instead of divine grace). By October 1636, Governor Winthrop, now reelected, began to view these beliefs as damaging to the stable and clergy-dominated society of Boston.

At about that time Hutchinson hinted to her admirers that in all of Massachusetts only two churchmen, John Cotton and her brother-in-law John Wheelwright, were under a covenant of grace and therefore fit to preach. If she had given this opinion to only a handful of listeners, she might have only been censured by her pastor. But by late 1636 her house was being jammed three times a week by up to eighty eager auditors, many of them merchants disgruntled with clergy controls on trade and profits, and even more members of other congregations all over the colony who trekked great distances to see and hear this bold woman speaking out against the black-robed, all-male power structure. As historian Edmund Morgan has put it, "more was at stake here than the welfare of the Boston church."

When Hutchinson's mentor, John Cotton, applied to become teacher of the First Church of Boston, which had the largest congregation in the colony, Winthrop could not stop him. But when John Wheelwright, whose views were no different from Cotton's or his sister-in-law's, was proposed as a teacher at a church meeting on October 30, Winthrop saw his chance to block Anne's growing influence. Most recent among her followers was Sir Henry Vane, the new Puritan governor out from England. Winthrop opposed the appointment of Wheelwright, "whose spirit they knew not and [who] seemed to dissent in judgment," as the church's third minister. Despite the fact that Wheelwright had the support of most of the congregation, Winthrop was even more popular as the man who had led and shaped the Puritan colony over the years. And now he was putting all that influence at risk to rouse the entire colony to the threat posed by Anne Hutchinson.

By early 1637, the colony was divided into two hostile factions, the town of Boston versus the surrounding countryside. In January, the worried General Court, the colony's ruling body, declared a day of fasting and prayer, a compulsory holiday. John Cotton preached. When he finished, Wheelwright rose from his bench and criticized anyone adhering to the idea of a covenant of works: "The more holy they are, the greater enemies they are to Christ. . . . We must kill them with the word of the Lord." Speaking figuratively, Wheelwright no doubt thought that most of the clergy and magistrates were dead wood, but someone took down his words. At its next session, the General Court charged him with sedition, convicting him but deferring sentence until after the annual May election. When the General Court sat again, John Winthrop was back in power. He had moved the court and the elections out of Boston into the countryside, to remote Cambridge, where he had the support of orthodox country clergy. He therefore succeeded in ousting Governor Vane, who soon sailed back to England. To buttress his position further, Winthrop again put off sentencing Wheelwright and called a synod of ministers in late summer to examine the doctrines his informants told him were coming from Anne Hutchinson's parlor. In the meantime, to keep the dissenters' numbers from swelling further, Winthrop sponsored a General Court order forbidding anyone to entertain strangers for more than three weeks without permission of the magistrates. The order was pointed at new immigrants from England whose views accorded with Mrs. Hutchinson's. America had enacted its first immigrant-screening law, aimed at stifling religious dissent.

Indeed, the year 1637, the ninth year of the Massachusetts Bay colony, was the year in which Puritan New England lost its innocence. Massachusetts troops used the murder of a New England trader as an excuse to destroy the main stronghold of the Pequot Indians near Stonington, Connecticut; they then slaughtered the escaping remnants near New Haven.

On August 30, ministers converged from all over Massachusetts and Connecticut for twenty-four days to define orthodox Puritan doctrines and to spell out for each other the implications of some eighty-two "erroneous" doctrines that witnesses said were coming from Anne Hutchinson's parlor. Anne's old mentor, John Cotton, fell into line with the orthodox majority; only John Wheelwright dissented. When the General Court reconvened in November, Wheelwright refused to recant and was banished from the colony; he was expected to go off to Rhode Island to join Roger Williams, himself banished the year before and now starting a new colony among the Indians. Then on November 12, the General Court, having already made up its collective mind that Anne Hutchinson must be silenced, tried the midwife and lay teacher, forty-six years old and five months pregnant, on charges of sedition and contempt.

The New Town (as Cambridge was then called) courthouse was unheated, stark, and crowded with some two hundred people when Hutchinson, dressed in black, was escorted in and told to stand facing the bench, a long table at which gowned and wigged General Court officials sat flanking Governor Winthrop.

There was no jury, although this was a civil case. Only the judges had footwarmers with hot coals inside. Anne heard the charges read to her for the first time. She was accused of eighty-two "errors in conduct and belief," including "consorting with those that had been sowers of sedition." Did they mean her own brother-in-law Wheelwright? In England, all Puritans were nonconformists by definition; in New England, nonconformity had just become an indictable offense. She was also accused of breaking the fourth commandment. The Bible was the law book, and "Honor thy father and thy mother" now meant that the governors of the colony were the fathers and all women their dutiful children, who must honor and obey them. Her third offense was to claim revelation of God's word directly, and her fourth that she had misrepresented the conduct of the ministers.

Legally, the court was on slippery ground, handicapped by Anne Hutchinson's caution. She had written nothing down and had never spoken in public. Furthermore, Winthrop could accuse her only of "countenancing and encouraging" Wheelwright's seditious circulation of a petition to reform the clergy: she had not actually signed it. To hold home meetings had never been a crime in England or New England before: it was the bedrock of the persecuted underground Puritan tradition. Only the charge of traducing the authority of the ministers seemed serious.

Without a lawyer, Anne ably conducted her own defense. Standing and parrying the governor's questions for seven uninterrupted hours, with a devastating combination of nerve, logic, and expert knowledge of the Bible, she often reduced lawyer Winthrop to exasperated outbursts of pique: "We do not mean to discourse with those of your sex." Called on to justify teaching crowds in her home, she quoted the Bible to show that older women were required to teach younger women. When Winthrop would not accept two biblical sources as grounding for her meetings, she answered sarcastically, "Must I show my name written therein [in the Bible]?" One clergyman after another was brought in to testify that she had belittled and insulted the ministers. Winthrop seemed to prevail on this charge, but only after introducing notes from an off-the-record pretrial meeting with Anne.

The first day's grilling paused only when the pregnant Anne fainted after not being allowed to sit, eat, drink, or leave the courtroom for natural relief. That night, slipped notes by a supporter, she found discrepancies in the testimony of her principal accuser, her pastor, Reverend Wilson. The next day, she insisted that all witnesses be put under oath, including the clergy, nearly setting off a riot. One final witness was her old friend, John Cotton, who rebutted the testimony of Reverend Wilson that Anne had admitted accusing the clergy of being "under a covenant of works" (unsaved). The case against Anne Hutchinson collapsed.

In her moment of unexpected triumph, Anne blurted out that she had known from a revelation at the start of her trial that she would prevail. And then she went even further: "And see this scripture fulfilled this day in mine eyes. . . . Take heed what ye go about to do unto me. . . . God will ruin you and your posterity and this whole state." This public challenge was too much for Winthrop and his all-male panel of judges and clergy. Winthrop asked Anne how she knew "that it was God that did reveal these things" and Anne, condemning herself under the colony's biblical laws against claiming immediate revelation, replied, "By the voice of His own spirit to my soul."

Deliberating only briefly, the court agreed Hutchinson's words were enough grounds for banishment. And when Anne asked to "know wherefore I am banished," Winthrop gave her only a curt, high-handed answer: "Say no more, the court knows wherefore and is satisfied."

Ordered held under house arrest in the isolated manse of a clergyman safely away from Boston all winter, Anne still refused to recant. In March 1638, she was excommunicated and ordered to leave the colony. At her sentencing, the Reverend Hugh Peter summed up her principal offense: "you have stepped out of your place, you have rather been a husband than a wife." And Reverend Wilson, her nemesis, after noting, "you have so many ways troubled the church," added, "I do cast you out and deliver you up to Satan." Immediately after Anne's November 1637 hearing, the court had stripped Captain John Underhill, hero of the Pequot War, of his militia rank and had disfranchised him for supporting Wheelwright and Hutchinson. Twelve days after sentencing Anne Hutchinson, the court ordered fifty-eight Bostonians (William Hutchinson was third on the list) disfranchised and stripped of their guns, powder, and lead—seventeen others from other towns were punished similarly. Six more women were tried and expelled in 1638.

With eighteen inches of snow still in the woods, Anne, now nine months pregnant, and her children made the sixty-five-mile journey from Boston to Aquidneck by horse, canoe, and on foot over Indian paths. It took eight days. Her husband had gone ahead with twenty of her faithful adherents to build log cabins. By March 1639, Anne was preaching again, her following growing. But as excommunications continued in Boston and John Winthrop raged that Massachusetts would soon seize Rhode Island, Anne felt she could not stay there. After her husband died in 1642, she moved to New York province with several other families. Far from the reach of John Winthrop, she built a house on Pelham Bay on the outskirts of the Dutch settlements.

Anne Hutchinson did not believe in war or firearms. Her Boston adherents had refused to fight in the Pequot Wars; now, on the frontier, she steadfastly refused to defend herself as a new war against the native tribes broke out in 1643. When she opened her gate one day to a group of young braves who asked her for cold water from her well, they rushed in and killed her and all of her daughters except one, who was taken into captivity. Unsympathetic even at the hour of the family's tragic death, the Reverend Thomas Weld, in whose house Hutchinson had been held under arrest, gleefully reported her death back to England: "Thus the Lord heard our groans to heaven, and freed us from this great and sore affliction."

TEEDYUSCUNG,
OR
BROTHER
GIDEON

AS THE STRUGGLE AMONG EUROPEANS FOR
control of North America intensified in the mid-
eighteenth century, the New World's native inhabitants were
forced to take sides. The competing networks of European forts
and trading stations gradually entangled most native tribes
south of Hudson's Bay and east of the Mississippi River. The
tribes came to depend on the settlers from the Old World even
for the weapons they needed to hunt for food and hides. They
became habituated to factory-made kettles, knives, hatchets,
coats, trousers, trinkets, liquor—all provided in exchange for
the furs so much in demand in Europe. Treaty alliances and
bribes of trade goods corrupted existing tribal power relation-
ships. The Delawares of New Jersey and Pennsylvania, for instance, became pawns of the Six Nations Iroquois Confederacy
of New York in its lucrative dealings with the confederacy's
military allies, the British. Not all tribes were willing to sit still
for the new arrangements.

Surrounded by a graceful ring of hills, the Lehigh Valley
had become the heartland of Moravian settlements in eastern
Pennsylvania. Even in the drought-ridden 1750s, it was rich in
corn and wheat, thick with dairy herds. Earlier, whenever the

intermittent colonial wars had broken out, only pacifist Pennsylvania had seemed immune to the bloodshed. Founded by Quaker William Penn, this sylvan island of tranquility was a magnet for European as well as English pacifists, as some 250 sects of German pietists alone settled in the fertile valleys between the Quaker settlements on the Delaware River and the Susquehanna, one hundred miles west. The Moravians, German forerunners of the Methodists, had purchased most of the Lehigh Valley from William Penn's sons. There they established unarmed towns with biblical names (Bethlehem, Nazareth), built missions, and preached Christian salvation to the native "heathen." They alone of the peaceful Pennsylvanians methodically studied the tribal cultures and dialects.

At the heart of their wilderness utopia was Bethlehem, a settlement that boasted a hospital, colleges for men and women, woolen mills, shops, grist mills that served the surrounding valleys, running water from the first waterworks in America, apothecary gardens, and a cocoonery for producing silk. The Moravians were housed in dormitories according to age, sex, marital status, and occupation. For recreation, they loved to sing in *a cappella* choirs, the well-scrubbed women in long black dresses and white caps, the brethren in starched white linen roundabouts and linen trousers. On summer evenings, violin and French horn, oboe and trombone music floated out to members of the Delaware tribe who came to visit and pray.

On November 25, 1755, there was no music. In the chilly early dawn, Bethlehem awakened to the doleful tolling of the town bells. The Moravian bishop told his people of a massacre at Gnadenhütten, the principal Moravian mission twenty miles up the Lehigh River. There, on the west bank, was the principal Moravian language school, a church, dormitories, stores, barns. Over on the east bank, the Delawares had only recently been given separate quarters in a new village of stone cottages. About one hundred, mostly women and children, remained in the village while the older boys and the men were away on the annual winter hunt. Even with the men gone, the mission was crowded. Sixteen Moravians were at the old mission as the last glow of twilight disappeared on November 23. When the dinner bell rang, they stopped their chores and gathered in the main mission house. After asking for grace, they passed the food around and spoke German softly. John and Susanna Partsch, who had recently arrived, ate together. Martin Kiefer, the blacksmith, sat next to linguist George Fabricius. Martin Nitschmann, a missionary, sat with his wife, Susanna. Gottlieb Anders was serving his wife, Johanna, who was nursing their infant daughter. Five single men sat near the front door.

One of them, seventeen-year-old Joseph Sturgis, was the first to hear footsteps on the snow-crusted ground outside. As he unlatched the door and swung it wide, he saw the black, blue, brown, and green painted faces of Munsee and Shawnee warriors, heard the first shrieking war cry, and saw the flash of muskets. Then he fell, shot in the face. Another ball hit Nitschmann, killing him instantly. A dozen attackers burst into the room and fired. Three men were hit; Susanna Nitschmann was wounded as she shoved other women ahead of her up the stairs into the women's dormitory. When she fell, two warriors dragged her outside. She cried out, "Oh, brethren! Brethren! Help me!" The other attackers dragged out the three bleeding, dying men and scalped them.

In the dormitory upstairs, Anna Sensemann sank to the edge of a bed, sobbing, "Dear Savior, this is what I expected!" Johanna Anders wrapped her baby in her apron and bent down over her as the warriors pounded on the trapdoor. All the women could do was scream for help through the garret window in the hope of attracting Delawares on the other side of the river. Downstairs, the surviving men looked for makeshift weapons—they had no guns. Suddenly, it was quiet outside. It seemed the warriors had gone. But when Joachim Sensemann came out and ran toward the new Delaware village, he saw that the attackers had surrounded the mission house with bundles of brush and were setting them afire.

From a second-story window of the single men's house nearby, Peter Worbas, who was ill, watched helplessly. He had seen Susanna Nitschmann dragged away and the three men scalped. His horror increased when he saw a half-dozen warriors ignite the piles of dry wood. Joseph Sturgis, bleeding from wounds in the face and arm, jumped from a window, landed safely, and ran into the woods. Susanna Partsch jumped next: she also made it to the woods. George Fabricius was less fortunate: when he stepped through the window, four warriors fired. They scalped him. As the flames burned higher, seven more Moravians died. Martin Presser was the last to get out: four months later, he was found and identified by his clothing. He had died lying on his back, his hands folded in prayer.

The twelve Munsee and Shawnee raiders stripped the food from the stores, butchered sixty cattle, set the other buildings afire, and then cooked a feast before making off with their plunder and the wounded Susanna Nitschmann. She died after several weeks at the Munsee Indian stronghold of Tioga. A year later Captain Jachebus, her pro-French captor, was strangled to death by a Delaware chief who had been baptized by the Moravians. His name was Teedyuscung.

Born east of Trenton in the New Jersey Pine Barrens around 1700, Teedyuscung was one of six sons of an outspoken Delaware known to his white neighbors as Old Captain Harris. He called himself a Lenni Lenape, "one of the original people." The whites named his tribe the Delawares after Lord De la Warr, who had been granted much of the region by the king of England. Teedyuscung's father spoke English and could remember the arrival of thousands of English Quakers in the 1680s, when they started to hem in his people, a change that forced them to give up their ancient way of life as farmers and to become fishermen and hunters. As game became scarce, they had to range farther and farther from their longhouse villages to find food and pelts for clothing. These long absences began to undermine the old native skills: turning pottery; cutting stone; making leather garments, bows and arrows, utensils of bark and bone; and turning into ornaments the oyster and clam shells from the annual summer migration to the Jersey shore. Instead, the Delawares became dependent on white traders to supply their guns and ammunition for the hunt that gave them hides and furs to barter for copper kettles and steel knives and shoddy, factory-made blankets and clothing. And the long hunting trips were always followed by rum, drunken brawls, and trouble with the resented white neighbors.

Little is known of Teedyuscung before age thirty except that he married, had a son, and considered himself one of his tribe's natural leaders. He was tall, powerful, and terribly fond of rum. He could drink a gallon of it and stay sober enough to make eloquent speeches, but totally lacked the decorum on which his tribe prided itself in official councils if he had had anything to drink. By the time he was thirty, friction between whites and Delawares in West Jersey province had grown so acute that Teedyuscung's family, which never did get along well with their white neighbors, decided to leave their homeland. They crossed the Delaware River to the Lehigh Valley, sixty miles north of Philadelphia, a rugged country of mountains and fast rivers where no whites lived. Teedyuscung's family was welcomed by local Delawares, and his father became the chief man of Pocopoco in the Lehigh Gap, near present-day Nazareth.

But within only three years, white settlers began to intrude here, too, so many of them by the mid-1730s that the Delawares protested to the Penns in Philadelphia. Teedyuscung was present when they met at Durham in 1734. James Logan, lawyer and secretary to the family's proprietary government, claimed that the Penns had already bought the land. Teedyuscung would never forget the moment when Secretary Logan warned the Delawares to leave the Forks of the Delaware and the Lehigh and stop impeding the white settlers. If they did not go peaceably, they would be cut off from trading with Philadelphia. Logan followed up his threat by circumventing the Delawares and sending emissaries to the Six Nations Iroquois in western New York, who considered themselves the overlords and powerful protectors of the Delawares. Logan's maneuver divided the tribes: the Iroquois were staunch allies of the British, the Delawares increasingly hostile to them. The Iroquois sent a chief to berate the Delawares and ordered them to leave and go to rental lands they owned to the north that they had set aside for dispossessed native peoples.

When more white settlers came, the Delawares refused to move away from the Forks. By 1740, more than one hundred white families had moved in, ignoring the Delawares' protests. On November 21, 1740, the Delawares sent a petition to Bucks County justices of the peace, denying that they had sold their lands and warning that intruders would be met with force. When the next white man tried to settle at the Forks, a recently dispossessed New Jersey Delaware attacked and nearly killed him.

But Pennsylvania officials were determined. That same year, as evangelist George Whitefield preached his Great Awakening revival from Boston to Savannah, the Pennsylvania Land Office sold his agents five thousand acres as the site of a school for freed blacks. But the project failed and was abandoned. Whitefield's agents resold the land to Moravian immigrants seeking to establish an American religious colony, an asylum from decades of persecution by Protestants and Catholics. When their leader, Count von Zinzendorf of Saxony, visited the Forks, he did not consult with the Delawares. Instead, on Christmas Eve, 1741, he founded the Moravian settlement called Bethlehem. When the count visited his father's village, Teedyuscung was impressed by his first exposure to a white man preaching. The German-speaking pietists led lives of spiritual simplicity in their new settlement that Teedyuscung came to admire. For the rest of his life, he would be inextricably tied up with the Moravians in a turbulent, twenty-year relationship. The Moravians' communal life resembled the native tribal belief in sharing, not ownership. Anything they produced on church-owned lands was contributed to the common good. They took their meals at common tables; they slept in dormitories.

As the first whites moved into the Lehigh Valley in 1740, Teedyuscung moved his family deeper into the hills farther south to a place called Memolagomeka; but when the Moravian Frederick Hoeth and his family moved into the valley in 1750,

Teedyuscung and his relatives were forced to evacuate. This time he did not resist but decided to join the whites. In the spring of 1750, homeless for the third time, he moved to the new Moravian mission for the Indians at Gnadenhütten ("The Huts of Grace"). At age fifty, on March 12, 1750, wearing a white robe, he was baptized a Christian and took a new name, Gideon. In the mission journal, Bishop Spangenburg noted, "Today I baptized Tatiuskundt, the chief among sinners." One week later, Teedyuscung's Munsee wife was baptized, taking the new name of Elizabeth. Within a year, his eldest son joined the Christian fold, and his wife's sister married a leading Moravian missionary.

As a Christian tribe, the Delawares wore distinctive garb. They stopped shaving their heads and wore their hair shoulder length, donning caps and long shirts and trousers. Instead of carrying their guns under their capes Indian-style to keep the priming dry, they slung them over their shoulders in imitation of the whites as they went off to hunt for the game needed by the mission. For the next four years, Teedyuscung and his followers lived as whites at Gnadenhütten. Styling himself a sachem, he emerged as the spokesman and leader of the Forks Delawares, even in his self-imposed exile among the Moravians.

There was a canny side to Teedyuscung; his people remained among the Moravians through a long drought that brought famine, weakness, and disease to the natives of Pennsylvania. During this period, thousands of Delawares, unhappy with Pennsylvania land policies and seeking a surer supply of game, migrated four hundred miles west to the Ohio Valley. By April 1754, however, Teedyuscung, too, had had enough of Moravian life; with seventy followers he led an exodus from the Moravian mission, where five hundred Delawares now lived, to the Wyoming Valley, to the site of present-day Wilkes-Barre.

Shortly after Teedyuscung staked out his new town, Iroquois chiefs representing the Great Council of the Iroquois signed a deed giving the Penns a vast new territory west of the Susquehanna River encompassing the Wyoming Valley. Only five days later, several of the same Iroquois chiefs secretly sold a large tract between the Delaware and Susquehanna Rivers, also including the Wyoming Valley, to the rival Susquehannah Company of Connecticut. To confuse matters further, the Iroquois encouraged Teedyuscung and his kinsmen to stay in the valley to act as a buffer between white settlers and the southeastern rim of Iroquois lands. For a short time during that summer of 1754 there was peace in the valley. When four Moravian missionaries visited Brother Gideon, they found his people once again living their ancient farming way of life. They kept horses, hogs, and cattle; grew corn; fished in the river; and hunted the abundant game in the woods.

But the bucolic interlude was shattered later that year when a twenty-two-year-old Virginian, Colonel George Washington, bent on claiming thousands of acres of Pennsylvania land for veterans of King George's War, triggered the longest and bloodiest struggle to date between the French and British by trying to build a fort in French-dominated territory. Within a year, a British army commanded by General Edward Braddock marched toward present-day Pittsburgh. After its rout, French-led Indians from the Ohio Valley—including one of Teedyuscung's sons—raided British settlements all over the settled eastern half of Pennsylvania. From the Delaware Water Gap to Maryland, men, women, and children were killed as hundreds of farms were burned. The destruction of the Moravian mission at Gnadenhütten in November 1755 brought the raids within twenty miles of the Delaware River. Almost all of Pennsylvania had fallen to the French.

In this climactic power struggle, every tribe was forced to take a side. The Iroquois, traditional allies of the British, expected Teedyuscung and his Delawares to join them, and hold the Wyoming Valley against French-instigated attacks by other tribes. Until the massive raids into Northampton County in November 1755, Teedyuscung tried to stay neutral, though tending to side with the British. After all, he had every reason to fear attack by the French-led Shawnees from the Ohio Valley. After more than a dozen years of trying to accommodate the whites, he now tried to assert himself as a native leader. When he appealed to Pennsylvania authorities in Philadelphia for help, however, he received no answer. He waited a tense month, meanwhile sending a series of requests for advice and aid to the Iroquois. He met with Scaroyady, a Six Nations chief acting as go-between from Pennsylvania to the Iroquois, giving him a black wampum belt. "This I am now going to send to the Six Nations," he told the old chief. "If they send an answer, well and good. If they do not, I shall know what to do." When no answer came, he decided to break with the British and cast his lot with the apparent victors, the French-led Shawnees. He sent a large belt of wampum to the Ohio Valley with the message, "I am in exceeding great danger, the English will kill me, come and help me."

Teedyuscung began in his messages to assert himself as "sachem," and "King of the Delawares." He needed the prestige that came from battle to enhance his claims. For the first time in his life, at age fifty-five, he became a warrior. On December 10, 1755, he led the first Wyoming Delaware war party of thirty men, defying the Six Nations and seeking British scalps. In his party were three of his sons, three half-brothers, and a nephew. The Delaware family once called Harris was out to avenge half a century of indignities and humiliation at the hands of white settlers.

Skirting German settlements north of Kittatinny Mountain on December 31, Teedyuscung and three sons surrounded four whites working on the isolated farm of the Weiser family, shooting down the elder Weiser and Hans Adam Hess. Two younger men, Leonard and William Weiser, were captured by a second party of Delawares led by Teedyuscung's son, Amos. The next morning, the war party attacked two more farms, killing two hired men on the farm of Peter Hess and taking him and his son, Henry, captive. Next they attacked the farm of Hess's brother, killing two more laborers and seizing two more prisoners. Taking a few horses, they torched the farmhouses and barns and slaughtered the livestock. As they led their prisoners back toward the Wyoming Valley the next day, old Peter Hess began lagging. His captors stabbed him to death, stripped off his clothes, and took his scalp while his son looked on. On January

3, 1756, Teedyuscung and his war party reached their homes with their prisoners and scalps.

This was Teedyuscung's only act of war, but it made him the most respected leader of the eastern Delawares, a community of about one hundred. As a chieftain, he did not allow the torture or slow killing of prisoners. He continued to send out small raiding parties of half a dozen warriors to take scalps and prisoners, whom he needed for diplomatic bartering with the whites when peace came. His daring raids briefly brought him honor among the tribes and even attracted runaway slaves to his ranks. At one point he considered persuading one runaway to foment a slave insurrection, an insight that made him one of the first tribal leaders to see the plights of native peoples and African-Americans as linked.

After 1756 newly built forts along the Pennsylvania frontier protected British settlers from further Indian raids, and a series of conferences between tribal leaders and Pennsylvania government representatives began at Easton in July 1757, lasting off and on for nearly five years. Teedyuscung enjoyed the solid support of the Quakers and their anti-Proprietary group in the Pennsylvania Assembly. The Quakers blamed the Indian attacks on the avarice of the Penn family, especially on their fraudulent claims to have deeds proving they had bought the area around the Forks of the Delaware in the late seventeenth century.

When the Easton talks began, Teedyuscung arrived with one hundred of his followers, warriors, and councillors. The British officers and Philadelphia Quaker merchants saw a tall, heavyset man, his face painted bright red, wearing a suit of English tailored clothes, complete with vest and shiny buttons, and English riding boots. He stood to address them in English in a speech a Quaker schoolteacher quickly took down:

> We desire you will look upon us with eyes of mercy. We are a very poor people. Our wives and children are almost naked. We are void of understanding and destitute of the necessaries of life. Pity us!

As usual, Teedyuscung had been drinking a considerable quantity of rum, but it only seemed to make him more logical and eloquent. In the course of the Easton treaty talks, the most elaborate in the history of Pennsylvania, he insisted that land disputes were not the principal cause of the alienation of his people from whites but "had caused the stroke to come harder than it otherwise would have come." What he and his people wanted, he said, was a permanent reservation in the Wyoming Valley of northeastern Pennsylvania

> and we want to have certain boundaries fixed between you and us and a certain tract of land fixed which it shall not be lawful for us or for our children ever to sell, nor for you or any of your children ever to buy.

Teedyuscung asked for help building white men's houses at the Wyoming reservation and for missionaries to teach his people "the Christian religion" and reading and writing (which he had never learned). He also asked that "a fair trade be established between us."

His visionary appeal met with only derision from Iroquois emissaries and resistance from the Penns, who demanded the return of all white prisoners before peace could be concluded. On August 3, 1757, Teedyuscung rose again.

> They should certainly be restored, but [the governor] must remember, they [the Indians] must first be satisfied for their lands.

The upshot of the conference was an agreement to allow the British government to investigate and mediate the conflicting claims. The Quaker-controlled Pennsylvania Assembly sent Benjamin Franklin to London on the mission. Pennsylvania authorities in turn sent Teedyuscung as an envoy to the Ohio Valley.

The five years after the cessation of fighting marked the high point of Teedyuscung's life. After he returned from his first visit to Indian country along the Ohio in the summer of 1757, he stopped off at Bethlehem for a few days. Moravian archives show that Bishop Spangenburg invited "the Apostate, who had raised himself to a King" and his family to have coffee with church leaders. The bishop recorded that "the King was animated and strictly attentive." Teedyuscung had begun refusing liquor before and during high-level meetings. "He is naturally quick of apprehension and ready of reply." Bishop Spangenburg tried once more to buy the Wyoming Valley for the Moravians. Teedyuscung refused.

After a year of almost ceaseless traveling and negotiating on behalf of the Delawares, Teedyuscung had the satisfaction of seeing fifty Philadelphia carpenters sent to the Wyoming Valley to build a white man's village of ten solid log cabins for his kinsmen. All but one cabin measured ten by ten by fourteen feet. His own house, built of squared and dovetailed logs, measured a substantial sixteen by twenty-four feet, larger than the average white settler's home. The settlement was also fenced with gardens plowed around it. For the first time since they had been dispossessed by the whites nearly thirty years earlier, Teedyuscung and his family could look forward to traditional Lenni Lenape lives of farmers—ensconced in the modern homes of whites.

For about five years it appeared that Teedyuscung had succeeded in his dream of bridging the gap between his and the white man's world. But the building of the new Delaware town at Wyoming aroused the jealousy of the Six Nations, who still claimed the valley, and of whites from already overcrowded settlements in Connecticut.

In the summer of 1762, Teedyuscung attended his last conference with the whites at Lancaster. He had come to hate these treaty conferences. His wife had just died in a dysentery outbreak after a parley brought natives and whites together during an epidemic. He had the great satisfaction of receiving orders from the Six Nations to remain in the Wyoming Valley. Tom King, a Seneca chief, handed Teedyuscung's band a belt of wampum and said, "By this belt I make a fire for Teedyuscung at

Wyoming." And Pennsylvania authorities had something for him, too, presents valued at £200 sterling (about $8,000 today). Most of the Wyoming Delawares had traveled all the way from Wilkes-Barre to Lancaster on foot for the great peace conference.

Only seven Delawares remained at home, not enough to resist the force of 119 armed settlers from the Susquehannah Company who chose this moment to assert their claim to the Wyoming Valley deeded to them by the Six Nations Iroquois. They ignored the handful of Delawares and cut down their hay. The settlers then began building three blockhouses, made huts for themselves, and sowed grain. On September 22, Tom King and the Six Nations delegation arrived on their way home to New York and surprised the Connecticut workmen. The angry Iroquois warned off the Yankees: he had just told the Lancaster conferees that the Six Nations would never permit the Susque-hannah Company to have the Wyoming Valley. The workmen, who had finished their tasks, agreed to leave but said they would be back next spring with a thousand armed men and cannons.

When Teedyuscung and his entourage arrived a week later, the Iroquois chieftain advised him to "be quiet" while the Six Nations conferred with Connecticut authorities to prevent the Susquehannah settlers from returning. But all that autumn, more Connecticut settlers came, fourteen to build a sawmill near Teedyuscung's house, then eight more who stole Teedyuscung's horse. Teedyuscung received a gift horse in return and rode it to Philadelphia, where he received assurances of government protection. He returned home.

On the evening of April 19, 1763, as Teedyuscung lay asleep in his cabin, someone set it afire. Simultaneously, all twenty houses in the growing Delaware settlement went up in flames. Within minutes, the Delaware village of Wyoming burned to the ground. The survivors fled to Moravian settlements, but Teedyuscung died in the lodge his Pennsylvania brethren had built for him. Two weeks later, the first permanent settlers from Connecticut arrived, bringing herds of cattle. Planting fields of corn and arming massive blockhouses, they named the place Wilkes-Barre. When their descendants wrote the local history, they claimed that Teedyuscung had been drunk and that it was the Iroquois who had burned his settlement. But the Iroquois officially condemned the act, accusing the Connecticut men.

The Delawares had no doubt who had murdered Teedyuscung. Six months later, under cover of Pontiac's War, his son, Captain Bull, led a war party from the tribe's new home on the Ohio River all the way to the Wyoming Valley and killed twenty-six Connecticut settlers. By the end of 1763, no white men and no Delawares remained alive amid the ruins of Teedyuscung's experiment in assimilation in the Wyoming Valley.

TOM QUICK
THE INDIAN
SLAYER

As the European settlements in America expanded during the eighteenth century, they put pressure on native tribes and their food supply, often changing ways of life and patterns of hunting. These tribes, in turn, were pitted against each other and increasingly relied on the whites for their weapons. The Six Nations Iroquois, for instance, became loyal British subjects; the Hurons depended on the French.

The Tuscarora and the Delaware, whose settlements once extended from present-day southern New York to northern Virginia, became so decimated by disease, war, and encroachment, that they fought each other and finally were appended to the Six Nations Iroquois for protection. But many of the Delawares resented the tricky deals and endless treaty-making conferences that only stripped them of their traditionally communal lands. They headed west, shifted their allegiance to the Hurons and their French allies, and, during the French and Indian War of 1754–1763, struck deep into their former homelands. In one regard, this desperate effort only gave whites such as Tom Quick the excuse he needed to launch his own campaign of extirpation.

Tom Quick grew up strong and agile and cunning as any tribal warrior in the elm forests of northeastern Pennsylvania. From his earliest childhood, he played with Delaware children around his father's house in Matchepeconck ("beautiful valley" in the Lenni Lenape dialect), near present-day Milford. His closest friend was Mushwink, son of a Delaware chieftain. While Tom's father ground grain or cut timber that floated to his sawmill, where the Van de Mack creek met the Delaware River, Tom explored neighboring hills and woods with Mushwink. Tom learned to track like his friend, with great skill and daring, trapping bear and snaring partridges and hunting elk and deer with either bow or musket.

Tom's parents, who were Dutch, had come from New York in 1733 to build their first log house at Milford. By then the Delawares, a defeated tribe paying tribute to the Iroquois, had settled into a rather sophisticated civilization, side by side with their British allies, in a way of life that their leader, Teedyuscung, hoped would endure. This peace was marred only by periodic depredations by French-led renegade warriors. The population of the six-tribe Iroquois Confederacy, known also as the Six Nations, was never more than twelve thousand, including the estimated two thousand coastal Delawares, who hunted and fished from the top of the river after which they were named to the bottom of the bay of the same name. They spent their winters in the forests of Pennsylvania and New Jersey, migrating to the shore each summer to gather shellfish for food and shells from which to make wampum, their medium of exchange and diplomacy.

The Delawares and their cousins were well organized in battle, moved quickly and quietly, struck with ferocity, and did unspeakable things to their prisoners. Before the British settlers arrived, they were generally left alone to till corn and squash, dry fish, string beads, and puff calumets in the smoke-filled, elm-bark longhouses of their stockaded towns. They could afford to be generous and hospitable, since they inhabited land that was unimaginably rich—land that produced tender ears of corn up to twenty-four inches long and squashes the size of pumpkins.

Thanks to the Delawares' hospitality, the colony of Pennsylvania, peopled by pacifist English Quakers, had grown up without a shot being fired in anger in its first three-quarters of a century. Shortly after the first hundred shiploads of immigrants had arrived in 1682, William Penn, leader of these political and religious refugees, wrote back to potential colonists in London:

> The soil is good, air serene from the cedar, pine and sassafras with the wild myrtle of great fragrance . . . I have had better venison [here], bigger, and more tender, as fatt as in England. Turkeys of the wood I have had of 40 and 50 pound weight . . . flowers for color, largeness and beauty excel.

Penn's promotional literature and his policy of religious toleration packed Philadelphia with immigrants of every faith, even if his judgment in appointing governors to rule in his place was less than wise. One governor distinguished himself chiefly as a barroom brawler; with friends, including William Penn, Jr., he severely beat up the town constable. His successor bickered with the Assembly so regularly that its members refused to pay his salary. Infuriated, this governor left the province, but not before kicking a judge. Fifty years were to elapse, however, before Pennsylvania politicians caused any lasting problem.

The Delawares were generous to the New Yorkers migrating into their domain, among them the Quicks. As the couple produced children—ten of them, enough to make the elder Quick hustle about his gristmill and later his sawmill—the neighboring Delawares taught the family how to farm and hunt, brought them presents of fur, and taught them their language. Young Mushwink, son and heir of the local chieftain, virtually grew up at the Quick homestead, eating and playing and sleeping with the eldest Quick boy, Tom, Jr.

Young Tom was only three when William Penn's sons, hard pressed by creditors, sought to add to their real estate inventory by invoking an old promise made to their late father: He could extend his settlements "as far as a man can walk in a day and a half." In the first "Walking Purchase" in 1701, the elder Penn —strolling along with the Delaware chieftains, pushing branches aside, stopping often, smoking the calumet, exchanging pleasantries in their native tongue—had covered fifteen miles. This was the distance that the Delawares expected his sons to cover.

But now, in 1737, the Delawares were dealing with lawyers. The bargain did not specify which man should make the walk or exactly what route he should follow. The young Penns ordered a wide pathway cleared through the underbrush. They hired and trained the three fleetest white couriers in the colony and provided relays of horses and riders to take them food, drink, and fresh moccasins. Leaving Wrightstown in Bucks County at dawn on September 19, 1737, the whites, heeling and toeing furiously, quickly outdistanced their Delaware escorts.

By noon, the fastest woodsman had already covered twenty-one miles and had crossed the Lehigh River. Halting only fifteen minutes for a meal, he set off briskly and duly reached the end of the prepared road. After a short night's sleep, he was handed a compass, and he struck off to the northeast, taking a well-worn warrior path along the Delaware River to Milford at the present-day border with New York. By the time he stopped at midday, he had covered nearly seventy-two miles and had virtually doubled the Penn real estate holdings.

The Delawares honored their pledge. Slowly, mournfully, resentfully, they began to move farther west, many of them migrating over the next twenty years to the Ohio River valley, where they mixed with other displaced tribes and waited to take revenge on the British. Only at the top of the Delaware River, near the Quick homestead, did they linger in any significant numbers, around their family burial grounds.

The cycle of revenge and reprisal called the French and Indian Wars broke out in its final and bloodiest spasm in 1754, when a detachment of Virginia militia led by the young George Washington tried to construct a fort at the forks of the Ohio, Allegheny, and Monongahela rivers, only to clash with the French and be driven, humiliated, from the area.

In July 1755, seventy-five years of peace between whites and Indians in Pennsylvania ended when a British army led by General Edward Braddock trudged into a bloody three-hour crossfire near its destination on the Monongahela. Already the Indians, annoyed by the Penn land deals, had begun to listen to the promises of food and clothing made by the French, who were building the massive Fort Duquesne—now Pittsburgh—close to the site of Braddock's defeat. Chief Logan, the Iroquois Six Nations' representative to the Pennsylvania government, had warned a few months earlier:

> Whosoever of the white should venture to settle any land belonging hitherto to the Indians will have his creatures killed first, and then if they do not desist, they themselves would be killed, without distinction, let the consequence be what it would.

When no retaliation for the defeat of Braddock's army came from the pacifist Quakers, the French and their new allies sent out small raiding parties to attack isolated targets.* Then they became bolder. By October, bands of up to 250 Delawares were ranging east from Fort Duquesne. One large party struck at Penn's Creek on the Susquehanna River, within one hundred miles of Philadelphia. Postmaster Benjamin Franklin relayed word to London:

> Just now arrived in town an express from our frontiers with the bad news that eight families of Pennsylvanians were cut off last week. . . . Thirteen men and women were found scalped and dead and twelve children missing.

On October 11, in the first raid east of the Susquehanna, 120 warriors attacked farms just west of Reading. After killing fifteen men and women and scalping three children (who survived), they set fire to scores of houses and destroyed large

---

* Among these raiders was one son of Teedyuscung.

numbers of cattle and horses, as well as quantities of grain and fodder. In November another war party attacked the Moravian mission at Gnadenhütten, killed or captured the missionaries, and sacked and burned this symbol of integration with the Christian settlers. The Quick family and their white neighbors fled across the Delaware to a fortified stone house in New Jersey's Sussex County. There, in December, Thomas Quick and his eldest son, now twenty-one, joined Captain John Van Etten's company of militia.

Colonel Benjamin Franklin, chairman of the Pennsylvania Assembly's Defense Committee, ordered Van Etten to help build a series of small forts in the fifty-mile stretch of the Pocono Mountains between Milford and the Delaware Water Gap, the area ceded after the 1737 Walking Purchase. The company stayed on active duty for about a year and a half, basing itself in the Minisink Valley just south of Milford. Each man was paid six dollars a month plus one dollar for the use of his musket and blanket, since pacifist Pennsylvania had no munitions to issue.

In their flight, the Quicks and their neighbors had managed to carry off only enough grain for a month. After the militia members had built stockades and cut gun slits, they stood guard as the settlers harvested and threshed their corn and as the Quicks milled it and stuffed it into heavy grists before hauling the sacks to canoes and transporting them to the Sussex fort. On Colonel Franklin's orders, most of the militia then began patrolling the five miles of hills to the outpost of the next fort to the southeast. Among Franklin's orders, which carried the authority of Governor Robert Hunter Morris, was permission to scalp Indians:

> You are to acquaint the Men that, if in their ranging, they meet with, or are at any Time attacked by the Enemy, and killing any of them, Forty Dollars [the equivalent of six months' pay] will be allowed and paid by the Government for each Scalp of an Indian Enemy so killed, the same being produced with proper attestations.

Under a new moon at the end of November, the Delawares attacked all along the line of settlements planted since the Walking Purchase. In the Minisink region alone, scores of farms were laid waste, houses and barns burned, and at least twelve farmers killed. At Easton, Franklin was rallying and training the survivors.* On Christmas Day he described the devastation in a report to the governor:

> The Country all above this Town for 50 miles is mostly evacuated and ruined. . . . The People are chiefly fled into the Jerseys. . . . The Enemy made but few Prisoners, murdering almost all that fell into their Hands, of all Ages and both Sexes. All Business is at an End. . . . The few remaining starving inhabitants . . . are quite dejected and dispirited.

Inside the stockade on the Delaware River, hunger and illness grew worse as the weeks dragged. Late one afternoon in early February 1756, Thomas Quick, his son Tom, and a son-in-law strapped on snowshoes, hoisted heavy grists of corn onto their shoulders, and headed for the mill, which stood about a mile away across the frozen Delaware. All night they labored, grinding the corn into flour, until at dawn they recrossed the ice. The elder Quick, fallen behind under the weight he carried, had just reached midriver as shots rang out and he dropped. His attackers yelled and rushed toward him, but young Tom reached him first and began to drag him away.

"I'm a dead man," whispered his father. "I can go no farther. Leave me. Run for your lives."

Reluctantly, Tom and his brother-in-law escaped across the river and stumbled up the bank. They could hear the chilling cries of the Delaware warriors and make out their faces. Tom recognized his boyhood companion, Mushwink, bending over his father.

---

* Franklin had the help of his son William, a captain in the Grenadier Guards in King George's War of the 1740s.

Mushwink, now a full-fledged chief, had been selected at a tribal council to lead the attack on his native Matchepeconck. He had given the Milford settlers a single warning to leave, kidnapping Tom Quick's young niece and then freeing her unharmed. Now Mushwink and his warriors scalped Tom's father, rifled his pockets, and cut off his silver sleeve buttons and shoe buckles.

The shooting had alerted the militia, which came to cover Tom's escape. After the attackers left, he went back and retrieved the mutilated corpse of his father. Whether it was that day or soon thereafter, Tom Quick vowed to avenge his father's death by killing one hundred Delawares. In family papers, his oath was recorded: "The blood of the whole Indian race is not sufficient to atone for the blood of my father."

Over the next forty years, Tom made hunting down and killing Delawares his profession and obsession. Setting about his mission of vengeance with grim precision, he equipped himself with "Long Tom," a Pennsylvania rifle with a fifty-eight-inch barrel that he could aim with deadly accuracy at long range. Nobody knows the name of the first Delaware man or woman he killed or just how much money he claimed for the grisly proof of his handiwork that he bore to the Pennsylvania authorities, but the scalping bounty remained $40 until the end of the French and Indian War in 1763. The same year, when the uprising led by Chief Pontiac swept from the Illinois country to the Pennsylvania frontier, Governor John Penn, grandson of the first Quaker proprietor, increased the scalp bounty. Any Indian male above age ten who was captured alive fetched a $150 bounty. Scalped, he was worth only $134. A female over ten brought only $30.

At a time when many Americans were coming to hate Indians absolutely and generally, Tom Quick became celebrated as Pennsylvania's foremost Indian killer. One story circulated that during Pontiac's Rebellion he even ambushed women and children. He would sometimes lure Delawares to his campfire for a hot supper and a warm night's rest—and then kill them in their sleep. He invited unsuspecting braves to hunt with him, then pushed them off cliffs. He set up elaborate little massacres that sometimes bothered even his calloused neighbors. After butchering one Delaware's entire family, he was asked why he hadn't spared the baby. "Because," he said, "nits make lice."

Scouring the mountains of Pennsylvania, New Jersey, and New York for his quarry, Tom Quick soon became quarry himself after Delaware councils began to notice that entire parties were not returning from hunting trips. He was captured five times but always managed to escape, taking more scalps as he went. One Delaware prophet cast this divination: "The missing braves have fallen victim to the rifle of Tom Quick, who haunts the forest of the Delaware like an evil spirit."

Three of Mushwink's young warriors volunteered to track Quick down and bring back his scalp. When they finally found him after a year's search, Quick detected their ambush and set one of his own, shooting two braves as they glided by in a canoe. Quick allowed the third man to escape so that he would take back word of the humiliation. In the warriors' canoe Tom found his father's Meerschaum pipe, engraved "TQ 1724."

Tom Quick and Long Tom eventually triggered an uproar in official Philadelphia, as aggrieved Quaker merchants demanded an end to his depredations. After the French finally surrendered in 1763, Philadelphia firms negotiated trading rights with tribes throughout Pennsylvania and the Ohio Valley. Now the tribesmen were to exchange their pelts for guns and powder, hatchets and knives, clothing and trade goods made in Britain instead of France. But such commercial considerations did not sway Tom Quick from his revenge.

Late in 1764, he found himself at Christopher Decker's tavern on Neversink Mountain near present-day Reading, Pennsylvania. There, one evening shortly before the end of Pontiac's Rebellion, a Delaware came up and offered to drink with him. Maybe Tom Quick recognized him in the dim, guttering candlelight of the tavern but probably he did not, for it had been nearly ten years since his father's murder. In any case, Quick refused. The Delaware, very drunk, persisted.

"You hate Delawares," he said in English. "I hate you."

Quick still refused.

"You kill Delawares. I kill your father."

"Prove it."

Staggering to him, the man pulled out the silver sleeve buttons cut from Tom's father's coat. "See?"

Quick jumped up and grabbed a musket off the tavern wall. "March," he ordered, shoving Mushwink ahead of him out the door. "You will never kill another white man." Moments later, there was a shot.

Mushwink's murder deep inside Pennsylvania in peacetime finally brought about Tom Quick's arrest. It was not so much the murder of Mushwink—who had probably been as drunk when he scalped Tom's father as he was when Tom shot him— as the fact that it occurred after the peace treaty, to the detriment of business as usual. So long as Tom Quick preyed on them, the Delawares were understandably reluctant to come out to trade. A Berks County justice of the peace issued a warrant, and a platoon of militia arrested Quick, who was bound, tied to a sled, and driven south to stand trial for murder.

But Tom Quick had many friends. At Milford, Daniel Van Gordon learned of Tom's destination and dashed back to Decker's tavern to tip off the townspeople. When the prison cavalcade halted at the tavern, where Quick had killed Mushwink, the whole town turned out, feigning a celebration to honor the militia for capturing the feared Indian killer. Decker played his fiddle, women danced with the militiamen, and barmaids distributed free hot toddy—and meanwhile someone cut Tom Quick's ropes and helped him from the sled. Dashing for the river, Quick plunged through the ice and swam to Pinckney's Island, where a hundred-man posse somehow failed to find him. In several weeks Quick resumed his quiet miller's life at Milford, with only occasional outings to hunt Delawares far away. No further attempts were made to arrest him.

As the years passed, the opportunities to kill a Delaware close to home became increasingly rare. For Tom Quick, the biggest problem was that as a result of a series of treaties with the British colonial authorities in the late 1760s, the Delaware nation had withdrawn west of the Ohio River. He nevertheless continued to pursue the Delawares, ranging as far as four hundred miles from home, until the Revolution intervened.

Tom Quick's name does not appear on any Revolutionary War muster roll. His services, if he did in fact offer them to the Revolutionary army, might have proved an embarrassment, since the Delawares were the first northern tribe to sign a separate peace treaty with the Continental Congress. It was their mistaken understanding that at the war's end they would become the fourteenth state.

Tom Quick's personal war with the Delawares undoubtedly contributed to the deteriorating relationship between settlers in the remote frontier valleys and the tribes that sided with the British. His unappeased appetite for revenge fueled the ferocious cycle of reprisal and counterreprisal that ultimately destroyed the entire Iroquois Confederacy. Much as he may have wanted to, Tom Quick did not choose—or perhaps was not allowed— to play a part in the final eradication of Indian power in New York and Pennsylvania. That is a story that grows out of, and belongs with, his.

By the summer of 1778, the American Revolution had settled into a long stalemate; for the first time, George Washington could turn to dealing with the Indian problem on the frontiers. His relations with the Indians had never been good, and war exacerbated them. The Iroquois had aligned themselves with their old allies, the British. Loyalists from the Mohawk Valley in New York escaped to Fort Niagara and persuaded the Iroquois tribes of the Mohawks, the Cayugas, and the Senecas to rally to the standard of George III. With Loyalist rangers under Major John Butler and his son, Walter, they raided frontier villages for hundreds of miles, pillaging, burning, and scalping. Early in June, a force out of Niagara destroyed the settlements in the Wyoming Valley near present-day Wilkes-Barre, Pennsylvania. John Butler reported taking 227 scalps and only five prisoners.

The Wyoming massacre shocked and terrified the frontier and spawned numerous atrocity stories. For example, it was said that Queen Esther, the half-breed Seneca, had arranged fifteen

victims in a ring and, circling and singing a dirge, had tomahawked them one by one.

Led by Mushwink's son, a band of renegade Delawares
fighting alongside the British struck farther east and succeeded
in capturing Tom Quick and his seventeen-year-old niece, Mag-
gie, while the pair were canoeing. Two of the Delawares were
appointed to march them off to certain torture and death. But
one night, as their two captors were bending over a fire, cooking
the day's catch of trout, Quick got loose and sprang, killing
both men with their own hatchets. It was the last time anyone
tried to bring Tom Quick to account.

When more joint Loyalist-Indian expeditions raided German Flats on the Mohawk River (below Utica) in September
1778 and struck Cherry Valley, only fifty miles west of Albany,
in November, Washington decided to detach enough Continentals in the spring to destroy the Iroquois homelands of the
Finger Lakes and the Genesee Valley of western New York. He
chose Major John Sullivan of New Hampshire and gave him
terse, carefully formulated orders. "The immediate objects are
the total destruction and devastation of their settlements. . . .
[The Iroquois lands] may not be merely overrun, but destroyed."
Tom Quick would have approved.

Sullivan was to lead a three-pronged attack, assembling his
main force of 2,500 Continentals at Easton, Pennsylvania. General James Clinton of New York was to start from Albany with
1,500 Continentals and proceed to the headwaters of the Susquehanna River at Otsego Lake and descend the river to meet
Sullivan at Tioga. A third column was to set out from Fort Pitt
(the former Fort Duquesne) with 600 regulars, under Colonel
Daniel Brodhead. In all, Washington had detached 4,600 Continentals, nearly one-third of his regulars. Sullivan was also to
take artillery. The Iroquois, in all of their century-long wars
with European colonists, had never faced cannon. Washington
stipulated that Sullivan's men were to attack with bayonet and
war whoop, "with as much impetuosity, shouting, and noise as
possible."

Three months of delays for supplies and road building for

1,200 pack horses, 100 officers' mounts, and 700 cattle for "beef on the hoof" brought Sullivan's main force to Tioga by August 11, 1779. The Seneca stronghold with "Queen Esther's Palace" was deserted. Deserters had alerted Loyalist John Butler to Sullivan's expedition, but the British commander at Quebec, the Swiss-born General Frederick Haldimand, shrugged off the report: "It is impossible the Rebels can be in such force as has been represented by the deserters." But green-uniformed Loyalist rangers roused the Indians to prepare to defend their homeland.

Meanwhile, General Clinton had assembled his 1,500 men at Canajoharie, forty miles west of Albany on the Mohawk, with two hundred bateaux, or flat-bottomed boats. He cut a twenty-five-mile road over a high ridge and downhill to Lake Otsego. Hauling his boats by wagon to the lake's northern tip and rowing them to present-day Cooperstown, he camped and waited for Sullivan. He was chagrined to find out how low the Susquehanna River was as it flowed out of the lake. Ingeniously, he ordered a temporary dam built. Six weeks later, on August 9, when a courier brought word from Sullivan to begin moving south, Clinton breached the dam, and the bateaux floated thirty miles in one day. En route, the New York troops burned deserted Indian villages. At Onondaga, a Loyalist settlement, they torched a Christian church and some log houses with stone chimneys and glass windows. When they rendezvoused with Sullivan, a military band sent along by Washington "played beautiful" as artillery fired a salute.

The delays now proved fortuitous. The Indians' ripe crops awaited as the troops attacked Chemung two days later. Fields full of corn, beans, squashes, and pumpkins either fed the New York troops or were destroyed. The Indians fled, sniping from the woods while the soldiers gorged. One soldier wrote that he ate ten ears of corn, a quart of beans, and seven squashes. The troops marched off with pumpkins impaled on their bayonets.

On August 27, 1779, Sullivan's four-thousand-man combined expeditionary force moved north with nine fieldpieces, including four six-pounders, four three-pounders, and a cohorn

—a small, easily portable mortar that was also called a "grass-hopper." The packhorses hauled solid shot and canister shot (the latter was timed to explode in the air and shower the enemy with small projectiles).

Many of Sullivan's officers blamed the artillery for slowing down the march. Major Jeremiah Fogg recorded in his diary, "The transportation . . . appears to the army in general as impractical, and absurd as an attempt to level the Allegheny Mountains."

But when Sullivan's army struggled up the narrow, steep Chemung Valley defile and approached the Indian village of Newtown on August 29, the artillery proved welcome. Sullivan had brought along several Oneida scouts. One of them climbed a tree on a 700-foot hill and made out painted Indians crouching behind a log breastwork camouflaged with green branches. With the Loyalist-Iroquois force in position, a thousand Indians under Chief Joseph Brant, as well as 250 of Butler's rangers and fifteen British redcoats, awaited Sullivan's advance.

Sullivan halted his column, sending a strong force to attack the hilltop detachment from the rear. He placed his artillery and opened fire on the breastwork with solid shot, spraying the defenders with canisters loaded with grapeshot and iron spikes. The terrified Iroquois endured the cannonade for half an hour, but the shells bursting behind them convinced them that the enemy had outflanked them. They ran, the Loyalists with them. On the hilltop, the Indians and Continentals seesawed in hand-to-hand combat until Brant signaled them to flee. Sullivan had lost only three men killed and thirty-six wounded; twelve Indian men and one woman died. The men were all scalped. One Continental officer skinned two Indians from the hips down to make two pairs of leggings, one for himself, one for his major.

While casualties on both sides were light at the Battle of Newtown, the artillery barrage was decisive. The terrified Iroquois never again put up a fight. Sullivan's army was unopposed as it burned a swath from Elmira—where the men cut down eighteen-foot stalks of corn—to the Saint Lawrence River and the southwest into the Genesee country. Detachments raided and burned Indian settlements in the Mohawk Valley, on the west side of Seneca Lake, and on both sides of Cayuga Lake. Typically, in a principal Indian riverside village southwest of present-day Geneseo, the army collected an immense amount of corn, packed it into more than a hundred well-appointed, "very large and elegant" houses, and then burned them all. At Aurora they girdled and destroyed 1,500 peach trees. In all, Sullivan's army of four thousand (Brodhead's column had turned back for want of shoes) destroyed forty villages and an estimated 160,000 bushels of corn, plus immeasurable quantities of other vegetables and fruits.

Marching back to Elmira, the army celebrated its five-hundred-mile expedition to the roar of triumphant fireworks and an ox roast, with a bull and a barrel of rum for each brigade. A few days later, back at Tioga, they put on war paint. Led by an Oneida sachem they joined in a war dance, each step ending with a whoop. Finally demolishing their forts, they returned to the Wyoming Valley. They had lost only forty men and had virtually eliminated the Iroquois Confederacy. Its survivors crowded into Fort Niagara and, as Washington had hoped, consumed precious British supplies all winter.

Tom Quick survived the Revolution, and at some point notched his ninety-ninth Delaware. In the end he fell victim as had thousands of Indians—to the white man's disease, smallpox. In 1796, at age sixty-two, Tom Quick lay dying in his substantial stone home in Milford, his family gathered around him. A daughter later recorded his dying wish: that a final, hundredth Delaware be brought close enough for him to fire Long Tom, though its stock was all but worn away. But there were no Delawares left for three hundred miles. Tom Quick died disappointed.

❧

NEARLY A CENTURY LATER, in August 1889, near the site of the scalping of Tom Quick's father, a crowd gathered for the dedication of a handsome, eleven-foot monument. It was

erected to the memory of Tom Quick, the Indian slayer . . .
the Avenger of the Delaware . . . and of his father Thomas
Quick, Sr.—the latter the first white settler and the former the first white child born on the site of the present
Borough of Milford.

There was no list of the victims of this serial killer. Nobody
knows the name of the first person he killed or of the ninety-
ninth; only his boyhood friend, his betrayer Mushwink, earned
a place in the family records.

The monument in Centre Square was dedicated in an oration
by a young hometown politician, Gifford Pinchot, recently
graduated from Yale and later to become the famed conserva-
tionist governor of Pennsylvania, and another by William Bross,
lieutenant governor of Illinois. A descendant of Tom Quick,
Bross had published *Legend of the Delaware: An Historical Sketch
of Tom Quick,* a local best-seller. About two thousand people
packed the town for a day of speeches and celebrations. The next
morning the *New York Times* carried its own paeans of praise,
under the headline "In Honor of Tom Quick."

GOVERNOR
WILLIAM FRANKLIN,
LOYAL SON

*F*OR THE FOURTH ICY JANUARY DAY SINCE
they had left the fortified town of Bethlehem, the Pennsylvania militiamen slogged northwest along the Lehigh River. Hunched under sodden wool coats, they bent into the blistering cold wind, their muskets hanging heavily in the hard, slanting rain. Aware that the natives were spying them out, they scanned the thick rocky cover to the left, and the bushes, boulders, and trees to the right. As they trudged along the narrow wagon road, their boots crunching through ice-crusted puddles, they covered no more than a mile an hour, occasionally looking up for signals from the officer at the head of the column.

Captain William Franklin, the only seasoned officer on the march, rode the lead horse, his scarlet grenadier's uniform a conspicuous target for Indian snipers. He had deployed his 172-man force with an eye to avoiding the fatal mistakes made by General Edward Braddock, whose campaign to Fort Duquesne had so recently ended in disaster, with half the British troops killed in battle and four hundred settlers dying in subsequent raids. Here, Franklin strung out twenty-two cavalrymen behind him to give the appearance of a much larger force. Behind them, single file, marched the Pennsylvania militia, ready to take cover quickly. A small contingent of scouts shielded the main body against ambush, probing thickets and ravines and occupying hills as the column approached. Bringing up the rear were heavy Conestoga wagons pulled by six-horse teams. Halfway back in the column, clad in a great blue coat, rode Benjamin Franklin, colonel of the militia and father of Captain Franklin.

The two men in charge of the grim little column personified the changes sweeping war-torn America as 1756 began. Benjamin Franklin, at fifty, had already lived through two wars between the British and French colonial empires. Half his age, William, his illegitimate son, had already been hardened by years of military service on the frontier, by long canoe trips into the wilderness. He had been at home on horseback since he was ten.

In a typically succinct piece of New England crackerbarrel wisdom, John Adams once said that his father had worked the soil so that he could study law so that *his* son could be a poet. No clearer example of this American evolution can be found than the Franklin family. From Josiah, wool dyer turned soap chandler, to Benjamin, printer turned statesman, the Franklin family continued to evolve. Benjamin's son grew up a tradesman's son with gentlemanly pretensions, learning French, limning poems in Philadelphia's genteel provincial society, and yearning to go to London.

William Franklin was self-assured, having assimilated all his father's hard-bought knowledge, wealth, and position, and he was determined to find new ways to shape the world his generation would inherit. The two men were unusually close, together attacking any enemy, political or military, who threatened either of them as vehemently as they would later oppose each other.

Sadly, William Franklin's contributions to his father's successes—political, military, and scientific—for twenty-five years before the Revolution have been all but forgotten. After they became enemies, Benjamin all but expunged his son from his famous autobiography. Only a few telltale reminders of how close they had once been remained unedited. Franklin's famous memoir began, "Dear Son." And when he wrote thirty years later about their dangerous fort-building expedition on the Pennsylvania frontier, Benjamin acknowledged that William had been "of great use" to him.

◄≡►

UNTIL HIS DYING DAY, William Franklin was apparently unsure of the date of his birth, although he always referred to Deborah Read Franklin as his mother. Benjamin Franklin remained silent on the subject and on the question of who William's mother was, even to his own family, for twenty years. In 1750, he told his own mother that William was just nineteen—when William had already been away from his Philadelphia home for four years, including two as an army officer. It was not a likely story, but Benjamin was clearly ashamed to tell his parents the full truth. He never revealed the identity of William's mother, ever since then a subject of political and historical speculation.

There was nothing luxurious about William's early childhood as he grew up above the Franklin printing shop and general store. Benjamin had an almost spiritual attachment to meager meals served plainly. Deborah helped long hours in the shop, ran their house, took care of William, made all their clothes, and destroyed her eyesight by hand-sewing bindings on books and pamphlets at night by candlelight. Six years after Benjamin took Deborah as his common-law wife, she bore Benjamin another son, Francis, who died of smallpox.

In the time of William's boyhood, growing up in Philadelphia meant following the seasons: kite flying in spring, swimming and fishing in summer, skating and sledding in the long winters. Young Franklin also took part in activities frowned on in the Quaker city, such as amateur theatricals in a warehouse, or horse racing on Race Street. But long periods of boredom intervened, and ships arriving with goods from as far away as India made William restless. They came up the Delaware laden with prizes from King George's War. Their crews carried sacks of gold to spend freely in the shops and taverns. It was only a

[48]

matter of time before William did as his father had done and tried to run away to sea.

Like so many fathers, Benjamin Franklin was too busy during the boy's adolescence to notice subtle changes in his son. When Benjamin was not in his print shop or at the State House copying down debates, he was traveling on Post Office business or running meetings of the numerous societies he founded to improve city life. His conversations must have been sprinkled with bits of wisdom that rarely probed a boy's problems or even called for an answer. If there were problems in the rented house on Race Street they had recently moved to, Benjamin Franklin was unaware of them.

At fifteen, William ran away. Franklin hurried from ship to ship, looking for him. In his memoirs Franklin recalled:

> My only son left my house unknown to us all and got on board a privateer, from whence I fetched him. No one imagined it was hard usage at home that made him do this. Everyone that knows me thinks I am too indulgent a parent as well as master. When boys see prizes brought in and quantities of money shared among the men and their gay living, it fills their heads with notions that half distract them and put them quite out of conceit with trades and the dull ways of getting money by working.

Until then, Benjamin had devoted little thought to his son's future. William had been tutored in math, cast his father's meteorological charts for *Poor Richard's Almanac,* read proof, kept the books for his business, and helped to supervise the apprentices. His father had talked, briefly, about founding a college in Philadelphia, but that dream was realized too late for William. It did not seem possible for William to continue his education as his friends had done. For lack of money, his formal education was over. If the young man wanted adventure, Benjamin reasoned, let him join the troops enlisting for the latest British expedition against French Canada. The privations of military life would surely make him eager to return to the comforts of a tradesman's life.

To Franklin's surprise, William did not hurry back. He thrived on the dangers of frontier war. He learned drill and discipline, tactics, weaponry, and fortifications. In August 1746, after French-led Indians attacked and burned Saratoga, New York, and then surrounded Albany, William, fitted out in a red ensign's uniform, rode north with a company of German-born laborer volunteers called "pioneers." The Pennsylvania troops found themselves surrounded by a large and determined force. William's regiment was slowly decimated by wounds, disease, and desertion. Hunting parties sent from their crude stockade were ambushed, and on one occasion, sixteen men were killed. Men who went out to fish were tomahawked. Yet William didn't complain—and he didn't hurry home. The youngest of the Pennsylvania officers, he was promoted to the highest provincial rank, captain, and he was praised in official dispatches for his conspicuous bravery on patrols. But Benjamin did not mention his own son's promotion in his newspaper, the *Pennsylvania Gazette*.

Captain Franklin's dreams of a military career did not die naturally: they were killed by lack of money. To become a career officer in the British military establishment meant buying a commission from the colonel of a regiment when a post became vacant. When the war ended, there were more officers available than regular army commissions. Even though William had gained personal distinction and cultivated prominent connections, his father showed no interest in laying out the large amount of cash needed to buy him a commission.

Unwilling to return to his father's shop, William, who had learned of a major expedition by Philadelphia merchants into Indian country, signed on as representative of the Pennsylvania Land Office to make the trek with Pennsylvania Indian agent Conrad Weiser. Appointed official courier, William attended the Treaty of Lancaster of 1748, where fifty-five Indian leaders offered Philadelphia merchants the exclusive franchise for fur trading. When Weiser, leader of the first Pennsylvania trade mission to the Ohio Valley, left Lancaster to plant the British flag west of the Alleghenies for the first time, he asked Captain Franklin to go along as Land Office agent. As the first British officer to carry the Union Jack across the mountains, he sensed the great promise of the West and his own place in it.

Young Franklin returned from his thousand-mile trek by horse and canoe something of a celebrity, but his father was unimpressed:

> Will is now nineteen years of age, a tall proper youth, and much of a beau. He acquired a habit of idleness on the expedition, but begins of late to apply himself to business, and I hope will become an industrious man. He imagined his father had got enough for him, but I have assured him that I intend to spend what little I have, myself, if it please God that I live long enough.

In William's years away in the army, he missed his father's first experiments with electricity, but he quickly made himself invaluable as his father's laboratory assistant. When the elder Franklin traveled, he left instructions that electricity from thunderstorms passing overhead should be gathered in great glass bottles. When Benjamin was ready to test his lightning rods, William scaled the roofs to install them. And when Benjamin was ready for his climactic experiment to draw lightning from the clouds with the aid of a kite and a key, it was William who designed and built the kite. Three times he raced across a cow pasture in an electrical storm to get the kite aloft while Benjamin stood sheltered in a shepherd's shed.

The Franklins' kite-and-key experiment proved that lightning was electricity, but establishing from what direction the current came was a more difficult question to resolve. Benjamin assumed that it came down from electrical storms, but in July 1753, William was able to demonstrate that the opposite was true. Benjamin was in Boston on postal inspections one night when a heavy dark cloud passed over their workshop during a downpour. Lightning flashed through a three-story house nearby, blasting out bricks, boring holes in the woodwork, melting lead sashweights, singeing roofing shingles. William, clambering over the roof, prying into every corner of the house, took notes and made drawings in a long, excited letter to prove to his father that the lightning had passed *upward*. Nearly ten years later, when Oxford University awarded Benjamin an honorary doctorate, university overseers voted William an honorary master's degree for his contributions.

※

As BENJAMIN FRANKLIN devoted more time to politics, he gave William a share in this work as well. Elected to the Pennsylvania Assembly in 1751, he turned his paid post of Assembly clerk over to his son. When he became deputy postmaster general for North America, he appointed William postmaster of Philadelphia and comptroller of the North American postal system, a job requiring skill in accounting, tact in collecting money, and patience in making detailed reports.

At age twenty, William decided to pursue a legal career. He went to work as a clerk in the law office of Joseph Galloway, a member of the town's elite group. Benjamin had a low opinion of lawyers. "God works wonders now and then./ Behold, a lawyer, an honest man," wrote Poor Richard. Yet Franklin promised his son that when he had completed the customary three-year term of clerkship in the office of a leading lawyer, he would send him to England to study at the Inns of Court, the ancient law school in London.

The personable young William, on good terms with all factions of Philadelphia society, contributed to the success of the elder Franklin's political and civic efforts. Yet each year he was becoming less attracted to his father's artisan friends and more closely linked to his father's rivals. Joining a circle of aristocratic young friends, William danced with the daughters and wives of the Penn political faction as a founding member of the Philadelphia Dancing Assembly. And when French and Indian attacks came in 1755, he organized the best-equipped, best-trained horsemen into a cavalry unit, helping his father to raise the rest of the five-hundred-man militia.

With four-fifths of Pennsylvania controlled by the French, the Franklins led a relief expedition to fortify the frontier towns from Lancaster northeast to Bethlehem, Easton, and the Pocono mountains on the New York border. The Franklin plan called for building standardized frontier forts fifty feet square armed with small swivel guns—taken from ships in Philadelphia harbor—to be manned by sharpshooters firing from platforms and twin blockhouses. Indians rarely attacked a fortified place; and a log fort, though rickety, was safe against an enemy who had no artillery. Forts were to be built every ten miles along seventy miles of mountains to shelter frontier families. Ranger companies, organized and trained by Captain Franklin, were to patrol constantly between the forts to guard against surprise attacks. It was William, acting as his father's aide-de-camp, who did all the training and wrote out all the orders, drawing on his British army training. In seven weeks of building a fort every five days, the Franklins, never closer in all their twenty-five years of collaboration, spiked the French and Indian winter offensive.

⊰⬒⊱

THE DASHING VETERAN of the French wars met seventeen-year-old Elizabeth Graeme, daughter of Dr. Thomas Graeme, a member of the governor's council and one of Benjamin's political rivals, at the Assembly balls in the late winter of 1756. It did not please Benjamin that his son was dancing every week with the daughter of a political enemy. When he founded the Pennsylvania Hospital and, as president, hired its first staff, Franklin did not hire Graeme. Graeme never forgave him. Opposition from both armed camps did not deter William from courting Betsy and, one year later, proposing marriage to her. Their engagement came at a time when Benjamin was determined to break the Penn family's control of Pennsylvania.

Appointed the Assembly's agent to Parliament in London, he had his son appointed the clerk of the mission. William wanted to know why he should leave the promise of a marriage that assured not only his happiness but his success. To win over his son, Benjamin offered to pay the young man's expenses to study law at the Middle Temple, assuring that he would be admitted to the London bar and become a leading American lawyer. He also wrote a new will, making William his heir and executor as well as leaving his son a legacy equal to five years of his own current income, a house, a town lot, Benjamin's extensive library, and all his scientific apparatus. These tempting opportunities proved too much for William. When he proposed a secret marriage, Betsy, apparently afraid to infuriate her father, declined. They postponed their wedding until he returned. After he reached London, their letters grew shorter, fewer. Then William stopped writing to Betsy altogether.

DURING HIS FIRST YEAR in London, William crammed massive doses of law. By the end of the autumn term of 1758, he was ready to stand before the Masters of the Bench at Middle Temple Hall for a grueling oral examination. On November 10, after processing with his classmates down the aisle of Westminster Abbey, William Franklin, bastard son of a provincial printer, was called to the English bar. That evening at the Middle Temple, William Franklin, Esquire, took his turn at the dark little table made from a hatch cover of Sir Francis Drake's flagship, *Golden Hind,* and signed the call book. Then he was invited up to the Bench. He had become an English gentleman.

England's foremost publisher, William Strahan, described William as "one of the prettiest young gentlemen I ever knew." William went to work in the law office of the influential barrister Richard Jackson, who introduced him to influential friends. He accompanied Jackson to fashionable Tunbridge Wells spa with his good friends Dr. Johnson, Mrs. Thrale, and the actor David Garrick. William, Benjamin, and "Omniscient" Jackson, as he was known, collaborated on *An Historical Review of the Government and Constitution of Pennsylvania,* an incendiary anti-Penn book that verged on libel and sedition. In private, Benjamin gave William much of the credit: "Billy afforded great assistance and furnished most of the materials," he wrote. Benjamin was clearly pleased by the effort. He shipped five hundred copies back to Philadelphia for sale in his bookstore and then had William pack several dozen copies into their carriage for distribution to influential politicians as they toured England and Scotland together in the summer of 1759, a time that Benjamin considered "six weeks of the *densest* happiness I have ever met with in any part of my life."

But for William, now twenty-nine, living and working at such close quarters was beginning to gall. He wanted a career and a private life of his own. In London the young Franklin sought both; giving up the idea of marrying Betsy Graeme, he joined wholeheartedly in the society of Northumberland House. Next to a direct royal summons to the Court of Saint James, an invitation there was a sure sign of Court favor, of a young man's chances to rise in the new imperial society and find a substantial post in the expanding colonial service. It must have been at one of the Friday evening parties there that he met a golden-skinned, languidly gracious beauty named Elizabeth Downes, daughter of a Barbados sugar planter. By the spring of 1761, as a new king, George III, waited to be crowned and the whole kingdom seemed to angle for his favors, William and Elizabeth became fixtures in London society, dancing at balls, strolling in Saint James's Park, frequently attending the theatre in Covent Garden.

So high was William's star rising that he was invited to the coronation of George III. William marched in the royal procession into Westminster Hall and to an assigned seat while Benjamin had to stand outside. Three weeks afterward, a new prime minister, the Earl of Bute, began a shakeup of royal posts. On August 20, 1762, Lord Bute informed the Board of Trade that the king "was pleased to appoint William Franklin, Esq. to be Governor of Nova Caesarea, or New Jersey." For the rest of William's life, it was his glory that he was the first royal governor appointed by the new king. But at this hour of his son's greatest triumph, Benjamin Franklin left England without him, also skipping William's marriage. Four days before he was sworn in as governor, William married Elizabeth Downes.

※

ON THE ICY MORNING of February 25, 1763, a gay cavalcade of sleigh-riding aristocrats rode out to welcome William and Elizabeth Franklin into the eastern capital of Perth Amboy, one of the province of New Jersey's two government centers. Indeed, as the townspeople managed a swirling welcome, there was little to hint that Franklin, already a career politician, would remain in the Jerseys any longer than it had taken his predecessors to find more lucrative posts elsewhere in His Majesty's service. If he planned to base his career on his first experience administering a colony, there were challenges enough in governing the 70,000-odd farmers and townspeople. Sixty years of royal rule had done little more than unite the two provinces of East and West Jersey on paper. The colony still had no governor's residence, no government buildings, no acceptable boundary line, few good roads and bridges, no thriving seaport, and only one incipient college at Princeton. Worse still, from Governor Franklin's standpoint, winter and summer the governor was obliged to curry favor among penny-pinching legislators to have his salary renewed, hopefully at no decrease, for it was cynically assumed he would find some device for enhancing his meager allowance.

If he succeeded in keeping the delicate peace among liberal western Quakers, conservative eastern gentry, and thousands of riot-prone Scots-Irish squatters in the north, if he somehow followed the outdated, unsympathetic, yet dreadfully precise instructions of the remote commissioners of trade in London, William could expect, in a reasonable number of years, advancement out of the colony. At first it appeared that young Franklin faced the additional handicap of his shadowy birth. "It is no less amazing than true," wrote irate Pennsylvania proprietor John Penn to his friend William Alexander in New Jersey, "If any *gentleman* had been appointed it would have been a difference

. . . I make no doubt but the people of New Jersey will make some remonstrance upon this indignity put upon them."

If the legislators assembling in the western provincial capital at Burlington in May 1763 objected to the bar sinister on the new governor's coat of arms, they did not show it. They increased his salary by a healthy two hundred pounds sterling and voted him a housing allowance. Apparently, many were pleased with his good sense in passing up the invitation to reside in the eastern capital at Perth Amboy; the nearly completed proprietary palace there was a symbol of friction between poor rural voters and land-rich proprietors.

Instead, Franklin chose the bustling river town of Burlington, a seat of Quaker dominance only seventeen miles upriver from Philadelphia in neighboring Pennsylvania. He began buying up real estate. He built a handsome three-story brick house of his own. He could sit on the columned porch, look out over the broad lawn to the sycamore-lined Delaware River, and ponder the problems that had plagued every governor in the colony's history: insufficient currency, almost no foreign exchange, simmering feuds over land titles, and no way to pay official salaries without—in his view—groveling before the Assembly. From his veranda, he could see a possible solution to this last problem. In the Delaware River were unclaimed islands with rich farmland. It occurred to him that this land might be annexed by the Crown, rented back to farmers, and the income thus realized earmarked to pay official salaries. He communicated this scheme to London at once.

While there was no guarantee that the Assembly would abide such a barefaced grab for its power over the purse strings, it was nevertheless ominous for Franklin that the commissioners of trade in London ignored his request and left his administration at the mercy of the Assembly. Without support from London on this key issue, it would be virtually impossible for him to untangle the colony's growing fiscal problems, which multiplied as the economy deflated after the French and Indian War.

Although New Jersey had suffered minor casualties at the

hands of marauding Indians along its exposed northwest frontier, it had gained great dividends in the war. Great Britain had poured in troops, who freely spent hard money. Parliament had paid subsidies to the Jerseymen—funds that were applied, in an early example of revenue sharing, to eliminate provincial taxes. The hungry war machine had exchanged hard coin of the realm for hemp, black oak, and pine for shipbuilding; wheat, corn, and cotton; barrel hoops and staves; anything, in fact, that could assist in the worldwide struggle. In a temporary lapse of mercantilism and the royal prerogative, the British had even allowed the Assembly to issue paper money, which debt-ridden colonists shrewdly sent to creditors back in Britain to retire long-standing accounts.

But with the signing of the Treaty of Paris in 1763, the boom swung back, the artificial prosperity deflated, and the second smallest populace in any colony in America woke up to a debt of £300,000, the highest in America. While the American colonial debt averaged eighteen shillings—slightly less than one pound—in New Jersey it amounted to fifteen pounds for every male between eighteen and sixty, rivaling the eighteen-pound burden on the mother country, where, as the depression deepened, Parliament seized the moment to reassert its right to regulate colonial currency. In February 1764 it outlawed paper money as legal tender. Parliament also claimed the absolute power of taxation, serving notice of its intent to impose a colonial stamp tax—similar to that in Britain—on all newspapers and legal instruments to help defray the cost of maintaining a garrison ten-thousand-strong in America. Jerseymen groaned at the news.

One trained observer, Woodbridge printer James Parker (erstwhile partner of Benjamin Franklin), denounced the stamp tax in a letter to Attorney General Cortlandt Skinner:

> There is such a general scarcity of cash that nothing we have will command it and real estates of every kind are falling at least one-half in value. Debtors that were a year or two ago responsible for £1000 can not now raise a

GOVERNOR WILLIAM FRANKLIN

fourth part of the sum. . . . There is an entire stop to all sales by the sheriffs for want of buyers, and men of the best estates amongst us can scarce raise money enough to defray the necessary expenses of their families. . . . Under the insupportable distress we are now called upon for many thousands of pounds sterling to be paid by a stamp duty.

Parker, secretary of the British postal service in America, issued the first revolutionary newspaper, the *Constitutional Courant,* sharply criticizing British policies, on September 21, 1765. The radical paper, which was distributed on the streets of New York City and along country roads by post riders, was quickly suppressed.

Again setting the pattern for other colonies, New Jersey's lawyers met on September 19, 1765, in Perth Amboy and agreed to conduct no business requiring the obnoxious stamps, which meant no business at all. Five months later, when they met again, many were suffering hardships from their protest. All were under pressure from the presence of eight hundred antitax Sons of Liberty. The lawyers voted to suspend business until April 1, when, if the law was not repealed, they would break it and resume practice without using stamps, giving in to the wishes of the radicals.

All over New Jersey, there were protests. When the stamps arrived off New York on the *Royal Charlotte,* Governor Franklin, on the advice of William Alexander, a member of his executive council, refused to let them be landed, saying there was no safe place on the entire coast. The stamp commissioner, William Coxe, was refused the rental of a house unless he could guarantee it would not be pulled to pieces by the mob. He resigned before the Stamp Act took effect, forfeiting a £3,000 bond. To make sure he did not reconsider, the New Brunswick Sons of Liberty followed him all the way to Philadelphia, coercing him into taking an oath not to handle the stamps.

Pleading that he had no clear instructions from London, Governor Franklin, who apparently was no less surprised than most Americans, exhibited uncommon diplomacy during the crisis. Since there was no collector for stamps and no armed place in New Jersey to protect them, he arranged to have a British troop contingent on alert in New York and then had the stamps transferred to HMS *Sardoine,* anchored in the harbor off Perth Amboy. When the captain asserted that he had to put the ship into dry dock and strip it of its guns for the winter, Governor Franklin stalled, appealing to Lieutenant Governor Cadwallader Colden of New York for permission to store the stamps at Fort George. That would be impossible, Colden replied, because the fort was filled with troops and supplies. There simply was no room. Turning to the Royal Navy again, he persuaded the *Sardoine*'s captain to take the stamps wherever he planned to keep his ship's stores for the winter, reasoning shrewdly that the citizens of one colony would not attack the stamps of another.

Despite Franklin's efforts at discouraging the Assembly, the legislators met at Sproul's Tavern in Perth Amboy after he had dissolved the House and voted to send delegates to a continental Stamp Congress in New York. When New Jersey Speaker Robert Ogden refused to sign the resulting petition to the king, he was burned in effigy all over New Jersey and felt obliged to resign promptly from public life.

At this time, Benjamin Franklin's long involvement in Philadelphia politics bore bitter fruit. The Proprietary Party accused the Franklins of fostering the Stamp Act—and William in particular of trying to block the New Jersey delegates from attending the New York Congress. Forced to issue broadsides throughout the city, William hurried to the Franklin home in Philadelphia, where Deborah and his sister Sarah had armed and barricaded themselves along with friends against the menacing mobs.

By now William Franklin, thoroughly shaken, appealed to the public press. He was so widely respected that his absolute denial of any involvement in the Stamp Act swung the mob's wrath away from him. Fortunately, word reached Philadelphia of his father's brilliant defense of American rights before the

House of Commons. Young Franklin, somewhat aged by the affair, admitted he had feared his house would be "pulled down about my ears and all my effects destroyed." When news of the repeal of the Stamp Act reached Burlington, the governor and his lady joined the public celebration, firing off two small cannon on his lawn and joining in eighteen toasts, to everyone's obvious relief.

Young Franklin was sympathetic to the Whig-American cause. He referred to "the people" while other Crown officials deplored "the mob." He openly refused to support the hated Customs Service as the stamp crisis was followed by the Townshend Acts crisis and a burgeoning smuggling industry developed in Cape May, Delaware Bay, and Little Egg Harbor Inlet. Jerseymen were startled to find that they had a governor who was not afraid to compromise to uphold the Crown's prerogative, even if achieving the compromise meant that he often had to bully the Assembly. While he seems to have despaired of wringing a higher salary and living allowance from the legislators and dropped his plans for a suitable official residence in the face of widespread economic dislocation, he pushed vigorously for badly needed reforms. His welfare plan to feed and clothe destitute Sussex and Monmouth County farmers; his support of the Anglican Church's retired clergy; his espousal of a second college in the colony (Rutgers); his campaign for more and better roads and bridges built with the proceeds of public lotteries; and, most of all, his successful eleven-year battle for a loan office to issue paper money to alleviate the cash shortage and to self-liquidate government operational expenses—all were visionary pieces of liberal legislation years ahead of their time. And while each excited the wrath of various factions, they combined to free him to pursue a grander scheme.

When the British, by the Proclamation of 1763, took over the huge wedge of real estate bordered by the Ohio and Mississippi Rivers and the Appalachian Mountain chain, the land was designated as an Indian reservation under Crown protection. But part of the plan was to drive off thousands of white squatters and subsequently to sell the land, providing a large source of quitrents to reduce the British national debt and defray costs of the royal military establishment.

The Franklins, father and son, along with leading Quaker merchants in Philadelphia and Indian agents in New York, grasped the possibility of creating new provinces, one of which was to be called Vandalia, covering much of present-day Indiana and Illinois. Long before promoting the development of this colony, Governor Franklin had explored the territory with Conrad Weiser.

It was crucial to keep friendly relations with the Indians inhabiting the lands. The Franklins surreptitiously pursued this end with pen and sword, leading the unpopular protest against the Paxton Boys' massacre of Christianized Conestoga Indians in Lancaster County, Pennsylvania, in 1764, and the similar killing of peaceful Indians in northwestern New Jersey. Their plan was bold. It cost the elder Franklin his Pennsylvania Assembly seat in the bitter 1764 election and permanently antagonized frontier Jerseymen against William Franklin when he insisted on hanging the white murderers of Indians.

Meanwhile, Governor Franklin expanded his real estate holdings, buying up valuable lands in New York and New Jersey. Acquiring 575 acres of choice riverfront in Burlington county, he turned his country estate, Franklin Park, into a showcase scientific farm, where he conducted experiments in husbandry, tilling, and breeding that he evidently intended to practice on a grander scale farther west. That he was sure the great scheme would ultimately succeed is apparent from his outspoken stands before the Assembly, which he accused of neglecting the public welfare by ignoring his programs of public works and crop bounties. He obviously hoped to be royal governor of a new western province where he could draw a larger salary and grow rich on the fees paid for deeds and land patents.

After a decade of push and tug, Governor Franklin and the Assembly finally parted company in 1773 over the theft of the tax returns of East Jersey from a trunk in the home of Treasurer Stephen Skinner. Although Franklin had the Samuel Ford gang hunted down and two of its members confessed the theft of £7,854 from the treasurer's house, the Assembly insisted that the wealthy Perth Amboy aristocrat had been negligent. Refusing to investigate further, they demanded restitution from Skinner and his resignation. Franklin, angrily protesting this incursion on the royal prerogative, doggedly held on for five months until Skinner finally resigned. This public furor masked a deeper malaise, however, brought on by the increasing frequency of mob violence centered in Essex County. Many of its residents were transplanted New Englanders with radical views. For nearly thirty years they had intermittently rioted against the East Jersey proprietors, mobbed Crown officials, and managed to keep their leaders out of jail.

Governor Franklin saw the storm clouds gathering. By now the Vandalia charter seemed a distant dream. Officials in London went out of their way to destroy the Franklins. The younger Franklin, tarred as a radical along with his father, came under suspicion and was passed over for promotion to the governorship of Barbados, birthplace of his ailing wife. Late in 1773 Governor Franklin, angered that his father's politics had damaged him and irritated that his father thought him so subservient, took a bold step. Placing Franklin Park and his Burlington mansion on the market, he moved the seat of government to Perth Amboy, where he could be near his few close friends on the council as he confronted the growing crisis.

William's move to the magnificent Proprietary House, with its marble floors, rich paneling, and stables for twelve carriage horses, seems to have severed him from Whig affections. His loyalty to the Perth Amboy aristocracy brought him finally within the social and political circle of the very Tories who had once spurned him as a bastard but now sought the comfort and protection of his official presence. But by now his enemies were many, powerful, and determined to bring him down.

Sickened by the growing dissension, Governor Franklin urged his father to come home soon after hearing of his father's disgrace before the Privy Council in London. The men had drifted apart ideologically over the years. The younger Franklin remained the more moderate, whereas his father had by 1774 reached the following conclusion:

> Parliament has no right to make any law whatever binding on the Colonies. . . . I know your sentiments differ from mine on these subjects. You are a thorough government man, which I do not wonder at, nor do I aim at converting you. I only wish you to act uprightly and steadily, avoiding that duplicity which . . . adds contempt to indignation. If you can promote the prosperity of your people and leave them happier than you found them, whatever your political principles are, your memory will be honored.

Although it was evident that the two Franklins had parted politically, the son feared for the safety of his father. Writing to him December 24, 1774, he pleaded with him to come home:

> If there was any prospect of your being able to bring the people in power to your way of thinking, or of those of your way of thinking being brought into power, I should not think so much of your stay. But as you have had pretty strong proofs that neither can be reasonably expected and that you are looked upon with an evil eye in that Country, you had certainly better return.

By September 1774, as the First Continental Congress assembled at Philadelphia to protest the closing of the Boston port after the Tea Party nine months earlier, Governor Franklin and his good friend Joseph Galloway, Speaker of the Pennsylvania Assembly, had decided that what would make their people happiest would be peace. If Benjamin Franklin had abandoned all hope of reconciliation, the younger men must make the effort. Modifying a plan of union the elder Franklin had advanced in Albany twenty years earlier, Galloway argued passionately in the Continental Congress for a continental legislature coequal with Parliament, presided over by a supreme executive appointed by the king. The Congress tabled the plan by a narrow six-to-five vote, following a last-ditch attack by the New

England democrats, who bitterly opposed an Anglo-American commonwealth. But the plan was praised in New York and, after it was forwarded, in London.

As the determined Sons of Liberty enforced nonimportation in New Jersey, protest and recruitment flourished. Events now swept past Governor Franklin, leaving this erstwhile Whig moderate a dogged conservative in their wake. In January 1775, four months before the bloodletting at Lexington and Concord, he gravely addressed the New Jersey Assembly:

> It is not for me to decide on the particular merits of the dispute between Great Britain and her colonies, nor do I mean to censure those who conceive themselves aggrieved for aiming at a redress of the grievances. It is a duty they owe themselves, their country, and their posterity. All that I could wish to guard you against is the giving any countenance or encouragement to that destructive mode of proceeding. . . . You have now pointed out to you, gentlemen, two roads, one evidently leading to peace, happiness, and a restoration of the public tranquility—the other inevitably conducting you to anarchy, misery, and all the horrors of a civil war.

This sober appeal served to suspend New Jersey in the eye of the hurricane for many months until news thundered south over the old Post Road that farmers and redcoats had clashed bloodily outside Boston. Everywhere, instantly, militia met, marched, drilled. Citizens associated, swore oaths and enforced them, and seized and disarmed recalcitrant Tories, purging them from their ranks.

In a bitter falling out, Governor Franklin purged Lord Stirling from his council for accepting a militia command. Stirling, systematically raiding British mail dispatches, intercepted Franklin's "secret and confidential" official correspondence to London, and with the approval of the Continental Congress ordered a guard placed on the governor's palace at Perth Amboy at 2 A.M. on January 8, 1776.

In this climate, Governor Franklin prevailed on the New Jersey Assembly to instruct its delegates to the Continental Congress against independence and instead to petition the king legally, through him, for redress of grievances. The Assembly agreed. Alarmed, the Congress sent three delegates to Burlington to argue against a separate peace for New Jersey. The Assembly wavered and fell into line, "not wanting to appear singular." An angry Governor Franklin refused to forward their petition.

On receiving a special message of king and Parliament offering limited grounds for negotiation, Governor Franklin, now the last hope of reconciliation, summoned the Assembly to meet on June 10. The rebel New Jersey Provincial Congress, in urgent session, decided that this was in direct contempt of a Continental Congress resolution "that it is necessary that every kind of government under the Crown should be suppressed." The Provincial Congress ruled that the governor had "acted in direct contempt and violation of the resolve of the Continental Congress" and ordered his arrest.

For months, the courageous Franklin had stayed on in the face of personal danger, long after other royal officials had fled. His gallant stand, which he justified by saying he would not give the Congress the excuse of creating a government because he had left none, masked his fear. In a letter to Lord Dartmouth in September 1775, he wrote, "It would mortify me extremely to be seized upon and led like a bear through the country to some place of confinement in New England."

In June 1776, he was taken from his ailing wife, who was soon to flee to New York and die there without seeing him again. Only one month later, the great British fleet arrived off Perth Amboy, and the governor's father came to Perth Amboy to negotiate on behalf of the Continental Congress with the British peace commissioners. There is room to speculate what a difference the presence of both Franklins would have made at the parley.

By then, however, Governor Franklin had been tried by a court he refused to recognize. Its president, the Reverend John

Witherspoon, president of the College of New Jersey, spoke insultingly of his "exalted birth." The Revolutionaries guarded the royal governor so closely that he sometimes could not "answer nature's call." Then he was led off, as he had dreaded, to Connecticut and a succession of ever-worsening prisons. Two years later he was released after remaining 250 days in solitary confinement in Litchfield Jail without clean clothing, furniture, books, pen, or paper. In addition, he nearly starved and emerged, as he put it, "considerably reduced in flesh."

Before the long civil war ended, Governor Franklin stood accused of authorizing, as president of the Board of Associated Loyalists, the brutal retaliatory hanging of a rebel officer. In the ensuing furor, he was never allowed to testify and was bundled off to Britain, ostensibly to plead the Loyalist cause.

But the bitterest hour had already passed, as William's wife lay dying in New York and the Continental Congress refused him a pass from Connecticut to see her one last time. Certainly, it would have taken only a word from his father to ensure mercy for his only son. But Benjamin never would forgive William. He did all he could to chastise all Loyalists at the signing of the Treaty of Paris ending the war in 1783. And he went to his grave denouncing his son in his will. It seems ironic that William Franklin, who had much more to forgive, tried to heal the open wounds in his shattered family, and went to *his* grave in exile in London in 1813 writing of their dream of so long ago, the new land in the West he and his father had envisioned.

TADEUSZ KOSCIUSZKO
AND THE
IMMIGRANT ARMY

A HISTORY OF THE AMERICAN REVOLUTION
should present a rich ethnic tapestry, not an all-white,
all-WASP Pantheon. Among other things, it should have much
less of an English accent. Revolutionary politics and the ranks
of Revolutionary soldiers included Czechs, Poles, Hungarians,
Greeks, Danes, Swedes, Italians, Bohemians, Dutch, Germans,
Scots, Irish, Scots-Irish, Swiss, French, African-Americans, Native Americans, Protestants, Catholics, and Jews from many
countries.

The British Army was preponderantly made up of Irish,
Scottish, and German mercenaries, with more Germans than
Englishmen fighting on the British side. British Major General
James Robertson, who had served in the American colonies for
a quarter century, reported that half the rebels were Irish, an
estimate that accords with the testimony that Joseph Galloway,
a Loyalist Pennsylvanian, gave before the British Parliament. A
modern Irish historian has concluded that 38 percent of the
Revolutionary soldiers were Irish. Yet Galloway and Robertson
may not have been differentiating between Irish Catholics and
Protestant Scots-Irish like Charles Thomson, whose ancestors
had settled in Ireland temporarily and re-emigrated to America

in the first half of the eighteenth century after enduring frequent crop failures combined with increasingly repressive British laws and taxes.

Thousands of Scots-Irish came to America in the 1770s when the linen-weaving industry collapsed in Ulster. By 1776, an estimated 300,000 Scots-Irish had come to Britain's mainland American colonies. Many of them, like Patrick Henry, who became the first governor of independent Virginia, and Charles Thomson, who served as secretary of all the Continental Congresses, took active roles in the earliest protests against the British. Others, like John Rutledge, took part in the Continental Congress's debate over independence. Still others, like Henry Knox, Washington's chief of artillery, fought throughout the eight-year war. The Scots-Irish were only slightly more numerous than German immigrants. By 1776, at least 225,000 Germans of at least 250 different Protestant sects had migrated to America in the wake of European religious wars. Many of them left behind the constant warfare of Europe only to march off to the war for America, some with clergymen like Frederick Muhlenberg. Other Germans came not to settle but to fight beside the Americans, most notably Baron von Steuben, a Prussian professional soldier who drilled the American troops at Valley Forge into a tightly disciplined, highly maneuverable army. Steuben stayed in the new United States after the Revolution. So did 12,562 of the 29,875 German mercenaries rented out by their feudal overlords to fight on the British side, and brought mostly against their will.

What would today be called ethnic Americans took part in virtually every military engagement. Polish-American sailors in the crew of the American ship the *Bon Homme Richard* fought under a famous Scottish-American captain, John Paul Jones, lobbing grenades into the powder magazine of the British warship *Serapis* until it struck its colors. Thirteen-year-old Pascal de Angelis, an Italian-American, fought under Benedict Arnold in the naval Battle of Valcour Island on Lake Champlain that saved the incipient United States from being cut in two by British armies and navies in 1776. Twenty Hungarian hussars came to

America to fight under their Polish friend Casimir Pulaski, a dashing cavalry officer who did stunt riding outside Washington's headquarters at Morristown to attract the commander in chief's attention and then commanded four cavalry regiments in the South until he was killed. Greek knights journeyed to America and fought as volunteers under the French Marquis de Lafayette in Virginia; at least half a dozen Greek-American patriots suffered the horrors of imprisonment on the disease-ridden British prison ship the *Jersey*.

The Italian Filippo Mazzei, Thomas Jefferson's next door neighbor in Virginia, took a musket and marched off as a private in 1776. Then he went to Italy as Virginia's diplomatic agent to drum up financial and political support for the American cause in Florence by writing pamphlets and books published in Italy. Subsequently, two regiments of Italians recruited in their homeland fought under the French flag at Yorktown. Joseph Vigo, an Italian who left his Piedmont home, came to New Orleans with a Spanish regiment and became a leading Mississippi Valley fur trader. When George Rogers Clark captured Vincennes and British troops recaptured it, Vigo found himself caught between the lines. He carefully observed British troop strengths and gun positions. Released because of his Spanish citizenship, Vigo supplied vital information to Clark in time for the American counterattack—as well as badly needed money and excellent credit that helped the Americans recapture Vincennes. By pledging his entire fortune to help the American cause, Vigo helped to extend American territory into the modern-day Midwest.

North and South, African-Americans fought on both sides, with both sides offering them freedom if they survived. An estimated 7,500 blacks fought under Washington, while more than double that number fought on the British side.* And all

---

* Among the black revolutionary soldiers was a teenage James Forten. African-Americans in the British forces were evacuated, some of them being settled in Sierra Leone as the first phase of the recolonization of Africa, against which Forten later spoke out.

through the war, Jewish Americans fought, suffered, and often gave all they had to keep the Revolution and its army and navies alive. Many Revolutionary leaders had no income while they served in the Continental Congress, relying on the generosity of richer Patriots. Wrote James Madison, "When any member of the Revolutionary Congress was in need, all that was necessary was to call on [Haym] Solomon" and receive an immediate loan or outright gift. Bernard and Michael Gratz equipped the 150 Virginians who made the original surprise attack on the Old Northwest under George Rogers Clark. Moses Levy, as Robert Morris's partner, built and paid the crews of privateering warships that captured and destroyed British shipping. The Jews of Charleston, South Carolina, marched off in the Jews Company to defend their city against invading British and German forces. Colonel Mordecai Sheftall acted as commissary general for the southern Continental Army and was held prisoner with his sixteen-year-old son for two years on a British prison ship, where sanitary conditions were horrible and food inadequate. Jacob Pinto of New Haven, Connecticut, a member of the town's Revolutionary Committee, fought beside his brother, Benjamin, in the Seventh Connecticut Regiment of the elite Continental Line.

Only days after the fighting had started at Lexington in 1775, a crowd gathered in Montreal, Canada, where King George III's bust had been smeared with a coat of black paint. Young David Salisbury Franks, who later became Benedict Arnold's aide-de-camp, admitted his handiwork and British soldiers dragged him off to jail. When Arnold led an American invasion of Canada later that year, Franks did everything he could to organize French Canadians to fight on the American side. When the Americans retreated south, he went with them and enlisted in a Massachusetts regiment. Arnold's treason meant a court-martial for Major Franks, but he cleared his name, and at war's end Congress honored him by asking him to carry the signed treaty of peace to Paris.

One of the many unsung ethnic heroes of the Revolution was Tadeusz Kosciuszko, the impoverished son of Polish gentry who had fled his homeland after he tried to elope with the daughter of a nobleman, who then ordered him arrested. After studying at the French royal military academy, Ecole Militaire, in Paris, and the royal artillery and engineering school at Mézières, he specialized in river and harbor defenses. Kos, as the American officers called him (Washington misspelled his name eleven different ways), came to Philadelphia in 1776 as a volunteer military engineer. He quickly showed a genius for river fortifications and thorough grounding in European warfare. The Continental Congress commissioned him as colonel of engineers for the Northern Department. But before he could ride north, Benjamin Franklin, in charge of defending Pennsylvania, commandeered Kosciuszko's talents. Together, they planned the elaborate network that was supposed to impede the expected British attack on the American capital. More than five thousand men—one in five Philadelphians—joined the gigantic defense-building effort that began in the summer of 1776 and lasted until the British attack came in October 1777.

On the New Jersey shore just across from present-day Philadelphia International Airport, Kosciuszko laid out two forts on the marshy banks of the Delaware River. Fort Billings, the first parcel of federal land, was purchased by Congress on July 5, 1776. Kosciuszko created a large, 180-foot-square redoubt with strong points at the corners, parapets for riflemen, the walls pierced for eighteen heavy guns. On the land side, he laid out earthen breastworks and a deep ditch, or *fosse,* filled with felled trees, their branches sharpened to impede infantry attack.

The main purpose of Kosciuszko's defenses at Fort Billings was to protect the downstream end of *chevaux de frise.* These were barricades submerged in the river to pierce the hulls of ships passing over them and immobilize the ships while the fort's guns poured cannon fire into them. Gangs of revolutionary volunteers floated 239 extremely tough hemlock timbers, fifteen to twenty inches thick, to the assembly area at Gloucester, New Jersey, where they lashed pine timbers to the bottoms and sides to form giant cribs sixty feet long. Then they attached damaging iron-tipped prongs, some of them seventy feet long, and braced them with iron straps and angles. The cribs were rafted down the Schuylkill River on barges from the quarries of Conshohocken, Pennsylvania, floated out into the channel, and then loaded with thirty tons of rock. When plugs were removed from their sides and bottoms, they sank. Submerged with their iron-tipped pikes six or seven feet below the waterline, they spread out into a deadly fan, sixty feet wide. In all, seventy of these uncharted *chevaux de frise,* were spread over eight miles of river between the guns of Fort Billings and Fort Mercer, the second fort built by Kosciuszko.

Fort Mercer, at Red Bank above present-day Woodbury, New Jersey, showed Kosciuszko's dual genius as both engineer and artilleryman. Its guns could fire down from a bluff forty feet high to link up with gunfire from Fort Mifflin across the mile-wide Delaware, both guarding the approaches to the *chevaux de frise.* Any British ship that slowed down to pick its way through the underwater trap came under heavy fire from Fort Mercer, whose elevation put it above the reach of British naval guns. The fort was also virtually impervious to amphibious assault by British marines because of its formidable landward defenses.

To the north of the fort, a dirt road ran due west from Deptford and Haddonfield, New Jersey. The road was flanked by heavy woods to the south and swamps to the north. Kosciuszko ordered orchards cut down to make a clear field of fire and had deep trenches dug around the fort's walls, which ran 350 yards from north to south. Then he laid out long, low breastworks for 200 yards to protect infantry along the river bluff. A moat filled with the standard *abatis* of sharpened trees and protected by breastworks made up the outerworks. It was to be manned by sharpshooters to slow down attack on the main fort, a solid-looking earth-and-log redoubt with walls fifteen feet high and twelve feet thick.

General Washington, headquartered farther upriver at Whitemarsh, sent two French officers from his staff—his aide, Marquis de Lafayette, and his chief engineer, Chevalier Mauduit du Plessis. They found the fort lightly garrisoned by two companies of Rhode Island Continentals, black troops (three-fourths of them slaves who had been promised their freedom in exchange for military service), and black freemen under the command of a tough former Quaker, Colonel Christopher Greene. The black troops, Lafayette reported to Washington, were waiting grimly behind eighteen heavy guns. At Mauduit's suggestion, Colonel Greene built another embankment between the inner and outer works on the north side to conceal another artillery battery. Here, on the New Jersey shore, a decisive battle was about to take place, pitting against each other forces that were almost exclusively non-British.

The British attack came soon enough. On October 11, a combined land-sea attack by two thousand British regulars encircled Fort Billings downriver. Only six cannon had arrived inside the fort. They all faced the river and were quite useless against the British land attack. During the night, the 350-man garrison of New Jersey militia spiked these cannon so that they would blow up if the British tried to use them. They blew up the bakehouse, barracks, and stockade and retreated toward Fort Mercer. The British, in turn, came under fire from Pennsylvania Navy galleys anchored at the foot of the bluffs under Fort Mercer's guns. While the Pennsylvania vessels—small, open boats propelled by oars and sails—would be no match for the British warships in a real battle, they managed to deter an amphibious landing.

The brunt of the British attack came from the land side. The assault was entrusted to Hessian mercenaries led by thirty-seven-year-old Count Karl Emil von Donop, an able field commander still smarting from his defeat by Washington at Princeton the winter before. Some 3,400 Hessians marched from their base at present-day Camden to Deptford, where they rested for the night. There they were observed by an American named Jonas Cattell, a fleet-footed courier who ran nine miles from Deptford to Fort Mercer that night to warn the garrison. Until then, the attack had been expected from the water. All that night, the black soldiers from Rhode Island sweated as they hauled the big guns around to the land side—and set their trap. Posting sharpshooters inside the outer breastworks, Colonel

Greene placed two heavy guns, double-loaded with grape-sized shot and canisters of shrapnel, inside the tree-branch-and-brush-camouflaged inner embankment.

Drums beating and bugles blaring, the Hessians paraded down the lane at noon the next day. They fanned out to form a cordon that extended from swamps to a flat plain south of the fort. Swinging down from his brown stallion, von Donop handed the reins to an aide and told him to carry this message to Greene: "The King of England orders his rebellious subjects to lay down their arms and they are warned that if they stand the battle, no quarters [mercy] whatsoever will be given."

Greene shouted back his reply: "We'll see King George damned first! We want no quarter and we'll give none."

Hessian axemen attacked from north and south under a galling fire from the walls of the fort. They hacked through the sharpened *abatis* as grenadiers bayoneted their way through the thin line of black skirmishers in the south ditch. Then hundreds of screaming Hessians charged the walls. A few made it to the top before they were riddled with point-blank fire. On the north side, at the first Hessian volley the black Americans, as planned, fired once and then dropped back. Charging and huzzahing wildly, the Hessians poured over the outer breastworks and into the inner defenses, racing toward the high north wall.

Then, yanking away tree branches, the hidden American gun crews fired. Count von Donop, leading the charge, was shot in the hip, chest, and face at such close range that the cannon's cotton wadding was embedded in his face. Blinded, he fell, as did scores of his German veterans and fifteen other officers. From the river, the Pennsylvania Navy gunboats (many of their crewmen also free blacks from Philadelphia), opened a crossfire against Hessians attempting to scale the west wall. More German grenadiers were mown down.

Within fifteen minutes the Battle of Fort Mercer was over. The surviving Hessians ran back to the woods and jettisoned their cannon in a creek, pausing only long enough to fashion stretchers with their muskets for wounded officers before fleeing back to Woodbury. They left 414 dead and dying on the field, in the ditches, sprawled all over the fort. Count von Donop died slowly and painfully in a house nearby after being nursed for nine days by Chevalier Mauduit. Numerically, it was the greatest American victory of the Revolution. Only twenty-four Revolutionaries were killed or wounded, nineteen of them when a carelessly swabbed cannon exploded while being loaded.

The furious British Navy command that night tried to maneuver its sixty-four-gun flagship, HMS *Augusta,* and its eighteen-gun escorting sloop-of-war, *Merlin,* through the upper *chevaux de frise* to avenge the defeat. Both ran aground. At dawn, the black Americans inside Fort Mercer discovered the British ships' plight and poured in more than one hundred cannonballs, many of them heated in a special furnace. Both warships were set afire. The powder magazine of the *Augusta* exploded with such force that windows shattered twenty miles away upriver at Washington's headquarters. The *Merlin* was so badly damaged that it had to be scuttled. It would take the British forty more days before they could clear out the river and settle down, stunned, in Philadelphia. Never once during that whole crucial winter of 1777–1778 did they attempt to crush Washington's army starving in the nearby hills of Valley Forge.

Indeed, already by late October the British had more bad news. Kosciuszko had gone north and had helped to lay another trap at Saratoga, New York. For weeks, the American army had been slowly retreating in the face of a British invasion from Canada. Sent to strengthen the American fortifications at Fort Ticonderoga on the southern tip of Lake Champlain, Kosciuszko had been ignored when he urged the placement of artillery on the highest hill overlooking the fort. The British, promptly seizing this high ground, had forced the Americans to withdraw precipitously. By early September 1777, Kosciuszko, at the side of General Benedict Arnold and under the command of General Horatio Gates, was seeking the perfect place to lure the British into battle on American terms. Kosciuszko chose hilly ground around Saratoga, on the west bank of the Hudson River.

Stretching off to the west were high bluffs and steep, forest-covered hillsides dropping off into deep ravines. If proper fortifications were built here, the British could not get around the Americans to the west nor past them down the Hudson River to link up as planned with a British army supposedly marching north. The narrow pass at Saratoga would be a perfect place to build strong works and make an all-out stand. The British would have to try to outflank the Americans by attempting to circle to the west of the American line, but in the thick, hilly forests their artillery and dragoons, indeed all their advanced European battle tactics, would be useless. They would be forced to fight American-style in the woods or, if they mounted a frontal attack, to risk being beaten piecemeal.

Kosciuszko took paper from his portfolio and penciled in redoubts, earthworks, bivouacs, company streets. Arnold placed the troops, interspersing battle-seasoned Continental units among inexperienced New York and New England militia. Making free use of artillery taken from captured British forts in the Lake Country, Kosciuszko heavily fortified the American right wing overlooking the river. He placed more cannon to protect *abatis,* strengthening earthworks and redoubts that he stretched fully a mile west to block any British flanking attack. By the time the British arrived, the American defensive position was virtually impregnable.

Despite a series of attacks and artillery barrages over the next month, Kosciuszko's defenses held. Finally, a deadly American counterattack on Hessian redoubts led by Arnold convinced the weary British that they should withdraw. Pursued and battered, the British surrendered. The first great American victory of the Revolutionary War persuaded the French government that the Americans would fight on and could actually win. The war would drag on for four more years until Franco-American combined forces won a second decisive victory at Yorktown, Virginia. But Kosciuszko's timely help in introducing state-of-the-art European warfare to a raw American army had helped to prevent the rout of the American colonists by the British redcoats, among the best soldiers of their age, in the critical early stages of the war.

The Polish colonel served out the rest of the war performing equally important engineering feats almost routinely. He fortified the bend of the Hudson River with a series of overlapping-fire fortresses at West Point; he sustained the beleaguered southern army in the field by perfecting pontoon transport across the South's many deep, narrow rivers; and always he kept the Americans a few steps ahead of an exhausted, exasperated British enemy in a new kind of guerrilla warfare. He fought and was wounded at the head of freed black American soldiers in the last battle of the war, outside Charleston. His mission complete and his reputation assured, Kosciuszko then returned to Europe. With a final departing flourish, he wrote the cavalry handbook used for half a century at West Point. And then he freed the slave he had been given as a token of appreciation for building the impregnable American fortress that became the United States Military Academy.

Napoleon chartered Kosciuszko to form a Polish Legion, and the Pole went on to lead his own country's revolution. But his army proved unable to hold out against an alliance of much larger powers when Poland was partitioned by Prussia, Austria, and Russia. The general sailed back to America in 1797, where he petitioned Congress for a pension and land. Unfortunately, a political division between President John Adams and the new party formed by Thomas Jefferson,* combined with fear of French revolutionary ideas, soon led to the nation's first anti-immigration laws. The Alien and Sedition Acts decreed that immigrants had to wait fourteen years (instead of five) before becoming citizens, and made them liable to summary deportation. Turning his pension claim over to Jefferson, Kosciuszko departed America for the last time. For most of the next twenty years he farmed in France, dying in 1817 after a fall from a horse.

Given the importance of Kosciuszko and numerous other Revolutionary fighters of varied ethnic backgrounds, why has the reality of this complex mosaic of the American Revolution

---

* Jefferson's meetings in New York and Albany en route to the Lake Country in 1791 seem to have been part of his party building.

remained so long dominated by a WASP myth? Perhaps the view of the Scots-Irish Charles Thomson offers an explanation. Thomson came to America a destitute orphan and became the protégé of Benjamin Franklin. He organized Philadelphia's radical Sons of Liberty, and grew to be a wealthy merchant. Yet despite serving as secretary of every Continental Congress from 1774 to 1789, he was excluded from the new federal government.

Thomson declined to write a history of the Congresses he had served after repeated importunings by many of the Founders. One of the reasons they hoped he might write one was that Thomson had been gathering vast numbers of state documents and private papers from members for all those years, suggesting that he was going to use them to write a history of the United States.

But finally he wrote to Benjamin Rush, saying, "No, I ought not. Let the world admire the supposed wisdom and valor of our great men. Perhaps they may adopt the qualities that have been ascribed to them, and thus good may be done. I shall not undeceive future generations."

MARGARET SHIPPEN
ARNOLD:
FOR SERVICES
RENDERED

UNDER THE ENGLISH LEGAL DOCTRINE
enunciated in 1765 by Sir William Blackstone in his
Commentaries on the Laws of England, married women had few
legal rights: what rights they had were bound up in their husbands, who alone had a legal existence. A married woman could
not hold property (even if it was inherited from her parents),
could not enter into contracts so long as her husband lived
(unless he gave express written approval), could not keep any
money she earned, could not vote or hold office. Women were
legally much better off single or widowed, but even a widow
could hold property only until her firstborn son came of age,
when it was transferred to him. Blackstone's conservative views,
first articulated at Oxford University in his Vinerian Lectures of
1758, were widely adopted in colonial America and became the
legal gospel of the new republic, where his three-volume set was
a best-seller.

If married women had few rights, they had all the disabili-
ties of the matrimonial state, especially in wartime, when they
had no right to dissent from their husbands' political decisions.
Yet women made vast contributions to the Revolutionary cause.
They melted down the great lead equestrian statue of King

George III from New York City into some 42,088 bullets in workshops in Litchfield, Connecticut. They traveled with the army, cooking, serving, and washing in the camps and winter quarters. They made the uniforms and the bandages and ran the farms and the newspapers and the stores.

But in the long civil war called the American Revolution, if they were opposed to the Revolutionary cause, like Philadelphia Loyalists Grace Growden Galloway or Elizabeth Graeme or Margaret Shippen Arnold, they could be evicted from their fathers' houses, stripped of their inheritances, and banished from their homelands. Chained to their husbands' destinies, their successes or failures, the women of Revolutionary America could look forward either to sharing in the final victory with their husbands —or to being expelled, reviled, and exiled forever for beliefs and actions not necessarily their own.

⌑

ALL HER LIFE, Peggy Shippen was surrounded by the turmoil of an age of wars and revolution. She was born on July 11, 1760, as the British Empire was coming into being, only weeks before the French surrendered all of Canada. Before her third birthday, British America had grown by conquest from a strip of small coastal colonies to nearly half of North America. The town of Philadelphia, where her father, Judge Edward Shippen, held a lucrative array of colonial offices, was the largest seaport in America. A center for trade and its regulation, it was a natural target for protests when resistance to British revenue measures flared in the 1760s. By the age of five, she had seen riots in the streets outside her father's handsome brick townhouse.

The revolutionary movement grew all during Peggy's childhood. At fifteen she listened at her parents' dinner table as their guests argued politics. George Washington, John Adams, Silas Deane, and Benedict Arnold were among the American patriots who dined at the Shippens', as did British officials and officers such as General Thomas Gage and the intriguing John André. By the time Peggy was seventeen, the British army had occupied

Philadelphia in its struggle to quell the colonial insurrection, and she was being linked romantically with this young British spymaster. After the Americans reoccupied the city, and before she was nineteen, Peggy married the military governor, Benedict Arnold, and helped him to plot the boldest treason in American history—not only the surrender of West Point and its three thousand men but the capture of Washington, Lafayette, and their combined staffs.

Delicately beautiful, brilliant, witty, a consummate actress and astute businesswoman, Peggy Shippen was the highest-paid spy of the American Revolution. Understandably, the Shippen family destroyed papers that could connect her to the treason of Benedict Arnold. As a result, for two centuries she has been considered Arnold's hapless and passive spouse, innocent though neurotic. But new evidence reveals that she actively engaged in the Arnold conspiracy at every step. She was a deeply committed Loyalist who helped persuade her husband to change sides. When he wavered in his resolve to defect, it was she who kept the plot alive and then shielded him, risking her life over and over. Ultimately expelled from the United States, she was handsomely rewarded by the British "for services rendered."

When Margaret Shippen was born, her father, who already had a son and three daughters, wrote his father that his wife "this morning made me a present of a fine baby which, though the worst sex, is yet entirely welcome." The Shippens were one of colonial America's richest and most illustrious families. The first American Shippen, Peggy's great-great-grandfather, the first Edward, had immigrated to Boston in 1668 with a fortune from trade with the Middle East. He married a Quaker who was being persecuted by the Massachusetts Puritans, and both were granted sanctuary in Rhode Island by Governor Benedict Arnold, the traitor's great-grandfather. The couple resettled in Philadelphia on a two-mile-deep riverfront estate. Shippen later became Speaker of the Pennsylvania Assembly.

Peggy's father, the fourth Edward in the line, was a conservative man who seemed constantly worried, usually about money or property. He followed his father's wishes and practiced law. He also held several remunerative colonial offices simulta-neously—admiralty judge, prothonotary, recorder of deeds—and was at first firmly on the British side in the long struggle that evolved into the Revolution. His tortured reactions to the almost constant tensions that accompanied years of riots, boy-cotts, and congresses in Philadelphia were the backdrop for his daughter Peggy's unusual childhood. When Parliament passed the Stamp Act shortly before Peggy's fifth birthday in 1765, her father read aloud to her about "great riots and disturbances" in Boston. He considered the Stamp Act oppressive, but he op-posed illegally destroying stamped paper. "What will be the consequences of such a step, I tremble to think. Poor America! It has seen its best days." By the time Peggy was eight and learning to read the leather-bound books in their library, her father's admiralty court had become the center of the storm over British taxation. When she was ten, his judgeship was abolished.

As the colonial crisis dragged on, Shippen lectured his favor-ite daughter on disobedience. Bad laws had to be repealed. Simply to ignore or resist them would open the door to anarchy. Despite his drawing-room bravery, however, Shippen refused to take a public stand, careful to avoid offending radicals or street mobs that might attack his property or harm his daughters. He burst into a rare fit of rage over Thomas Paine's book, *Common Sense*, which argued in favor of total separation from Britain. Shippen found *Common Sense* "artfully wrote, yet might be easily refuted. This idea of independence, though sometime ago ab-horred, may possibly, by degrees, become so familiar as to be cherished." No doubt Peggy had to learn the arguments against independence by heart.

Judge Shippen seems to have taken over Peggy's education from her mother. He was disappointed in his only son, Neddy (the fifth Edward), who showed himself early on to be inept at business and would eventually squander much of the family fortune. The judge decided to educate Peggy as if she were his son. Peggy curled up in a wingback across from her father to read Addison, Steele, Pope, Defoe, all the latest British writers.

Her mother saw to it that she was instructed in needlework, cooking, drawing, dancing, and music, but in none of her surviving letters is there any of the household trivia of her time.

Peggy had a distinctive literary style and wit, and like her father, she wrote with unusual clarity. A quiet, serious girl, she was too practical, too interested in business and in making the most of time and money for frivolity. By age fifteen, as the Revolutionary War began, she was helping her father with his investments. Years later, she wrote to thank him for "the most useful and best education that America at that time afforded." At her father's elbow, she learned the finer points of bookkeeping, accounting, real estate and other investments, importing and trade, banking and monetary transactions—and she basked in his approval. Peggy had also been studying her sisters' manners and social behavior. It was at the fortnightly Dancing Assemblies at Freemasons Hall that young men who danced with her older sisters began to notice Peggy. She was tiny, blond, dainty of face and figure, with steady, wide-set blue-gray eyes and a full mouth, which she pursed as she listened intently.

Judge Shippen would invite partisans of all stripes to his brick mansion on Fourth Street in Philadelphia's Society Hill section to air their views at his dinner table. In early September 1774, when Peggy was fourteen, her family entertained some of the delegates to the First Continental Congress. Few, if any, foresaw a war of revolution against the mother country; many expected to reconcile their complaints with Parliament peacefully. Of all the colonies, Pennsylvania was the most divided. The majority there were either Quaker pacifists or members of one of 250 German pietist sects, while the strong Penn Proprietary Party was loyal to the British.

That steamy September, Philadelphians agonized over the course of the New England radicals' confrontation in British-occupied Boston as post riders, delegates, militiamen, and redcoats came and went down the broad cobbled streets, making it increasingly difficult to remain neutral. Congressional delegate Silas Deane wrote to his wife that "this city is in the utmost confusion." Rumors of British invasion also were flying. During one panic, Pennsylvania militiamen drilled and marched past the Shippens' house even as the last redcoated British regiment in the middle colonies strode to the waterfront and boarded troop transports taking them north to reinforce Boston.

One young British officer who could have chosen to join them was Second Lieutenant John André of the 7th Foot, the Royal Welsh Fusiliers, who had arrived in Philadelphia just a few days earlier. Sent out from England to join his regiment, André was en route to Quebec. He had been a peacetime officer for five years and had never fought in battle but instead had pursued the life of a dilettante poet, playwright, and artist.

From the safety of England, André had taken the unrest in America lightly, but upon arrival he found Philadelphia in the grip of anti-British frenzy. It was not a safe place for a young, solitary British officer. Oddly, he decided to travel not aboard a British warship but alone on foot north to Lake Champlain. He sailed on to Quebec on a schooner, wrapped in a bearskin robe in the company of a black woman, an Indian squaw in a blanket, "and the sailors round the stove." It was the first of John André's strange and romantic journeys through an America he would never understand.

As André meandered north, thirty-three-year-old shipowner Benedict Arnold, who had arrived in Philadelphia with the Connecticut delegation to the Continental Congress, was accompanying his mentor, Silas Deane, to a series of political caucuses and dinners. A self-made man of means and long a leader of the radical Sons of Liberty in New Haven, Arnold was helping to plan the systematic suppression of antirevolutionary dissent. The purpose of the Congress was to protest British oppression, but Sons of Liberty from a dozen colonies were also discussing the elimination of Loyalist opposition.

Yet Arnold and Deane had time for dinners in Philadelphia's best houses. And the hospitality of one Loyalist family, the Shippens, stood out. Deane and Arnold were invited to the judge's dinner table, where Shippen introduced his daughters, including the youngest, the precocious Peggy. Although only fourteen, she was already one of the city's most popular debutantes. Flirtatious and quick-witted, she could talk confidently with men about politics and trade. Benedict Arnold met her for the first time at dinner that September.

Peggy heard Benedict Arnold's name frequently in the next few years as the Revolution turned to war and its leaders put on uniforms and fanned out to fight the British. Arnold's attack on Fort Ticonderoga, his heroic march to Quebec and daring assault on the walled city, his naval campaign on Lake Champlain, his injury, and his quarrels over promotion often put his name in the Philadelphia newspapers. A few blocks from the Shippen house, a new ship in the Pennsylvania Navy was given Arnold's name, and that was in the papers, too.

News of the war often touched closer to home. Peggy's oldest sister's fiancé, a rebel, was missing and presumed killed in the American rout on Long Island. Her eighteen-year-old brother, Neddy, decided on the spur of the moment to join the British army in Trenton for the Christmas festivities. When Washington attacked, Edward was captured. He was freed by the Shippens' erstwhile dinner guest, George Washington himself. All of Judge Shippen's careful neutrality was jeopardized. Stripping the youth of any further part in family business affairs, the judge turned his son's duties over to Peggy.

When the Americans invaded Canada late in 1775, the British made a stand at Fort Saint Jean on the Richelieu River, surrendering only after a long siege. One of the officers captured was twenty-five-year-old Second Lieutenant André. Freed on parole, he was sent south with the baggage of his fellow officers to house arrest in Pennsylvania. In Philadelphia, while he attended to provisions for his fellow prisoners, André had time to explore "the little society of Third and Fourth Streets," the opulent town houses of Peggy's neighborhood. The romantic young officer was ushered into the Fourth Street home of Judge Shippen and introduced to fifteen-year-old Peggy Shippen. Before he left for an indefinite term in captivity on the Pennsylvania frontier, he played his flute, recited his poetry, and asked to sketch her.

One year later, André was exchanged for an American prisoner. Then, in the autumn of 1777, British forces drove the Americans out of Philadelphia and marched up Second Street, two blocks from the Shippens'. André had recently given the orders for a British regiment to fix bayonets, remove the flints from their muskets, and attack a sleepy American unit at nearby Paoli. The increasingly callous young André tersely described the massacre in his regimental journal, calling the Americans a "herd" as nearly two hundred men were killed and a great number wounded. He noted they were "stabbed till it was thought prudent to desist."

Now an aide at British headquarters in Philadelphia, André decided to follow the example of his commanders and seek diversions from the toils of killing. He and his elegant friends reconnoitered in the best society they could find, and André began calling on the Shippens with his friends Captain Andrew Snape Hamond, of HMS *Roebuck,* and Lord Francis Rawdon, who considered Peggy the most beautiful woman he had ever seen.

Even a conquering officer, however, could not hope to escort a Philadelphia debutante to the incessant round of military balls without prior introductions. The first step was the morning visit to the drawing room of the intended partner. André, sketch pad under his arm, frequently came for obligatory cups of tea and chaperoned talks about the latest books, balls, and plays. In the evenings, André and his assistant, New York Loyalist Captain Oliver DeLancey, were hard at work turning a former warehouse on South Street into a splendid theater. They painted a waterfall and wooded scenes on the curtain and a brook meandering through a darkly shaded forest toward a "distant champagne country." For five months an entranced Peggy joined the resplendent crowd of redcoated officers and their Tory ladies.

That winter Peggy Shippen probably fell in love for the first time. But the charming Major André flitted from one drawing-room beauty to another, serious about none of them. Still, he liked to be with Peggy; he liked to sketch her, showing her as elusively elegant and poutish, sometimes turning away, sometimes fixing him with an enigmatic smile. He enjoyed breakneck sleigh rides with her at his side, her friends crowding in with them under heavy bearskin rugs.

But when Peggy stepped out for the evening, it was more often on the arm of Royal Navy Captain Hamond, who later said, "We were all in love with her." One of the season's highlights was a dinner dance aboard the *Roebuck*. Peggy was piped on board the ship, which was illuminated with lanterns for the occasion. She sat down at Hamond's right for a dinner served to two hundred invited guests and then danced until dawn.

By late April 1778, the British officers learned they were to withdraw to New York City and prepare for the arrival of the French, the Revolutionaries' new ally. Philadelphia was too exposed. A new British commander was coming, and General Howe was being recalled. John André volunteered to prepare a lavish farewell, a Meschianza, including a waterborne parade, a medieval tournament, a dress ball, and an enormous dinner party. No other effort of André's ever approached this opulent festival. He designed costumes for fourteen knights and their squires and "ladies selected from the foremost in youth, beauty and fashion." For the ladies, he created Turkish harem costumes evoking the Crusades. He designed Peggy's entire wardrobe and sketched her in it. André's own glittering costume featured pink satin sashes, bows, and wide baggy pants.

Peggy's father grumbled, but he shelled out enough gold to outfit three of his daughters. As Peggy rode home the next morning, a Quaker diarist wrote, "How insensible do these people appear while our land is so greatly desolated." Before André left a few weeks later, he gave Peggy a souvenir that showed how close they had become: a locket containing a ringlet of his hair. Though parted, they wrote each other secretly, through the lines, at great risk to Peggy, directing the letters through a third party.

In May 1778, as the British evacuated Philadelphia, the new American military governor of Philadelphia, Major General

Benedict Arnold, the wounded hero of Quebec, Ticonderoga, and Saratoga,* drove into the city in his coach and four with his liveried servants, aides, and orderlies. From their brick mansion, the Shippens could see the American light horse ride by. Arnold's duties as military governor included evenings filled with social activities. Once a poor orphan, General Benedict Arnold moved freely in Philadelphia's elite circles. Soon he, too, was keeping an afternoon round of tea sipping with the Shippens, the Robert Morrises, and other wealthy merchants and hosting many members of Congress at lavish dinners at his headquarters. Arnold often encountered Peggy at these gatherings. As the summer progressed, she became known as the general's lady. Frequently, his carriage was seen parked in front of the Shippen house, where British officers had come to call only a few months before. At first, resentment that the American hero of Saratoga was courting the Loyalist belle of British officers' balls was confined to a little sniping in Congress. Arnold's insistence on inviting Loyalist women to Revolutionary social events brought increasing criticism; yet Arnold seemed oblivious as he spent more and more time with the eighteen-year-old Peggy.

In September 1778, Arnold declared himself a serious suitor in two letters, one to Peggy, one to her father. One of Peggy's relatives wrote that "there can be no doubt the imagination of Miss Shippen was excited and her heart captivated by the oft-repeated stories of his gallant deeds, his feats of brilliant courage and traits of generosity and kindness." Peggy seemed especially touched that he paid for the education and upbringing of the four children of his friend, Dr. Joseph Warren, who had been killed at Bunker Hill. But Peggy had other reasons for falling in love with Benedict Arnold. He was still young, thirty-six, ruggedly built despite his wounded leg, animated, intelligent and witty, strongly handsome, and sometimes charming. It was obvious that a life with "the General," as she always called him, would not be dull.

* Arnold's battlefield leadership and the fortifications of Tadeusz Kosciuszko are credited for this victory.

Judge Shippen did not say yes, but he did not say no. He wrote to his father to seek advice. But the more Arnold was publicly criticized for his leniency to Loyalists and his quite open love of one, and the longer the judge balked, the closer the two lovers drew together. Arnold had come to appreciate her "sweetness of disposition and goodness of heart, her sentiments as well as her sensibilities." He had faced few more implacable adversaries than Judge Shippen, who worried about his daughter's marrying an invalid. Finally, however, relatives persuaded the judge that Arnold was "a well-dispositioned man, and one that will use his best endeavors to make Peggy happy." The judge also liked the fact that Arnold planned to settle a £7,000 country estate named Mount Pleasant on her as a wedding present.

On the other hand, the judge didn't like what he was beginning to hear about Arnold's private business dealings, but months of attacks on Arnold by radical political opponents had made Peggy all the more determined to marry him. In the end, Judge Shippen seems to have consented to his daughter's engagement only when his continued refusal made Peggy, now thoroughly in love, hysterical to the point of fainting spells. The Shippens invited only family members to the wedding in their parlor. On April 8, 1779, Arnold's nineteen-month siege ended. He rode down Fourth Street with his sister, his three sons from a previous marriage, and an aide for the evening ceremony. In his dark blue American uniform, Benedict Arnold, thirty-eight, married eighteen-year-old Peggy Shippen. A young relative wrote that Peggy was "lovely, a beautiful bride" as she stood beside her "adoring general."

In May 1779, within one month of their wedding, the couple entered into a daring plot to make Arnold a British general who would lead all the Loyalist forces and bring the long war to a speedy conclusion. All through their courtship, there had been a mounting furor in the press about Arnold's alleged profiteering as military governor. No proof has ever been found that, up to then, he had done anything more than use his office to issue passes that helped Loyalist merchants, who in turn cut him in for a percentage of their profits; and he had once diverted army wagons to haul contraband into Philadelphia for sale in stores. Both were common practices, but Arnold was often stiff-necked and arrogant in his dealings with Pennsylvania Revolutionaries. When Pennsylvania brought formal charges against Arnold, George Washington, Arnold's comrade for years, refused to intervene and, far from supporting him, treated him with the same cold formality he reserved for all officers facing court-martial. Arnold had already endured years of censure and controversy, and Washington's aloofness, coupled with a ferocious attack by the Congress and in the newspapers, evidently drove him over the edge. Peggy seems not only to have approved of his decision to defect to the British but to have helped him at every turn in a year and a half of on-again, off-again secret plotting that, at least once, she alone managed to keep alive.

Both the Arnolds apparently decided, after the yearlong radical campaign against Benedict, that they did not want to live under the new Revolutionary government that had made Arnold's enemies powerful enough to force his court-martial by the army. When Arnold's prosecutors produced no evidence to convict him and when Washington, whose generals were preoccupied, was unable to bring about a speedy court-martial to clear him, the proud hero could tolerate the public humiliation no longer. On May 5, 1779, he wrote a drastic letter to Washington: "If your Excellency thinks me criminal, for heaven's sake let me be immediately tried and, if found guilty, executed."

Apparently that same day, Arnold opened his secret correspondence with the British, using Peggy's friends and Philadelphia connections. A china and furniture dealer, Joseph Stansbury, who was helping Peggy decorate the Arnold house, acted as courier through the lines to Major André at British headquarters in New York City, where Stansbury often went on buying trips. Peggy already had been sending harmless messages to André with Stansbury. She now worked with Arnold to encode the messages, using a cipher written in invisible ink that could be read when rinsed with lemon juice or with acid: a symbol in one corner indicated which to use.

On May 21, 1779, Peggy sat down with Arnold in a bedroom of their Market Street house and pored over the pages of the twenty-first edition of *Bailey's Dictionary.* (André had preferred Blackstone's three-volume *Commentaries on the Laws of England,* but they had rejected it as too cumbersome.) According to Stansbury, they used one of two copies of the compact dictionary: "I have paged for [them], beginning at A. . . . Each side is numbered and contains 927 pages." The Arnolds added "1 to each number of the page, the column, and of the line, the first word of which is also used, too. Zoroaster will be 928.2.2 and not 927.1.1. Tide is 838.3.2 and not 837.2.1." It usually took ten days for Stansbury to slip through to André in New York and as long to return. Late at night, he would send a servant to the Arnolds, and Peggy would carefully decode the message and encode Arnold's reply. Only rarely did the Loyalist Stansbury see the general, because almost always he dealt with Peggy. André had instructed Stansbury to deal with "the Lady." In October 1779, when the British at first failed to meet Arnold's terms after six months of negotiations, Peggy wrote a cryptic letter in code to André and kept the negotiations alive until the two principals struck their bargains. This time she sent her note with a British prisoner who was being exchanged and sent back to New York. She had become far more than a go-between, as historians have tended to portray her. She was now writing as an active coconspirator:

> Mrs. Moore [Moore was one of Arnold's code names] requests the enclosed list of articles for her own use may be procured for her and the account of them and the former [orders] sent and she will pay for the whole with thanks.

The shopping list, evidently not the first, included cloth for napkins and for dresses, a pair of spurs, some pink ribbon. André, who had feigned indifference in recent messages, became alarmed. He saw through Peggy's list. Although the negotiations with her husband had been fruitless so far, she was telling André that they were not hopeless. He put aside her shopping list and informed Sir Henry Clinton, the British commander in chief, that Arnold had finally stated his price. As Stansbury told André, Arnold wanted £20,000 if he succeeded, £10,000 if he failed. What Clinton wanted was detailed plans of West Point, the new American stronghold fifty miles up the Hudson from British lines. André sent the proposal back to Peggy, referring to Peggy's list as "trifling services from which I hope you would infer a zeal to be further employed."

It was late October 1779 before André received another coded note from Peggy:

> Mrs. Arnold presents her best respects to Captain André, is much obliged to him for his very polite and friendly offer of being serviceable to her.

To entice the British, the Arnolds sent much vital military and political intelligence through the lines in the seventeen months from May 1779 through September 1780. In June 1779 they tipped off the British commander that as soon as the first hay was harvested, Washington would leave his base at Morristown, New Jersey, and move north to the Hudson for a summer campaign. This leak gave Clinton time to strike first up the Hudson before Washington could reinforce his forts there. The couple disclosed that Congress had decided to all but write off Charleston, South Carolina, the largest and most important town in the South, if the British once again attempted to take it. (They did and succeeded.)

The Arnolds also informed Clinton about American currency problems and about congressional refusal to give agents in Paris full power to negotiate a peace treaty with Britain. The Arnolds believed the French alliance was shaky and that if it fell apart, the Americans would have to sue for peace. Arnold thought he could then be useful in bringing about a reconciliation between responsible Americans and the British. "I will cooperate with others when opportunity offers," he wrote, adding a postscript: "Madam Arnold presents her particular compliments."

Ironically, one of the Arnolds' early messages to the British led to the interruption of his court-martial in June 1779, soon after it finally began, when the British took his advice and attacked up the Hudson. As Washington and his army dashed north, Arnold lurked behind at headquarters, talking to other officers about Washington's plans for the season of war.

The Arnolds encoded top-secret information about American troop strengths, dispositions, and destinations. He was the first to warn the British of an American expedition "to destroy the Indian settlements" of Pennsylvania and New York. But his most devastating tips were dispatched on July 17, 1779. Arnold detailed the latest troop strengths, the expected turnout of militia, the state of the army, the location of its supply depots, the number of men and cannon on the punitive raid against the Iroquois, as well as troop locations, strengths, and weaknesses in Rhode Island and the South and the location and movements of American and French ships. Peggy Shippen met alone with Joseph Stansbury during these treacherous July 1779 negotiations as Benedict Arnold showed the British what he was willing to give in exchange for a red uniform and at least £10,000.

More months dragged by before Washington could spare general officers to convene Arnold's court-martial. Meanwhile, Arnold had resigned as military governor of Philadelphia. Not until December 1779 was he allowed to defend himself, and although the generals recommended a formal reprimand, the Arnolds did not learn of his conviction until April 1780, just weeks after the birth of their first child. Arnold never forgave Washington for publicly censuring him in writing. But Washington considered it only a minor affair and promptly offered Arnold another field command, this time as his number two general.

The Arnolds were determined to defect, and Arnold himself now put it in writing to André and Clinton that West Point would soon be his to command and his to betray to the British. But Washington insisted that Arnold join him with his troops. Peggy was at a dinner party at the home of Robert Morris when news reached Philadelphia that Arnold had been appointed to command the left wing of the Continental Army, not West Point. She fainted.

What Peggy did not learn for three weeks was that Arnold, pretending his old injuries had flared up, had finally persuaded a puzzled Washington to rewrite his orders, installing him as commandant of West Point, where he took command on August 4, 1780. He sent word to Peggy in Philadelphia to leave his sons by his first marriage in the care of his sister and to come by carriage with the baby and her two servants. Meanwhile, he went about weakening West Point defenses by deploying men so that they could not defend it against a British attack, and arranged the details of his defection with Major André, who had been promoted to chief of the British secret service inside New York City. Plans for a first meeting on the Hudson set for September 11, 1780, miscarried; Arnold was almost killed by gunfire from a British gunboat.

After two months apart from her husband, Peggy arrived at West Point, and their days and nights took on the added excitement of plotting their defection. Peggy's weeks without Arnold, the longest she had ever been away from him, had been one of the loneliest periods of her life, filled with desperate anxiety. But the same day she rejoined him, they received a letter cutting short the time they could expect together. Washington was coming north from his New Jersey headquarters, he wrote Arnold secretly. Arnold was to provide an escort and meet him as he rode without his army to confer with the French in Hartford. Realizing how vulnerable Washington would be, Arnold sent off an urgent message to André saying that if the British moved quickly, their warships on the Hudson, helped by a few hundred dragoons, could capture Washington and his generals as he crossed the river with a few score troops. In a bold military coup, Arnold would seize Washington and negotiate an American surrender that would quickly end the war. If the plot succeeded, Arnold could expect a dukedom from a grateful king and Peggy would be a duchess.

Peggy's first and only Sunday as the mistress of West Point, September 18, 1780, was a tense affair. Arnold's staff filed into the wainscoted dining room of Beverley, the commandant's house, to take their seats with Arnold's weekend Loyalist house guests. Dinner was served early so that Arnold could leave to go downriver with Washington's hand-picked escort. They were hardly seated when a courier arrived with two coded letters for Arnold from André, who was aboard the *Vulture,* a British ship twelve miles downriver. Trying not to betray his excitement, Arnold pocketed the letters. After dinner, he rode off with forty life guards to meet Washington. Circling back alone that night after his last meeting with Washington, Arnold waited for the British attack, but Clinton procrastinated and it did not come. But when Arnold learned that Washington would be inspecting West Point on September 23, he realized that the British would have a second chance. Three more anxious days passed at Beverley. Shortly before dawn on September 21, Arnold kissed Peggy goodbye and slipped off to meet André. Late that night, an open boat bearing André, wrapped in a navy blue caped coat, thumped ashore two miles below Haverstraw. At last the two men met. For two hours, Arnold and André conferred in a darkened grove of fir trees. Arnold turned over papers to André and returned to West Point.

While Arnold was gone, Peggy, still exhausted from her nine-day journey to West Point in an open carriage in the summer heat, had stayed with the baby in Beverley's master bedroom, a sunny, quiet place with big open windows and a balustraded porch. Now, on September 23, a Saturday, she stayed late in the room, planning to go downstairs later when Washington arrived. Arnold and his staff had just been served breakfast when a messenger was shown in, muddy and dripping. He brought word that John André had been captured. The papers André carried, in Arnold's handwriting, had been sent on to General Washington.

Excusing himself, Arnold hurried upstairs to Peggy, locked the bedroom door, and whispered to her that André had been caught, the plot discovered. Washington was expected any minute. Peggy must have reassured her husband that she and the baby would be safe; it is certainly unlikely that she tried to talk him out of fleeing for his life. She agreed to burn all of their papers and stall for time. Embracing Peggy and taking a last look at Neddy, Arnold hurried out, ordering an aide to saddle a horse. At the river, Arnold jumped into his eight-oared barge, drew his pistols, and told his crewmen he would give them two gallons of rum if they got him downriver. The boat lurched into the Hudson channel, Arnold in the stern. By the time Washington arrived a few minutes later, Arnold was on his way to the *Vulture* and the British lines.

Peggy's years of studying theatrics now saved her husband's life, even if her performance could have cost her her own. As Arnold was making his escape, she ran shrieking down the hallway in her dressing gown, her hair disheveled. Arnold's aides rushed up the stairs to find her screaming and struggling with two maids who were trying to get her back into her room. Peggy grabbed one young aide by the hand and cried, "Have you ordered my child to be killed?" Peggy fell to her knees, the aide later testified, "with prayers and entreaties to spare her innocent babe." Two more officers arrived "and we carried her to her bed, raving mad." The sight of the distraught twenty-year-old so distracted Arnold's staff that none of them thought to pursue their master until Washington arrived.

Peggy Shippen's world had exploded because of a plot she had encouraged, aided, and abetted. The sheer nervous tension of the day of discovery helped her to fool everyone around her completely. It would be the twentieth century before the opening of the British Head Quarters Papers proved what the eighteenth century refused to believe: that a young and inno-cent-appearing woman was capable of helping Benedict Arnold plot the conspiracy that nearly delivered victory to Britain in the American Revolution. When Peggy learned that Washing-ton had arrived, she cried out again and told the young aides that "there was a hot iron on her head and no one but General Washington could take it off." The aides and a staff doctor summoned Washington, the commander in chief, but when Peggy saw him, she said, "No, that is not General Washington; that is the man who was going to assist . . . in killing my child."

Washington retreated from the room, certain Peggy Arnold was no conspirator. A few days later, he sent her and the baby under escort to her family in Philadelphia.

When news of Arnold's treason spread throughout America, Peggy was ordered expelled from Pennsylvania. The same officials whose hounding of Arnold had provoked him into treason now unwittingly aided her escape through British lines to join the traitor in New York City. She arrived at Two Broadway, the house Arnold had rented next door to British headquarters, in time to learn that John André had been hanged by Washington after a drumhead court-martial for espionage. She secluded herself in her bedroom for weeks, rarely appearing with Arnold at headquarters functions.

The British commander dishonored his pledge. Instead of the £10,000 Arnold had been promised if the plot failed, he was paid only £6,350 (about $250,000 in 1997 dollars). Commissioned a British brigadier general, Arnold raised a regiment, the American Legion, made up exclusively of deserters from the American army—no British officer would serve under him. He led the regiment on bloody raids through Virginia. Arnold's troops sacked the capitol at Richmond, nearly capturing Thomas Jefferson, and also raided his native Thames River valley in Connecticut.

Peggy spent the last year of the Revolution, her last year in her native country, a celebrity in New York. She was pregnant much of the time with her second child. Some of her old Society Hill neighbors were also Loyalists living in British-occupied Manhattan; they kept tabs on her and wrote back news to Philadelphia. Peggy was grieving for André, even if her marriage to Arnold was serene. Mrs. Samuel Shoemaker wrote in November 1780 that Peggy now "wants animation, sprightliness and fire in her eyes." When she did appear in public, however, it was as the new favorite at British headquarters balls. Peggy "appeared a star of the first magnitude, and had every attention paid her," especially after she received a personal pension of five hundred pounds a year from Queen Charlotte.

After the British surrender at Yorktown, where American

troops celebrated victory by burning Arnold in effigy, the Arnolds sailed for England in a 150-ship convoy. They arrived on January 22, 1782, and according to the London *Daily Advertiser,* took "a house in Portman Square and set up a carriage." She was, wrote one nobleman, "an amiable woman and, was her husband dead, would be much noticed." The Arnolds' warmest reception was at the Court of Saint James, where they were introduced to the king and queen. Arnold, King George III, and the Prince of Wales took long walks together, deep in conversation. Queen Charlotte was especially taken with Peggy, and her courtiers, as one wrote, paid her "much attention." The queen doubled her pension to one thousand pounds a year and provided a lifetime annuity of one hundred pounds for each of her children. Since Peggy was to raise five, she eventually received far more from the Crown than Arnold did. Her pensions guaranteed that she could bring up her children comfortably and that, based on their mother's prestige alone, they would be introduced into society as English gentry. All four of the Arnolds' sons became British officers; their daughter married a general.

Arnold never got another farthing. When peace came, he became a half-pay pensioner and had to strap family resources to build a ship and return to the life at sea that had once made him wealthy. As her husband sailed to Canada, Peggy, twenty-five years old, suddenly felt the loss of her American home and family. Life with Benedict Arnold was hard on Peggy's nerves; without him, it was harder. Arnold was gone for nearly a year and a half, during which Peggy ran their business affairs, collected and invested their pensions, and fought lawsuits. When he returned, she had to pack everything up again—this time, they were moving to Saint John, New Brunswick, where Arnold had established a shipping business, had built a general store, and was buying up land. Late in 1787, only six weeks after they arrived in Canada, Peggy gave birth again.

For the first time since she left Philadelphia, Peggy was able to make close friends. She lived in a big gambrel-roofed clapboard house, elegantly decorated with furniture Arnold brought from England. There were blue damask-covered sofas and matching drapes and a mahogany table that seated twelve on blue damask-covered Sheraton cabriolet chairs designed by Arnold himself. After pouring her guests tea, she served them dinner (she was considered an accomplished cook) on Wedgwood giltware. But the house was an opulent island in a sea of deprivation. The new city was crowded with impoverished Loyalist refugees, and few people could afford to pay Arnold for his imported goods. He made new enemies as he faced frequent decisions about whether to sue delinquent customers or to put men in debtors' prison.

When Arnold's warehouse and store burned, there were whispers that he had torched them for the insurance. A former business partner was one of his accusers, and when Arnold confronted him, the man said, according to the court record, "It is not in my power to blacken your character, for it's as black as it can be." The insult directly resulted in the denial of Arnold's insurance claim—and in the first jury trial for slander in New Brunswick history. Arnold won, but instead of the five thousand pounds he sought, the judges based the award on the value of his reputation and gave him only one pound. At the same time, a mob sacked the Arnolds' home. Fortunately, Peggy and the children were away at the time. After five years in Canada, the Arnolds moved back to England.

Like many Loyalists, Peggy planned to return one day to live in the United States, where she kept her inheritance invested in Robert Morris's Bank of the United States. However, when she went to visit her ailing, aged mother in Philadelphia, the arrival of the traitor's wife, even as a convention was deliberating a new Constitution, stirred controversy. Her brother-in-law recorded that she was treated "with so much coldness and neglect that her feelings were continually wounded." Old friends said her visit placed them "in a painful position." Others whispered that "she should have shown more feeling by staying away." After a five-month visit, Peggy left her family forever, deeply saddened. She wrote back to her sister,

How difficult it is to know what will contribute to our happiness. . . . I had hoped that by paying my beloved friends a last visit, I should insure to myself some portion of it, but I find it far otherwise.

By early 1792, Peggy was back in London, unpacking after the Arnolds' third transatlantic move in ten years. Benedict Arnold's final years were occupied with a long string of business misadventures and also with his obsessive defense of his reputation. He expanded his Caribbean operations, in his last eight years sending or sailing thirteen different ships on trading voyages. Often offended publicly, he fought a duel with the Earl of Lauderdale, who had insulted him on the floor of the House of Lords. Peggy wrote to her father that the days before the duel were filled with "a great deal of pain." She "had not dared to discuss the duel with the silent general," fearing that she would "unman him and prevent him acting himself." The duel produced no casualties, but it "almost at last proved too much for me, and for some hours, my reason was to be despaired of."

As the Napoleonic Wars engulfed Europe, Arnold outfitted his own privateering ship to attack French shipping in the Caribbean. This time, he was gone eighteen months—agonizing months for Peggy, who learned that her husband had been captured by French revolutionaries and had managed to escape only shortly before his scheduled execution. When Arnold returned and she once again became pregnant, Peggy's health began to decline. On December 5, 1795, she wrote to friends in Canada, "For my own part, I am *determined* to have no more little plagues, as it is so difficult to provide for them in this country." For years Peggy lived in dread that the queen would die and her pensions would stop—a legitimate fear after her husband's captains defrauded them of some fifty thousand pounds and she had to sell her private investments to bail him out. In 1801, at age sixty, Benedict Arnold became dispirited and, after a four-month illness, died "without a groan." Peggy, oppressed by his creditors and stunned by his loss, lived for three more years, only long enough to pay off all his debts "down to the last teaspoon."

"Years of unhappiness have passed," she confided in a letter to her brother-in-law. "I had cast my lot, complaints were unavailing, and you and my other friends are ignorant of the many causes of uneasiness I have had." To her father, she wrote that she had had to move to a smaller house, "parting with my furniture, wine and many other comforts provided for me by the indulgent hand of [Arnold's] affection." Arnold had paid a final compliment to Peggy's business acumen by making her sole executrix of his estate, an unusual step at the time. Once she had cleared up the mess he had left and could see that her children would be provided for, she thanked her father for her fine private education: "To you, my dear parent, am I indebted for the ability to perform what I have done."

Years of anxiety and illness had exacted a terrible toll, and Peggy Shippen Arnold's quarter-century ordeal in exile ended on August 24, 1804. She had, she wrote, "the dreaded evil, a cancer." She told her sister she had "a very large tumor" in her uterus. "My only chance is from an internal operation which is at present dangerous to perform." Peggy died at forty-four. After she died, her children found concealed among her personal possessions a gold locket containing a snippet of John André's hair. Family tradition holds that Benedict Arnold never saw it.

A VIRGINIA
GENTLEMAN
IN THE
LAKE COUNTRY

*A*T THE END OF AMERICA'S FIRST CON-
gress in the temporary capital in Philadelphia,
Thomas Jefferson was still working hard. In addition to his
official duties as secretary of state, he was designing the new
nation's mint, establishing a system of weights and measures,
and helping to choose the site and supervise the design of a
permanent United States capital. He disliked the noise, dirt,
and crowds of Philadelphia, the boring routines of office work.
The past year especially had taken its toll, with Jefferson suffering recurring migraine headaches. He could find little peace in
his rented house on the main wagon route into the city. Jefferson
saw hope of a welcome respite when, on March 13, 1791, Congressman James Madison wrote to propose that they make a
tour in summer as far to the north as they could go and return
in a month.

Jefferson especially wanted to visit Vermont. The first new
state admitted after the thirteen colonies declared independence,
Vermont had applied for admission while Jefferson was secretary
of state. As champion of the frontier farmer, he thought of
Vermont as the ideal, a sort of Virginia unspoiled by slavery and
by entrenched tidewater aristocrats, a place where all settlers

would have a chance to own a home and land and make a good living by trading surplus crops for whatever else they needed.

Jefferson had an additional incentive to undertake the tour. In his free time, the secretary of state wore another hat, that of vice president of the American Philosophical Society, a circle of amateur scientists who included most of Jefferson's close friends. That spring, the society was pondering two questions: when the opossum's pouch disappears and how to stop crop damages caused by the Hessian fly. Jefferson had written his son-in-law, Thomas Mann Randolph, who was managing Jefferson's plantation, Monticello, to be on the lookout for opossums. On May 8, Jefferson informed the society that Randolph had observed that the "pouch of the opossum disappeared after weaning the young," and continued:

> Though a single observation is not conclusive, yet the memory remains strong with me that, when a boy, we used to amuse ourselves with forcing open the pouch of the opossum, when [it had] no young. . . . The sphincter was so strongly contracted it [was] difficult to find where we were to enter our fingers.

More serious was Jefferson's concern about the Hessian fly, which had been ravaging American wheat harvests. He asked his scientist friends to help him put together a list of questions he could ask along his vacation route. Such a questionnaire was quite advanced for the times. While the document does not survive, we can deduce its existence from the systematic way Jefferson recorded responses at every stop to questions he put to farmer, ferryman, local official, or tavernkeeper, as well as to the report he later circulated in the newspapers. He would note the year and extent of each Hessian fly infestation, asking about each of the last six years. Jefferson, a man of the Enlightenment, believed that the use of reason when applied systematically could lead to human progress. He believed such questions to be of paramount importance, especially when they related to anything that endangered the crops of his largely agricultural country.

Jefferson believed that the American future should belong to the independent farmer, not the city-dweller. He not only was uncomfortable in cities, he thought they bred crime and disease. He envisioned the dark urban landscape of the Industrial Revolution after only a single visit to the grimy factories and crowded tenements of London. He wanted to endow Americans instead with enough land to provide high nutrition and crop surpluses that they could sell or barter for whatever they themselves could not grow or make. In addition to putting into practice a carefully considered philosophy, he was combining his public and private offices. As secretary of state, he was also secretary of the interior and secretary of agriculture, since these offices had not yet been separated. Jefferson was using his unique position to carry out what was probably the first federal scientific study.

Thomas Jefferson liked to think about things in new ways. In the strictest sense, he was not an inventor. The only *device* he actually invented was a new kind of plow, but there were many other situations in which his innovative spirit stopped little short of invention as he put his mind to thinking about age-old problems in new ways. For example, he pondered the question of time, how and where to spend it, and travel, and how and when to put time and travel together into something entirely new: the summer vacation. (The word "vacation" as we now use it had not even been invented yet.) At a time when traveling for pleasure was almost unheard of except for the once-in-a-lifetime grand tour of European capitals made by a small number of wealthy young Englishmen and even fewer Americans, Jefferson had begun to take annual trips away from the press of official business. On half a dozen sojourns away from Paris, Jefferson turned himself into a scientific traveler, always following a carefully arranged and timed itinerary and carrying out a complicated agenda. Traveling without servants in a plain black suit in a carriage crammed with books and a portable writing desk, he made detailed notes of his studies of farming methods, soil conditions, weather, art and architecture, currencies, governments, trade, and nutrition. Shunning politicians, he interviewed farmers, merchants, shopkeepers, shipowners, and workers of all sorts as he traveled through England, France, Italy, the Netherlands, and Germany.

To his close friend, the Marquis de Lafayette, Jefferson confided on the eve of the French Revolution his belief that to govern a country with any degree of enlightenment, officials needed to get away from their capitals and go "absolutely incognito" to see firsthand how people live:

> You must ferret the people out of their hovels as I have done, look into their kettles, eat their bread, loll on their beds under pretense of resting yourself but in fact to find if they are soft. You will find a more sublime pleasure . . . when you shall be able to apply your knowledge to the softening of their beds and the throwing of a morsel of meat into their kettles of vegetables.

It had been seven years since Jefferson had made a long swing through the eastern United States en route to his diplomatic duties in France. To former aide David Humphreys he confessed, "I know only the Americans of the year 1784. They tell me this is to be much a stranger."

On May 9, 1791, Madison left Philadelphia for New York City to procure supplies and make travel arrangements. Jefferson sent him a proposed itinerary:

> When we tack about from the extremity of our journey, instead of coming back the same way, to cross over through Vermont to [the] Connecticut River and down that [river] to New Haven, then through Long Island to New York and so to Philadelphia.

Jefferson wrote to President Washington, who was touring the Carolinas, "I think to avail myself of the present interval of quiet to get rid of a headache which is very troublesome by giving more exercise to the body and less to the mind."

What weighed most heavily on Jefferson's mind were controversies with Secretary of the Treasury Alexander Hamilton. The in-fighting was about to become public. Jefferson opposed Hamilton's pro-British trade policies and was alarmed to see his old friend Vice President John Adams advocating stronger ties with Great Britain, writing under a pen name in a series of columns in the pro-Hamilton *National Gazette*. Jefferson was therefore elated to receive a copy of Thomas Paine's latest anti-British blast, *The Rights of Man,* just published in London. Jefferson wrote a note recommending publication in the United States and sent it off to a printer. He intended his comments to remain private. He was, after all, in Washington's cabinet with Adams and Hamilton. He was chagrined when the printer published his signed letter as the introduction to Paine's tract. That spring, scores of newspapers reprinted Jefferson's letter. Overnight, Jefferson became the spokesman for Americans disenchanted with Washington's policies. "I am sincerely mortified," he wrote Washington, "to be thus brought forward on the public stage against my love of silence . . . and my abhorrence of disputes."

But a note to son-in-law Randolph suggests a hidden political agenda. Jefferson sent him a copy of the *National Gazette,* describing its editorial policy as

> pure Toryism, disseminating [Hamilton's] doctrine of monarchy, aristocracy and the exclusion of the people. . . . We have been trying to get another weekly or half-weekly [newspaper] excluding advertisements set up, so that it could go free through the states in the mails and furnish [our] vehicle of intelligence. We hoped at one time to have persuaded Freneau [Philip Freneau, a New Jersey journalist, poet, and college roommate of Madison*], but we have failed.

Jefferson here was admitting in a private letter what he had been denying in public: that he was involved in an opposition

---

* Freneau had made his reputation as a poet with an account of his captivity on two prisoner-of-war ships of the sort on which James Forten was also confined.

faction within Washington's government and was backing his own partisan newspaper. His son-in-law was to forward Hamilton's paper each week via government mail to stops along his route. Jefferson and Madison would have the latest political news to discuss in the long days on the road, where they would have strictest privacy.

James Madison had long been a protégé of Jefferson in Virginia politics; the two planter-lawyers had battled for ten years to win religious freedom in the state. Lately, however, Madison seemed to be rising above his mentor in public acclaim. Jefferson's main contribution to the Revolution—drafting the Declaration of Independence—had been a state secret of the Continental Congress. In contrast, Madison was known throughout the new nation as a defender of the Constitution and the congressman who proposed its Bill of Rights.

Jefferson had not expected to remain in the United States in 1789 when he took home leave after five years as ambassador to Paris. But Madison had told Washington that, without his fellow Virginian in the first cabinet to speak for the farmer and for the worker, the government would be in trouble. The newly elected president had insisted that Jefferson accept the post of secretary of state. Just as they had been in Virginia, in Philadelphia Thomas Jefferson and James Madison were the closest of political allies.

SINCE JEFFERSON WAS, as usual, strapped for cash, he had to await the arrival of four hogsheads of Monticello tobacco to be sold for travel money. But when the shipment finally arrived, it was worthless, already smoked in a fire. It "cannot be sold here at all," he moaned. At first, Jefferson had offered to pay all Madison's expenses, but Madison insisted on dividing them. As it turned out, Jefferson would run out of money on the road and end up borrowing from Madison. As Jefferson's high, black carriage rolled out of Philadelphia on May 17, he wrote in a travel journal he kept on the back of his pocket almanac, "heard the first whip-poor-will." Two days later, Madison, in New York, wrote his brother that "Mr. Jefferson is here."

Jefferson checked into Mrs. Ellsworth's boardinghouse in Maiden Lane with Freneau, Madison, and John Beckley, clerk of the Virginia House of Representatives. Their meeting fanned reports from Hamilton supporters of political intriguing, but Jefferson and Madison remained silent. One of Hamilton's friends was George Beckwith, unofficial envoy of Great Britain to the United States. "I am sorry to inform your Grace," Beckwith wrote to the British Foreign Secretary, Lord Grenville, "that the Secretary of State's party and politics gains ground here. [They] will have influence enough to cause acts and resolves which may be unfriendly to Great Britain to be passed early in the next session of Congress. The Secretary of State, together with Mr. Madison, are now gone to the Eastern States, there to proselyte as far as they are able a commercial war with Britain." Alexander Hamilton's son, John, had no doubt that Jefferson was politicking. He flatly asserted that the Virginians were meeting secretly in New York City with newly elected United States Senator Aaron Burr, before going on to huddle with Governor George Clinton, a leading anti-Federalist, in Albany. Aaron Burr had just unseated Hamilton's father-in-law, Philip Schuyler, from the Senate.

If Jefferson and Madison were merely on vacation, they had no reason to conceal or to comment on visits to New York politicians. But if, as John Adams's son, John Quincy, later wrote, they were engaged in "double dealing," there was good reason for silence. It is likely that Jefferson and Madison called on Aaron Burr. Instead of using his own distinctive Monticello-made carriage, which was recognizable, Jefferson, according to his expense records, hired a coach for one day while in New York City. Even the possibility of such an alliance worried Hamilton's supporters. "They had better be quiet," wrote Robert Troup to Hamilton, "for if they succeed, they will tumble the fabric of the government in ruins to the ground."

Intrigues aside, the first thing Jefferson did when he reached a large town along the road was to buy books. He also sent out his manservant, the mulatto slave James Hemings, to buy fresh fruit and vegetables. James, who had been a servant at Monticello since he was nine and spoke French fluently, had shared Jefferson's travels for ten years. In his years in Paris, Jefferson had placed James in the kitchen of the Prince de Condé to learn French cooking. In Paris, Hemings's younger sister, Sally, was the servant of Jefferson's teenage daughter, Patsy. James and Sally were the half-brother and half-sister of Jefferson's wife, Martha Wayles Jefferson, sharing the same father.

Jefferson entrusted James with his carriage and enough travel money for him to go ahead on the Post Road to Poughkeepsie, New York, where the touring party would rendezvous. For all their obvious and substantial presence, slaves are usually invisible in early American history. Jefferson's expense records prove Hemings's presence on his voyages and give glimpses of his duties. "James for expenses to Poughkeepsie 6 (dollars)." In 1792, Jefferson would set James free. He was becoming convinced, as he wrote to the black mathematician Benjamin Banneker, that "nature has given to our black brethren talents equal to those of the other colors of men."

As the Virginians sailed up the Hudson they made an overnight stop at Conklin's Tavern. In addition to writing down the price of breakfast, Jefferson began to rate the inns along their route: a nondescript inn got no comment or "middling," a good inn, a plus mark or star, a bad one, a minus. Jefferson passed on this record to family and friends: thirty-five years later his granddaughter went to New England on her honeymoon, using Jefferson's travel recommendations from his 1791 vacation. Back aboard Captain Cooper's sloop, Jefferson began to keep yet another journal on a single seven-by-nine-inch sheet of paper, a botanical account of the tour. He recorded plants and trees he had not seen farther south. He wrote on his portable laptop desk:

May 22. Conklin's in the Highlands. Found here the Thuya Occidentalis, called white cedar, and Silverfir, called hemlock. . . . Also the Candleberry myrtle.

Botany was the cutting-edge science of the late eighteenth century. Jefferson had been keeping detailed garden records at Monticello for nearly twenty years. Here, he was keeping a detailed traveling botanist's record for the first time.

After three days aboard ship, Jefferson and Madison were ready for the comforts of Hendrickson's Inn in Poughkeepsie. Jefferson appreciated a good roadside inn:

> A traveler retired at night to his chamber in an inn, all his effects contained in a single trunk, all his cares circumscribed by the walls of his apartment, unknown to all, unheeded and undisturbed, writes, reads, thinks, sleeps, just in the moments when nature and the movements of his body and mind require. Charmed with the tranquility of his little cell, he finds how few are his real wants, how cheap a thing is happiness.

The next day, they rode north. Jefferson noted there were juniper trees with "berries used for infusing gin." They drove sixteen miles before breakfast; in all, they rode thirty-seven miles on horseback that first exhilarating day, Hemings driving the carriage behind them. It was at Lasher's Inn that evening that Jefferson conducted his first interview on Hessian fly damage:

> The Hessian fly remains on the ground among the stubble of the old wheat. At plowing time for sowing the new crop, they rise in swarms before the plow horses. Soon after the wheat comes up, they lay the egg in it. . . . [Conrad Lasher] supposes the old fly dies in the winter. In the spring they begin to grow. I saw them in the worm state, about as long as a grain of rye, and one third its volume. White, smooth and transparent. In June, the chrysalis

bursts and the insect comes out, brown like a flax seed, a little longer, and with wings. . . . He has counted 120 on one stalk, always under cover of the blade.

Jefferson noted that farmers nearby "have found a remedy," using a "new sort" of white bearded wheat with "a more vigorous stalk." The new variety of wheat was undamaged.

Hurrying on toward Albany, Jefferson noted a variety of azalea he had never seen before. He used one flower to describe the fragrance of another. The azaleas were "wild-honeysuckle rose-colored, on stems four feet high loaded richly with large flowers, of a strong, pink fragrance." In other words, they smelled like pinks.

If the two tourists indulged in politics in Albany, there is no record they visited Governor George Clinton. The Albany *Register* of May 30 recorded:

On Thursday last, this city was honored with the presence of Mr. Jefferson, Secretary of State, accompanied by . . . the celebrated Madison. . . . It is to be regretted that their short stay in this city deprived our principal characters from paying that respectful attention due to their distinguished merit.

Only John Hamilton insisted that Jefferson and Madison visited Governor Clinton and other anti-Federalists "under the pretext of a botanical excursion to Albany"; he remained convinced they were studying "Clintonia borealis."

⸎

ONE MAN in New York state was big enough to set politics aside when the two Virginians arrived. He was Major General Philip Schuyler, recently unseated from the Senate by Aaron Burr. Hero of the Revolution, Schuyler came from a family that owned the land on which several battles had taken place. He welcomed Jefferson and Madison and instructed his son, a Hamilton partisan, to do likewise. In Paris, Jefferson had been a close friend of Schuyler's daughter, Angelica. Their daughters had attended the same school. For the next few days, Jefferson and Madison toured overgrowing battlefields where British, German, French, and Americans had fought for control of the continent. Jefferson described these "scenes of blood" in a letter to President Washington.

Riding north into the Hudson Highlands, Jefferson and Madison visited factories: a canvas factory, where sailcloth was made; a plant where "1,000 barrels of salted herring [are] exported annually, a distillery from which 1,000 hogsheads of rum are annually exported." They "saw nails made by cutting them with a pair of shears from the end of a bar of iron." Making nails was a technology new to America, where houses and furniture were still joined by wooden pegs. Jefferson was amazed to see "120 [nails] cut off in a minute" with "very simple tools." Using slave boys, he later manufactured nails at Monticello.

Jefferson was struck by the serene beauty of what he called the "lake country." On May 29, 1791, Jefferson's journal burst with honeysuckle, wild cherry, black gooseberry, velvet aspen, cotton willow, paper birch, "bass-wood wild rose," and "abundance of sugar maple." Hemlock was draped with moss "a foot long" sometimes "4 [feet]." Strawberries were in blossom, bearing "young fruit." His account of their two days gliding over Lake George on a sloop includes geographic descriptions (the lake was 36 miles long and "very clear") as well as geological comments ("formed by a contour of mountains into a basin") and climatic observations ("healthy").

Jefferson and Madison did more than take notes: they went fishing. The "abundance" of fish "have added to our other amusements the sport of taking them," wrote Jefferson. They caught salmon trout "of 7 lb. weight," speckled trout, Oswego bass "of 6 or 7 lb. weight," rock bass, yellow perch. He noted wild ducks and seagulls "in abundance." They found rattlesnakes, "two of which we killed." As any visitor to the north country in late May quickly learns, there were "swarms of mosquitoes and gnats, and two kinds of biting fleas." Swatting, picking off the insects, he carefully noted he had been bitten by two different kinds of fleas.

Sailing on Lake George with the right "kind of leisure," Jefferson wrote letters. To his daughter, Patsy: "Lake George is without comparison the most beautiful water I ever saw." It was "finely interspersed with islands, its waters limpid as crystal and the mountain sides covered with rich groves" of evergreens "down to the water edge." As they approached Lake Champlain, his only complaint was the weather: it was as "sultry hot" as "could be found in Carolina or Georgia":

> I suspect indeed that the heats of Northern climates may be more powerful than those of Southern ones in proportion as they are shorter. Perhaps vegetation requires this. ... Here, they are locked up in ice and snow for six months. Spring and autumn, which make a paradise of [Virginia], are rigorous winter with them, and a tropical summer breaks on them all at once.

What struck James Madison, who was keeping a tiny diary, the hardest was finding a free black farmer, Prince Taylor, whose house in Ticonderoga township sat all alone at Lake George's north end, at what is still called Black Point. "He possesses a good farm of about 250 acres which he cultivates with 6 white hirelings." The "free Negro," a Massachusetts native and Revolutionary War veteran, had paid about $2.50 per acre

> and by his industry and good management turns [it] to good account. He is intelligent; reads, writes and understands accounts and is dexterous in his affairs. . . .

They trudged over the ruined ramparts of Fort Ticonderoga and enjoyed a French Canadian meal at Charles and Mary Hay's inn in the old King's Store, the only building left standing by the British. Their hosts had helped the Americans during the Revolutionary War attack on Quebec and had fled with them. Another traveler in the 1790s found that the Hays provided "a neat table and a comfortable light supper specially laid out for us." Jefferson's only comment was to rate the tavern "middling."

The next day, Jefferson and Madison sailed out onto Lake Champlain—into strong headwinds. Sailing on the mountain lake with its headlands, shoals, and crosswinds was tricky. After a full day in which they covered only twelve miles, they lodged at an inn at Chimney Point on the Vermont shore. The next morning, Jefferson "met with a small red squirrel, of the color of our fox squirrel with a black stripe on each side, weighing about six ounces generally." The squirrels were

> in such abundance . . . that twenty odd were killed at the house we lodged in . . . without going ten steps from the door. . . . We killed three which were crossing the lakes, one of them just as he was getting ashore where it was three miles wide and where, with the high winds then blowing, he must have made it five or six miles.

The next day they attempted to sail north again, but the wind was still adverse and the sea was high.

Now nearly a week behind schedule, Jefferson and Madison modified their plan to cruise north the full length of Lake Champlain and cross the Green Mountains. Instead of sailing to the Canadian border, they came about at Split Rock, only thirty miles up the 110-mile-long lake. Jefferson vented his frustration in his journal: "Lake Champlain is a much larger but less pleasant water than Lake George." Yet he admired the Vermont scenery, the "champagne" country of wheat fields rolling up to the Green Mountains. He wrote daughter Patsy that his journey was "prosperous and pleasant."

Hurrying south sixty-two miles by carriage in the next two days, they retraced their route to Saratoga, crossed the Hudson, and approached Vermont from the southeast. Riding over a rutted, bone-rattling dirt road to Bennington on horseback, they now had to stop every day at blacksmiths. As they left New York, Madison noted that the terrain changed from flat pine barrens as they crossed into Vermont to "7 or 8 [miles] of a fine fertile vale separating two ridges of low mountains." They were looking down on the close-packed rich farms of the Walloomsac River valley. The ground was "rich and covered with sugar maple and beech." In Vermont, unlike the New York side of Lake Champlain, the countryside was "closely settled." The fields were full of corn and potatoes, flax to make linens, wheat and clover and half a dozen grass crops for feeding livestock. From the sugar maples they now saw for the first time "some sugar is made and much may be."

That spring, Jefferson had been busy with an interesting agricultural question with political overtones. The British government's Rule of 1756 barred American ships from carrying British goods to and from British possessions in Canada and the Caribbean. Jefferson was determined to break American reliance on imports such as sugar grown on British plantations in the Caribbean. Sugar was the leading American import, a severe drain on hard cash. Americans drank many cups of tea a day, lacing it with expensive imported sugar. Searching for an American substitute, he came across maple sugar. Jefferson believed that Americans could produce enough maple sugar on their farms not only to meet their own domestic needs but also to export their surplus to Europe to compete with the British. And maple sugar could be tapped, boiled, and bottled by free men, women, and children on the family farm, with no need for slave labor. In 1790, Jefferson had instructed his son-in-law to plant maple seedlings at Monticello, but as he did not know enough about where to situate them or how to cultivate them, they all died. Before going on vacation, Jefferson wrote to another Virginia farmer, President Washington, the latest news about "the sugar-maple tree." He was a little worried that farmers would distill the maple juice into alcoholic spirits, drink the stuff up, and still need to import sugar. He had sampled the drink, "which is exactly whiskey."

As they crossed over into Vermont, Madison observed a fundamental difference in the people: Vermonters owned their own land. We can visualize him poking his head into farmhouses, asking, "Do you own your own house or do you rent it?"

Vermont farms, he recorded, "vary from 50 to 200 acres; in a few instances, they exceed 200." The Vermonters' way of life was extremely plain and economical, particularly in the table and ordinary dress. "Their expense is chiefly on their houses, which are of wood and make a good figure without, but are very scantily furnished within."

Stopping briefly at the scene of the Revolutionary Battle of Bennington (near present-day Hoosick Falls, New York), the road-weary travelers rode on to Elijah Dewey's Tavern (now the Walloomsac Inn) in Bennington, Vermont, the afternoon of June 4. They stayed only one night. Vermont's first U.S. Senator, Moses Robinson, learned they had arrived in town and insisted they stay with him. Until now, they had kept to Jefferson's plan of traveling through Vermont incognito, but they had not reckoned with Anthony Haswell, a fiercely republican fan of Jefferson's, who edited the *Vermont Gazette*. He had received his exchange copy of the previous week's Albany *Register* and had broken the story of this visit of the two highest U.S. officials ever to come to the new state of Vermont the day before they arrived.

The town of Bennington was couched in the middle of the richest wheat- and corn-producing area in the adolescent United States. Young couples who came to the Walloomsac Valley enjoyed probably the best prospects for prosperity in the new nation. An average couple could buy land, build a house and barn, and pay them off in only five years, exporting their surplus crops by wagon to New York and rendering any scrap wood into potash to be shipped in barrels up Lake Champlain to Canada. It was the perfect forum for Jefferson's doctrine of life, liberty, and land, and he was welcomed as a hero.

If the two Virginians had hoped to move on after a one-night stopover, however, they had not reckoned with a new Vermont blue law that forbade travel on the Sabbath. As a high government official, Jefferson could claim pressing business and, by applying to a magistrate, obtain an exception. But as secretary of state, the cabinet officer in charge of protocol, he decided to observe the newest state's newest law. They would again modify their route, staying over in Bennington until Monday morning.

Jefferson spent much of Saturday interviewing local citizens about the Hessian fly (there had been little damage this far north). In his memo for the American Philosophical Society, Jefferson noted, "Bennington. Had a few in 89, 90. Have not heard if there are any this year." That afternoon they moved to Senator Robinson's, where Jefferson was fascinated by a giant balsam poplar tree in the front yard. That evening, Senator Robinson gave a dinner and introduced his guests to the local gentry. Several at the table that night had represented Vermont as agents to the Continental Congress in its decade-long effort to enter the Union.

But this night, according to journalist Haswell, it was Thomas Jefferson bending Vermonters to his point of view. In his low, slow voice, he urged them to consider seriously a new cash crop: maple sugar. Haswell enthusiastically reported Jefferson's idea to make money from the sugar maples that abounded in Vermont. Bringing to the maple-tree-rich, cash-poor Vermont frontier a promise of dripping prosperity, Jefferson brought into being its maple syrup industry. The next year, as Jefferson promised, a Dutch company set up maple-sugaring operations in nearby Rutland. That autumn, using techniques long ago developed by Native Americans, Vermont settlers began their annual midwinter harvests.

Visiting Bennington on the Sabbath meant going to church. The "zealously pious" Senator Robinson took Jefferson and Madison along to the great gambrel-roofed Congregational meeting-house and ushered them to his family pew as the choir sang its favorite hymns. That afternoon, at Senator Robinson's house, Jefferson found peace for his favorite activity, writing letters. He took out several slips of birch bark he had cut from trees along Lake George and wrote his son-in-law a long letter describing the first four hundred miles of their tour. "The laws of the state not permitting us to travel on Sunday has given me time to write to you." He listed their battlefield tours and botanical discoveries, especially "an azalea very different from the nudi-flora with very large clusters of flowers, more thickly set on the branches, of a deeper red, and high pink fragrance. It is the richest shrub I have ever seen." When he returned to Philadelphia, Jefferson confirmed with botanist friends that he had discovered an as-yet-unclassified variety of azalea.

Jefferson then wrote another letter—to President Washington. Probably at dinner the night before, he had learned that the British, violating the Treaty of Paris of 1783, had built a blockhouse "something further south than the border," on North Hero Island in Lake Champlain, five miles south of the Canadian line. They had stationed a sloop-of-war named the *Maria* there and were forcing American ships to heave to, even in storms; as a result, two of them had sunk. Vermonters were nervous; two hundred militia had occupied a stockade nearby, and state officials expected trouble.

With a clock ticking now, before sunrise on Monday morning Jefferson and Madison slipped out of town, riding fourteen miles before breakfast. Madison's horse was becoming lame: they stopped at a blacksmith's. Jefferson tried to make light of the problem when he reported to Washington that they were having "cavalry troubles." They rode on, south along the Connecticut River, making overnight stops at Northhampton, Hartford, Guilford. Crossing to the north shore of Long Island, they toured farms and stayed in comfortable inns for five nights, arriving in New York City on June 16. In all, Jefferson calculated, they had travelled 900 miles, 236 by water, 664 by land.

In those last days on Long Island, Jefferson paused long enough to interview three old women of the Unquachog tribe, writing down 250 of their equivalents for English words. It was the first of fifty brief tribal glossaries he gathered, hoping in retirement to publish a systematic study of Native American languages. He also shopped for trees at a nursery at Flushing, ordering, at the top of his list, sixty maples for Monticello. They never produced any syrup or sugar, but Jefferson had learned another use for trees during their five weeks on the road. From that time on, when politics oppressed him, he took afternoon rides along the Schuylkill River in Philadelphia or the Potomac in Washington and sat a spell under a shade tree.

For the next twenty-five years Jefferson, Madison, and men they encountered in Philadelphia and New York would battle over the two highest offices in the land. In 1796 John Adams and Jefferson opposed each other for the presidency, with Adams winning and Jefferson becoming his vice president. Four years later Jefferson won the rematch, but only because Hamilton supported him over his running mate, Aaron Burr; through a fluke in Madison's Constitution, Burr might have been named president by the disgruntled congressmen of Adams's party. President Jefferson then named Madison his secretary of state. In 1804 Burr killed Hamilton in a duel. Jefferson dropped Burr from his reelection ticket, choosing Governor George Clinton of New York instead. (For much of his second term Jefferson tried to have Burr convicted of treason.) In 1809 James Madison became the fourth president of the United States, keeping Clinton on as vice president, and Jefferson happily retired to Monticello.

The vehemence of such partisan (and intraparty) strife seemed unimaginable in the Virginians' last days on Long Island in 1791, however. Thomas Jefferson had finally learned how to relax.

TECUMSEH
AND THE
INDIAN
NATION

*A*REASONABLE PERSON MIGHT BELIEVE
that contact between whites and American Indians
moved from being a rare but recurring event to an everyday
aspect of life in America. In fact, all such contact kept its novelty
for both sides for generations because the people involved kept
changing. Much subtler than the meeting of two, big, stable
populations, American settlement brought together newly arrived Europeans with many different tribes and from places
farther and farther west. Over time, prolonged contact did
change the stories that people told and how each side thought
about its opposite. The Indians learned that whites were not all
the same. The French for the most part left the culture of North
America undisturbed so long as they could hunt and trap to
promote their flourishing fur trade. The British strove for dealings that were correct in diplomatic and legal terms, trying to
find old agreements and documents to uphold their claims.
Then new people came, settlers who would promise anything to
get land.

Gradually, and in many cases reluctantly, the Europeans had
to change how they saw the American Indians. In the Southeast
in particular, where the Cherokees developed a system for writ-

ing down their language and had their own newspaper, portraying them as uncivilized no longer matched the reality of what many whites saw and knew. But even as their views of the different tribes changed, some whites felt no less greed for the land they occupied and saw themselves as entitled to seize it. Whites did not question or doubt what they expected to be the result of their contact: defeat of the native peoples and takeover of their land.

On their side, the various tribes showed new ideas that evolved within their own societies because of contact with whites. Some of their leaders took lessons from the generals sent to deal with them; others gave lessons. When the Shawnee chief Tecumseh went to talk with William Henry Harrison, military governor of the Indiana Territory and future president of the United States, he addressed the general as nearly his equal. "How can we have confidence in the white people?" he asked. "When Jesus Christ came upon the earth, you killed him." Not confident that translation could convey his message, he later relied on body language. He and Harrison sat on a bench. The chief steadily leaned against the general, finally crowding him so much he nearly fell on the ground. Without a word, Tecumseh had eloquently conveyed that he understood what policy the officer was carrying out. He made it plain that white settlers were humiliating his people and that no one could be expected to put up with such treatment.

⇥⇤

IF HE HAD NOT BEEN a Shawnee, Tecumseh would likely be remembered as a revolutionary leader and political thinker of vision and daring. In the proud and sad memories of his people, he was and remains a hero. Tecumseh ("Tecumtha" before whites changed it) was born a Shawnee and became an Indian. That shift gives clues to the extraordinary man who came close to achieving an Indian state within the still expanding United States. Harrison, one of his bitterest enemies, understood the greatness of this warrior, "one of those uncommon geniuses which spring up occasionally to produce revolutions and over-turn the established order of things." What he had seen of Tecumseh made Harrison speculate that if he had not lived within the territory of the United States, "he would perhaps be founder of an empire that would rival in glory that of Mexico or Peru."

For a time during the short life of Tecumseh, American Indians had greater hope than ever before or since. Tecumseh gave them a consciousness of themselves as one people more than members of just one tribe. He taught them that all tribes shared the challenge he saw, just as all tribes shared the native history he taught them. Few leaders before Tecumseh had preached the tragedy of the Pequot and the Narragansett, of tribes that were simply gone—as all their people would be, he warned, if they did not unite.

Tecumseh, whose name means "panther lying in wait," was born in March 1768 in Old Piqua, near Dayton, Ohio. Pucken-shinwe, his war chief father, and Methoataske, his mother, had come to eastern Ohio after wandering great distances. The Shawnee ("southerners") had migrated so much that they could be found all the way from South Carolina, where Europeans called them Savannahs, to Pennsylvania. Besides migrating, these tribes divided, with subgroups going to new regions. Be-cause native groups in disparate places called themselves Shaw-nee, white settlers and soldiers could not easily understand that they were one coherent people or nation. Some Shawnee groups had settled in Alabama, so Tecumseh's father did nothing un-usual by taking as his wife Methoataske, a Creek woman from the eastern part of Alabama. By the time they reached Old Piqua in eastern Ohio, where Tecumseh was born, the couple already had four children. In all there would be nine.

As a boy, Tecumseh learned that treaties could not be counted on for land and that white people could not be counted on for honor. Because he was born in 1768, Tecumseh always knew war, and especially border war. In 1774 friction between white settlers and the Shawnees worsened to the point of being called a war: Lord Dunmore's War, named for the royal governor of Virginia who led about two thousand settlers into Ohio and Kentucky. Many Shawnees and settlers died before the Shawnee leader Cornstalk decided to make peace, mainly to preserve Shawnee villages in Ohio. Making what he saw as a sensible bargain, Cornstalk gave up Shawnee lands south of the Ohio River and consented to open Kentucky to whites in return for his understanding that his people would retain their land north of the Ohio River.

The older males in Tecumseh's family, his father and his oldest brother Cheeseekau, both fought with Cornstalk and knew what the treaty promised. They resented the settlers who ignored the agreement and kept on coming into Shawnee land. Far worse, a group of whites found Puckenshinwe in the woods alone and shot him through the chest. He was not yet dead when Methoataske and her young son Tecumseh found him. Only a few years later the fatherless boy lost his hero Cornstalk. He, too, was violently murdered by whites the Shawnees saw as lawless liars. Land-seeking whites burned Old Piqua twelve years after Tecumseh was born there. The Shawnees of that settlement moved west to the Miami River to build a new settlement named Piqua ("village that rises from the ashes"). No one had to teach Tecumseh hatred.

Tecumseh would inevitably become a warrior, but not like his father. Part of his great intelligence expressed itself in very lucid self-awareness: "I am a Shawnee. My forefathers were warriors. Their son is a warrior. From them I take only my existence. From my tribe I take nothing. I have made myself what I am." The adult who characterized himself so starkly had in mind perhaps his unusual beginning of warrior life. In 1782 Tecumseh, aged only fourteen, came close to fighting for the first time when he and his brother Cheeseekau became involved in a small engagement with settlers in Ohio. His brother was wounded, causing the young Tecumseh to run away in horror. Later that same day, he suffered shame and disgust at his own cowardly reaction, vowing to himself that he would not show fear again.

While he honored the promise to himself, Tecumseh insisted on the difference between courage and brutality. As a teenager he did what other Shawnees did by attacking boatloads of settlers on the Ohio River. One day, the Shawnees burned at the stake a settler they had captured after a river attack. Tecumseh felt such revulsion that he took a stand and publicly spoke out against their barbarism. Winning had to do with honor and with land, he explained. And the speech worked. He made the Shawnees feel humiliated with him. That ability to move people with his words would develop as he matured into an orator of legendary power.

Because white settlers filled up land so quickly and had the protection of soldiers, some native tribes thought that resistance made no sense when there could be treaties. Aware of this reasoning and also aware of his own powers to convert people to his thinking, Tecumseh traveled great distances to win the support of more tribes. He went east to Tennessee, then south through what is now Mississippi, Alabama, and Georgia all the way to Florida. But while he was away from Ohio, a new army under Anthony Wayne headed north from Cincinnati. Wayne planned to stay. Rather than accompany soldiers or protect boats on the Ohio, he set out to build frontier fortresses. He spent nearly a year in one of these at Greenville, Ohio, before heading northwest in the direction of the Maumee River. In late August 1794, the tornado season, Wayne began advancing with three thousand men. Shawnees, under their chief Blue Jacket, decided that they would engage Wayne's forces. The place where they fought along the Maumee River was an open space where men could fight because so many big trees had been knocked down by a tornado. Later, that encounter would be referred to as the Battle of Fallen Timbers. The Shawnees under Blue Jacket put up a good fight, but in the end cavalry and bayonets in superior numbers forced them to flee. Tecumseh fought in Blue Jacket's forces that day and inspired others to fight.

Not until the following spring did the natives hear from Anthony Wayne. This time he called for a peace meeting. In answer to his gesture, leaders and representatives of as many as twelve different tribes went to see what was being offered. Blue Jacket went, but Tecumseh refused. Two months later the chiefs of the different tribes accepted the terms of what would be known as the Greenville Treaty. The United States won a great deal of land as a result of Fallen Timbers. Places important to the Shawnee, including Old Piqua, passed into American hands. Most of what is now Ohio became the property of the whites, as did good settlement locations that would in time become Detroit, Toledo, Peoria, and Chicago. For their part, the tribes were given promises, money, and goods worth something like $20,000. They were also promised annuities amounting to $9,500.

The chiefs at the conference saw these terms as valid, or at least they signed them. But Tecumseh, still furious, refused to acknowledge the agreement as legitimate. From his previous experience, he was convinced the whites would not respect their own terms. But what bothered him and many other tribal leaders, including, no doubt, some who had been at the conference at Fort Greenville, was the notion of treaties in general, not this one in particular. By the reasoning of the native tribes, treaties made no sense. The idea that words on paper could alter the relation of people to land struck them as foolish. For one thing, they had no concept of having acquired the land they called theirs. They belonged to it as much as it belonged to them, and that relationship was spiritual far more than legal. They lived from what the land gave them in their hunting and fishing. The bones of their ancestors belonged to the land. How could words on paper change any of that? Even chiefs who signed treaties did not necessarily understand that once they had deeded land over, they were expected to leave. If a paper opened land to whites, then whites were free to belong to the land as they did. Why could they not both belong to it? They probably wondered how it had been possible for so many whites to leave their own land on the other side of the ocean. What about the bones of their ancestors?

Tecumseh, with his talent for articulating what others believed, gave this terse analysis: "Sell a country. Why not sell the air, the clouds and the great sea, as well as the earth? Did not the Great Spirit make them all for the use of his children?" Even while the concept of owned land remained incomprehensible, Tecumseh could see the tide of settlers advancing from east to west, and he moved west.

Not all the tribes of the Northwest had sent representatives to Fort Greenville, and not all tribes accepted the treaty. Their discontent suited Tecumseh's plan to put himself at the head of a force of warriors from many tribes. He did not want to be a Shawnee war chief but a leader of red men. His gift for speaking depended on his ability to hold the attention of a gathering of people of any race. Almost every eyewitness account of him remarks that he was an unusually good-looking man. His fine features, light hazel eyes, and superb physique gave the tall Shawnee a strong visual presence that drew and held people's curiosity. To address a crowd he would sometimes stand before it in only his moccasins and breech cloth, displaying his strength. Then, when he began to speak, a powerful voice conveyed great conviction and, most of all, his authority. Even through the clumsiness of translations that survive, his poetic language comes through.

When he was around thirty, Tecumseh met a well-read farmer living in Ohio named Galloway who recognized and appreciated the Shawnee's language and inquisitive mind. More dramatically, Tecumseh also met Galloway's young, fair-haired, and beautiful daughter Rebecca. She tutored him, reading to him and with him. In time, Tecumseh's admiration for the young woman moved him to ask her father for her hand in marriage. Her wise father wanted the choice to be his daughter's. She told Tecumseh that she would gladly be his wife, provided that he leave his people and live with her as a white man. She wanted him to stop being Shawnee. Tecumseh recognized a grave decision and would not be rushed. A month later he gave Rebecca Galloway the answer that caused him much agony: he had to turn her down. He knew that he could not abandon his people.

QUITE OFTEN, chiefs who were talked into signing treaties, in particular those who were old and weak, ceded land that was not theirs. In his response to that injustice, Tecumseh showed the suppleness and originality of his thinking. Rather than resent the trickery of the ploy or the arrogance of the white view that *any* tribe could sign away the land of any other tribe, he seriously considered the notion of seeing all of them as part of the same race. That change in his thinking gave Tecumseh a vision that distinguished him from other tribal leaders of his time. He recognized that if groups saw themselves not as Creeks and Sioux and Choctaw and Miami but as one people resisting the whites, they had a stronger chance of succeeding. The tribes he visited recognized the power of this new, revolutionary idea. They must have had a sense of urgency about the new thinking, because they knew that the United States government was organizing ways to prepare land to be settled. In particular, they were preparing the territory west of Ohio, referred to as Indiana. The question for Tecumseh, and for everyone, was, what kind of state would Indiana be—white or red?

One strategy of preparing land for settlers used a new element in the white arsenal for weakening tribal resistance. At the very end of the eighteenth century the whites found that alcohol could bring willing chiefs to the negotiating table very quickly. In this campaign the tribes that stayed farthest from contact with whites withstood the best. Others, such as Chippewas, Piankashaws, and Weas, quickly degenerated from proud, socially coherent groups into pitiful, miserable stragglers living in poverty. When a tribe held its own land, poverty did not exist as a social curse. From hunting and fishing and from knowing the forest, people could provide for themselves and take care of their families. The tribe could grow. Without land, families became homeless, unemployed, and alienated with astonishing speed. Naturally, in no time the profound sense of loss led to hopelessness. The demoralized people with no more social identity could be counted on to sign white men's papers.

For the most part, Tecumseh kept alcohol from his Shawnee people by the force of his personality and by keeping white contact to a minimum. But his shiftless one-eyed brother, who made no attempt to hunt and fish and was given the degrading name of Laulewaskia ("The Idler"), did not show the same strength. The outcast showed no resistance to alcohol. But after white culture diminished him, it also offered him a way out. Contact with the Shakers, a Protestant sect whose followers swooned, trembled, and writhed in a spiritual dance, awakened Laulewaskia to the possibility of saving himself. Before long he experienced trances, which left him with the conviction that he must and could stop drinking because he had met with the Master of Life. The radical change that the Shawnees saw in him so convinced them of his spiritual powers that they freed him from his demeaning name and started calling him Tenskwatawa ("The Prophet").

Tecumseh needed no help in seeing the value of a brother with powerful medicine to help him in his cause of converting tribes to unified resistance to whites. Since "treaty chiefs," as they were called, tended to be old and tired of fighting, the warriors who were most easily persuaded to join Tecumseh were the strong and fierce young men of many tribes; the Sioux, Blackfeet, Arikaras, and Mandans wanted to follow the Prophet. The combination of a powerful new idea and strong spiritual backing needed to be controlled. The desire to get rid of chiefs and tribespeople who had too easily cooperated with whites created what modern times would recognize as a revolutionary purge. Only the faithful and the pure could be tolerated. The zeal of Tecumseh's converts started an internecine massacre that he personally had to stop.

News of the Prophet and his brother Tecumseh spread to whites. Thinking that he could fight words with words, the governor of the Indiana Territory, William Henry Harrison, started his own campaign to discredit the Prophet by mocking him. Sure that he had found a way to defeat an unimportant rival, Harrison sent a written challenge asking for proof of his prophetic powers. A real prophet, said Harrison, would be able to "cause the sun to stand still, the moon to alter its course, the rivers to cease to flow, or the dead to rise from their graves. If he does these things, you may then believe he has been sent from God."

Because he had a low opinion of native tribes in general, Harrison had never considered that other whites, including the British, might have talked to important tribal leaders. It was probably from them that Tenskwatawa knew what a solar eclipse was and was aware that there would be one on June 16, 1806. Staging it as an answer to the written challenge, the Prophet let many tribes know that he wanted a large gathering at Greenville on that day. (Choosing the location where a broken treaty had been signed enhanced the propaganda value of what he intended to do.) With a large crowd around him, Tenskwatawa let it be known that he would make darkness at midday. Just after 11:30 A.M. he called out with a large pointing gesture and ordered the sun to stop shining. Within minutes the shadow of the moon started to conceal an edge of the sun and then moved across its face. Dumbstruck, everyone there knew a challenge had been met. Before the awed assembly, the Prophet then summoned the Master of Life to make the light of noonday return. Moments later, the moon's shadow passed.

As news of that day spread, it was not individual warriors but entire tribes who came over to the side of Tecumseh and the Prophet. When Tecumseh went to speak to tribes, his riveting style usually assured his success. The Potawomis of Illinois joined his cause; the Sauk and the Foxes, great numbers of Menominees and Winnebagos in the North promised to help him. Some tribes, among them the Ottawas and the Kickapoos, said that they could be counted on in case of war. Tribes weakened and ravaged by alcohol—Piankashaws, Chippewas, Weas, and all the Wyandots—now took heart in the message of Tecumseh.

During Tecumseh's absence the Shawnee forfeited land through a treaty with William Henry Harrison. Even worse, the loss included some of their most valued hunting ground. From reports he had heard, Harrison thought that the Prophet led the uniting tribes. He did not know that his war chief brother Tecumseh had first gathered and then led the thousand warriors

who now stood ready to keep new settlers from coming into
Indiana. Making what he saw as a concession, Harrison sent
word that the Prophet was invited to Washington to meet the
president. Tecumseh and his brother sent word that they would
come to see Harrison in August 1810 at Vincennes.

Mutual distrust surrounded the meeting of Harrison and
Tecumseh. Arriving with several battle-ready warriors, Tecumseh gave no hint of being intimidated. In his mind, they met as
equals. Although Tecumseh could speak English, he made his
address in Shawnee. According to reports from witnesses, he
spoke with such conviction and speed that the translator could
not easily keep up with his pace. His words can accurately be
called a speech, even a lecture, and were clearly not at all what
Harrison had expected. Tecumseh gave a well-reasoned argument based on a careful chronology of grievances between his
people and whites. He recounted the many injustices and broken
treaties that they had suffered because of whites. His most important point had to do with unity. "The way, the only way to
stop this evil [of the whites] is for all the red men to unite in
claiming a common and equal right in the land, as it was at
first, and should be now—for it never was divided, but belongs
to all. No tribe has a right to sell, even to each other, much less
to strangers."

Harrison's reply could not have shown more contempt. His
words gave the impression that he had not even been listening
to Tecumseh. He spoke as if he had just arrived in the room,
having heard nothing. He objected strenuously to Tecumseh's
claim, saying that Shawnees came from Georgia, so how could
they have any say concerning land in Indiana? Insulted, Tecumseh accused Harrison of lying and nearly lost control of himself
as he reached for his tomahawk. To avoid a violent conclusion to
the meeting, Harrison announced the meeting was adjourned
and left. The next day Tecumseh sent his apologies. As further
proof of how poorly he understood the stature of the leader he
was facing, Harrison later felt sure that all his troubles with the
Shawnees could be explained by the meddling efforts of the
British in Canada. He could not imagine an intelligent antago-

nist, even after he had seen an outstanding leader of great political talent.

In November 1811, Harrison and an army of some one thousand men soundly defeated the Prophet's forces in what came to be called the Battle of Tippecanoe. The notoriety Harrison won from this success earned him the nickname "Tippecanoe." (In 1840, he would win the presidency campaigning on the slogan "Tippecanoe and Tyler, Too.") Having been away when the battle was fought, Tecumseh was enraged over his brother's decision to fight when their people were unprepared. Tecumseh banished his brother the Prophet, and saw his own dream of pantribal resistance fade.

Meanwhile, the United States and Great Britain had again been drawn into conflict with the outbreak of the War of 1812. Tecumseh was quick to side with the British, with whom he had excellent relations, partly because they listened to him. When a British officer astutely asked for his help, the result benefited both sides. Major General Isaac Brock, the lieutenant governor of Canada, got along well with Tecumseh, perhaps because they were alike and understood each other. When Brock arrived at Fort Malden, near present-day Detroit, he did not rely entirely on his staff. The tall and confident Brock acted on Tecumseh's advice, against that of all his officers except one, and attacked Detroit at daybreak. He sent a message to General William Hull, the American commander, asking him to give up. Hull, an aging hero of the Revolution, refused. Then Tecumseh and Brock proved themselves brilliant collaborators. Arranging for a scout to be captured, they planted the false information that five thousand braves were on their way from the lakes to the north to reinforce Tecumseh. To make the lie credible, Tecumseh went with his men to the woods and marched them single file past a small convoy of Americans under Captain Henry Brush. Then he took them back through the woods and marched them a second time and then a third. The trick worked. Men in the fort believed that the reinforcements had arrived. At that point, Hull did give up. Tecumseh and Brock were victorious without a fight.

That partnership, had it gone on, might have made the critical difference for Tecumseh and his cause. But Brock was killed in fighting near Niagara Falls. His successor could not have been worse, in Tecumseh's eyes. Colonel Henry Procter, the new commander at Malden, resembled Harrison rather than Brock in his low opinion of Tecumseh's people. Tecumseh wasted no time in letting the obese and arrogant Procter know that the low opinion was mutual.

When tribal warriors won a solid victory at the River Raisin against men from Kentucky, Procter was on the scene to assure the Americans that he would guarantee the safety of prisoners who had been captured. But he did nothing. Tecumseh's people marked the victory with excessive alcohol, which transformed tension into violence. While Procter remained absolutely passive, drunken warriors butchered unarmed captives. Indignant, Tecumseh criticized Procter severely. Besides the loss of life and his revulsion at such brutality, he knew that the massacre had set back his cause.

Inevitably, the River Raisin Massacre, as it was known, helped white settlers justify uncontrolled vengeance against the tribal warriors. Harrison came back to get even. Again, Tecumseh's forces defeated the whites, this time near the very recently built Fort Meigs, on the site of Fallen Timbers. And they started a massacre of captives after their victory, since no chief stopped them. Tecumseh, however, was nearby so that word could be sent to him. After twenty murders, Tecumseh arrived and stopped the massacre. Immediately, he asked Procter why he had not stopped the killing. The colonel's inept answer only placed blame: "Your Indians cannot be controlled." Procter's incompetence continued to hurt Tecumseh by eroding the confidence of his people. Procter lifted the siege of Fort Meigs. As Harrison advanced, his response was always the same: to retreat. In disgust, Tecumseh finally called him a "miserable old squaw."

Tecumseh knew exactly what would happen next. As he prepared his men to follow Procter retreating toward the Thames River, he told his men, "We are now going to follow the British, and I feel certain that we shall never return."

In his final battle at the Thames River, Tecumseh faced Kentuckians. Their battle cry, "Remember the River Raisin" must have pained the humane Shawnee chief. Outnumbered more than two to one, Tecumseh's people and the British lost to the American forces. Most of the day Tecumseh fought in the woods; he could be heard roaring like a wild animal and inspiring his men. By the end of the day, having been severely wounded and after continuing to fight with blood running from his mouth and from wounds, Tecumseh stopped shouting. The following morning Harrison's men felt disappointed, mystified, and afraid when they could not find his body. For years after that battle of October 4, 1813, white settlers still believed that Tecumseh roamed the woods.

His people, especially the Shawnees, had lost much more than a brilliant and gifted leader. They had also lost a dream.

THE
"NEW MEASURES" OF
CHARLES GRANDISON
FINNEY

CHARLES GRANDISON FINNEY HAD NEVER been a very religious young man. He came from an old New England Puritan family, but two years after he was born on August 29, 1792, his father, a Revolutionary War veteran named Sylvester, moved the family to Oneida County on the central New York frontier, where there were no churches. The land around Kirkland had been taken from the Six Nations Iroquois during the Revolution. In Finney's *Memoirs,* he says he grew up in what was "to a great extent a wilderness," where "no religious privileges were enjoyed by the people" and where "no Sabbath schools had been established." The settlers, mostly New England veterans of the Revolution, saw the urgency of setting up elementary schools, but there was "very little intelligent preaching" and "very few religious books were to be had."

Charles lived the rugged life of a boy on the frontier. He loved sports and prided himself on being able to outrun, outjump, outrow, outswim, and outwrestle all his friends. He also managed to get a good schooling. Later, he was proud that he went to school "summer and winter" until he was sixteen years old, an unusually intensive schooling for the son of a farmer. He seemed destined to become a schoolteacher, not a preacher. Very few of his neighbors professed any religion, and he thought little of the few sermons he heard: "when I heard any at all," he observed, they were "some miserable holding forth" by an "ignorant preacher" that left people with "irrepressible laughter" on their way home from meeting "in view of the strange mistakes" and "absurdities" they had heard. Just as a meetinghouse was built and young Charles began attending services regularly, his father decided to move again.

For two years, Finney was able to go to a private high school, the Hamilton Oneida Academy. He walked four miles each way to the school. The principal, Yale-educated Seth Norton, spotted great intellectual potential in the tall, blue-eyed pioneer boy. Six feet two, spare and athletic, Finney had a natural gift for both music and classical studies. Norton urged him to go to Yale.

When his parents moved again to start over in Henderson, on the Lake Ontario shore, the sixteen-year-old Finney taught school for two years. Then he took a teaching job in his parents' hometown of Warren, Connecticut, living with an uncle while he attended Warren Academy and prepared for Yale. He supported himself by working on his uncle's farm and running a singing school. A skilled cello player and choir director, he also taught music at the academy. The advice of his Warren schoolmaster, a Yale student, decided Finney against enrolling at Yale. He became persuaded that so much of college time was wasted that he could do all the work himself in two years. Moving to Mount Pleasant, New Jersey, Finney began teaching school in November 1814, a job he held for two years while he mastered the curriculum of Yale. He had learned Latin at Warren and taught himself Greek and, subsequently, Hebrew, but he never received a college diploma.

In those days, however, it was still possible to be admitted to the bar by serving a clerkship in a lawyer's office to prepare for the bar examination. Finney's decision to study law seems to have been half-hearted. His New Jersey headmaster had proposed that they go south to start their own academy. Finney had not seen his parents in about four years, and when he wrote them of this plan, they visited and urged him to come home to Jefferson County, New York, and clerk in a law office in the town of Adams. He did so, beginning his apprenticeship at the office of Benjamin Wright in 1818 at age twenty-five.

It was at this point that Finney began to study the Bible—as a law book. "In studying elementary law," he afterwards wrote, "I found the old authors frequently quoting Scripture and referring especially to the Mosaic institutes as authority for many of the great principles of common law. This excited my curiosity so much that I went and purchased a Bible, the first one I had ever owned." Finney began to take an interest in the Bible beyond his legal studies. He not only read it but began to meditate on it; "however," he noted, "much of it I did not understand."

He also began to attend church services in Adams, where the pastor was George Washington Gale (later the founder of Galesburg, Illinois, and of Knox College). Finney liked Gale personally but not his preaching. One Sunday after church, Finney said to Gale, "You don't believe what you preach. Were I in your place, holding the truth you declare I would ring the church bell, and cry in the streets, 'Fire! Fire!' " Reverend Gale got in the habit of dropping in on Finney at his law office and asking him what he thought of his latest sermon. The clerk "sometimes criticized his sermons unmercifully." Finney was just as outspoken in his critiques of the dogmas Gale taught; and he found that his clergyman friend was just as mystified by his preaching as his congregant.

Finney went on with his legal studies and was admitted to the bar, but as he attended church, listened to Gale, and studied the Bible more and more, he "became very restless." Something about religion "was of infinite importance." He became convinced that the teachings of the Bible had little to do with all the sermons and prayers at church. He once refused to allow the congregation to pray for him because none of their prayers seemed to be granted. He was popular enough to get away with openly criticizing the church services: "You have prayed enough since I have attended these meetings to have prayed the devil out of Adams if there is any virtue in your prayers." Studying the Bible more and more, he came to believe that his neighbors' prayers were not answered because they didn't expect them to be.

In October 1821, Finney relates in his memoirs, he had a two-day struggle with himself. He stopped by the church on Monday night, October 7, where Reverend Gale said to him, "You want to get something to make sport of." But Finney surprised him: he declared he had decided to "be a Christian." Years afterward, Finney asked Gale if the church had shaken as he knelt down with the others. "He trembled so that he thought the house shook," Gale recalled. The next night, Finney said later, "I felt almost like screaming." He went to the law office anyway, and later took a walk in a grove of woods north of town where he often strolled, but he could not relax. That evening, after work, he went into a darkened conference room at the law offices after everyone left. There, his conversion took place. He wrote in his memoirs that he then and there met God

> face to face and saw him as I would see any other man. . . .
> The Holy Spirit . . . seemed to go through me, body and
> soul. I could feel the impression like a wave of electricity,
> going through and through me. Indeed it seemed to come
> in waves and waves of liquid love . . . as the breath of God.
> . . . Immense wings . . . literally moved my hair like a
> passing breeze.

The next day, Finney went to work and began to ask the senior partner about "his salvation." The lawyer looked at him "with astonishment." Then a client came in and asked him if he was ready for his court case. Finney told the man, "I have a retainer from the Lord Jesus Christ to plead his cause and I cannot plead yours."

Finney left his law practice and decided to prepare himself to become a minister. His dramatic conversion experience at age twenty-nine led him to become a powerful preacher with a plain, direct message and style. He refused to go to Princeton seminary to study theology as Gale urged—even when he was offered a scholarship. He applied instead to the Saint Lawrence Presbytery as a candidate for the ministry but said he did not want to be put under the same theological influences "as they had been under." His friend Reverend Gale and the Reverend George S. Boardman were appointed to supervise his private studies, which lasted nearly three years. "After a great struggle with [Rev.] Gale," Finney finally was examined by the Saint Lawrence Presbytery and licensed in March 1824. Once again, Finney had proved extremely independent, aggressively opposing Gale's views on original sin and atonement, working out his own theology from study of the Scriptures. Gale's health was broken in the effort; he toured the South to recover before leaving for the West.

Three months after his ordination, in July 1824, the thirty-two-year-old lawyer-turned-minister married Lydia Andrews and began immediately to carry out his promise—to convert everyone else, starting with the people of New York state. Tall, handsome, with strikingly intense eyes and a powerful voice that he could project and modulate over a great distance, Finney introduced a new technique of preaching, what he called "new measures." His hold over an audience was so strong that when he described the descent of a sinner into hell, people in the back rows of a church stood up to watch the final fall. He singled out a poor "sinner" and called him by name to come and sit on the "anxious bench," the front row under the pulpit on stage, and berated his sinfulness in personal terms as the entire congregation witnessed the conversion struggle.

Religious revival meetings had been sweeping the country for a quarter century, but Finney now subjected them to rules and order. "A revival is not a miracle, it is a purely scientific result of the right use of constituted means." Casting aside the usual conventions of preaching, he used expressive language and colorful illustrations. He was shockingly direct and personal in his appeals to the conscience and in his prayers, so much so that he was threatened with tar and feathers and even with death. Emphasizing the terrible guilt and consequences of disobeying divine laws, he terrified his hearers. Rejecting the Calvinistic doctrine of predestination, he preached that everyone was responsible for his or her own salvation and, moreover, for the welfare of the community. Even writing a training manual for other revival preachers, he began a ten-year campaign of confrontation and conversion in the middle and eastern states that attracted nationwide attention.

Finney's methods and his message were so controversial that in July 1827, Presbyterian and Congregationalist ministers from all over New York state attended a convention called to consider his views. His followers, however, seemed to prevail, and he was permitted to go on preaching. But because the revival movement was not new, other practitioners objected vehemently to Finney's aggressive techniques and popularity. When Finney met Lyman Beecher at the New Lebanon Convention, Beecher told him to stay out of Massachusetts. If he dared bring his message of free will and salvation there, Beecher warned, "I'll meet you at the state line and call out the artillerymen, and fight you every inch of the way to Boston."

The religious revival that became known as the Second Great Awakening had begun, if its origin can be traced to any one location, on the Kentucky frontier in 1800, and had reached its climax at the Cane Ridge Meeting of August 1801, attended by an estimated 24,000 and resulting in a schism in the Presbyterian Church. In New England, the heated presidential campaigns of 1800 and 1804, in which 80 percent of the newspapers and most of the Congregationalist clergy attacked Thomas Jefferson as a Deist, masked a great struggle between Congregationalists and Unitarians. Unitarian scientist Joseph Priestley was one of the first to prophesy a millennium, which became a standard feature of the nineteenth-century revivals.

The revival movement had swept the nation's college campuses in 1802. Many Yale undergraduates boasted that they read deist books like Thomas Paine's *Age of Reason,* which mocked biblical "superstitions." Yale President Timothy Dwight challenged the campus radicals to debate and by his eloquence won students over. One of those students was Lyman Beecher, the son of a Connecticut blacksmith. By the time of Charles Finney's ordination a quarter century later, Beecher was the most famous evangelical preacher in the nation. Father of eleven children (including Harriet Beecher Stowe), he brought an almost fanatical energy to nearly every aspect of his life. His religious routine at home included taking his family to hear him preach twice on Sundays, to a weekly prayer meeting, and to a monthly "concert of prayer" where they prepared for the conversion of the world. By 1810, Beecher's evangelism would result in the formation, with help of other born-again Protestant ministers, of the American Board of Commissioners for Foreign Missions; in 1816, the American Bible Society; and in 1826, the American Tract Society. Together, they spread Bibles and tracts all over America. Soon, benevolent societies sprang up in hundreds of churches to promote Sunday schools and to provide ministries for sailors and for the poor. Revivalists concentrated their fire and brimstone along the "burned-over district" of New York and New England, a line that corresponded to the forty-second parallel running through the raw Erie Canal ports and teeming southern Massachusetts mill towns.

In 1826, Beecher became pastor of Hanover Street Congregational Church in Boston, where he attacked Unitarianism and its upper-crust Boston Brahmins. Unitarian theology, which denied the divinity of Christ and saw him only as a teacher and redeeming role model, was far too liberal and rational for Beecher; he called it a "halfway house on the road to infidelity." Beecher vilified the comfortable lives of Boston merchants, bankers, lawyers, and Harvard professors, denouncing as sinful their card playing and gambling. He crusaded to outlaw lotteries popular with lower-class Bostonians. He roundly condemned drinking and campaigned to shut down the grog shops on Boston Common. He also attacked the Roman Catholics who began to converge on Boston in the late 1820s, calling their priests and nuns operatives of the "Antichrist."

What Beecher advocated was the "New Haven theology" of his friend Professor Nathaniel Taylor of the Yale Divinity School. Like Finney's, this set of beliefs rejected the Calvinist doctrine of original sin, which held that the sin of Adam and Eve tainted human nature. Men and women sinned, Taylor said, but they were rational beings with free will who could choose to resist evil. The new evangelical theology rejected the predestinarian views of John Calvin and Jonathan Edwards, the belief that God sat in judgment on every human being before birth and decided that individual's eternal fate; to the instinctively democratic American, this was a harsh and unbelievable God.

The new evangelical theology, which Finney and Beecher popularized, preached that it was the duty of ministers to persuade sinners to choose by their own free will to accept God's gift of salvation. Over and over again, Finney insisted to his millions of listeners from Rochester, New York, to Glasgow, Scotland, that they were "moral free agents" who were "responsible for [their] own salvation" and for that of others around them. To the squirming occupants of the "anxious bench" and the teeming, crying, swooning congregations looking on, he thundered, "Do it!" Emotion was not only central to the new American religion: it was paramount. And if Beecher and his fellow ministers questioned Finney's methods at the 1827 New Lebanon Convention, Finney argued that the emotional outbursts of the sinners were preparing them to accept conversion. His success became his justification. If everyone cooperated with him, "if the church would do her duty, the millennium may come in this country in three years." Urging "the complete reformation of the whole world," Finney pushed onward his revivalist crusade, preaching not only personal progress but human "perfectionism." Christians should "aim at being holy and not rest satisfied until they are as perfect as God."

Finney's aggressive brand of optimism was nowhere more successful than in his attempt to convert the entire new city of Rochester, New York, during six months of daily preaching in 1830–1831. It had grown from a farming community of a few hundred people to the largest town in the American interior at the completion of the Erie Canal in 1824. By the time Finney arrived on a canal boat in the autumn of 1830, some twenty thousand people made their living from the half-million barrels of flour milled and exported as far as England every year. As the Genesee Valley became one of the world's leading grain-producing areas, merchant fortunes were made in Rochester and expressed in Grecian Revival mansions and tall-spired churches.

But there were two Rochesters: one the home of prosperous, churchgoing, middle-class merchants and proprietors of family businesses, the other a brawling frontier town of bars and fist-fights and poverty-stricken wives and children who watched helplessly as pay envelopes were emptied on whiskey and cards before wages made it home each week. In both Rochesters, there were thousands of men who had lost their moral bearings since they had left their New England homes to strike it rich in America's latest boom town.

Between September 1830 and the spring of 1831, Charles Grandison Finney and a team of four fellow evangelists waged daily war on sin in Rochester. They attacked alcohol, the circus, the theater, and other working people's entertainments that wasted time and money and distracted and delayed the coming millennium. Ignoring sectarian boundaries, Finney and his assistants mobilized the entire religious community and tapped its enormous economic power. While Finney was in Rochester, his rich evangelical converts organized a church for canal workers, transients, and the poor—the Free Presbyterian Church. Starting with 45 members, the church grew to 237 in one year. Church membership overall doubled in Rochester as a result of Finney's crusade. There were financial rewards to conversion: two-thirds of the workers who became church members improved their job status in the next seven years as employers came to insist on hiring only God-fearing, churchgoing men.

Aiming his crusade at women as well as male sinners, Finney grasped that the factory system deprived women of income and status when cash-paying traditional home crafts such as weaving were destroyed by the power looms. Women gained new status in Finney's revived churches, where they were urged to form women's associations to promote temperance, prison reform, abolition, and other reforms. Finney not only appointed women the guardians of the new morality, he gave them a church environment in which they were freed from their husbands' domination. Men and women were urged to pray together—and women could lead the congregation in prayer.

This new power and moral authority was a dangerous novelty for many men, implying as it did equality between the sexes. One Rochester gentleman was especially unhappy about Finney's practice of going door to door and handing out tracts to women. After a Finney visit, he complained, "He stuffed my wife with tracts and alarmed her fears and nothing short of meetings, night and day, could atone for the many fold sins my poor, simple spouse had committed." But what really bothered him was that "she made the miraculous discovery that she had been unevenly yoked. From this unhappy period, peace, quiet and happiness have fled from my dwelling, never, I fear, to return." When men resisted Finney's blandishments, their womenfolk could not all be persuaded to accept their own salvation. Finney records in his memoirs that one woman refused to be saved because she didn't want to go to heaven alone while her husband went to hell.

Finney's well-publicized Rochester revival—he introduced the use of newspaper advertising in advance of his sermons and visits—led to a prosperous church of his own in New York City the next year. In 1832 he became pastor of the Second Free Presbyterian Church in New York City, which held its services in the Chatham Street Theatre. Finney had attracted the backing of millionaire abolitionists Arthur and Lewis Tappan, who leased the theatre and helped him organize his own church, the Broadway Tabernacle. Withdrawing from the Presbyterian Church in 1836, Finney joined the Congregationalists and preached the New Haven theology with his own variations to a huge audience. His own newspaper, the *New York Evangelist,* published his lectures, and he also printed them in best-selling book form. By 1835, as his books sold widely, he took a decisive antislavery stand in public for the first time, but he was careful not "to make it a hobby or divert the attention of the people from the work of converting souls."

Finney's antislavery views attracted young seminarians who

left Lane Seminary because it placed restrictions on discussing slavery. At first, he agreed to teach them in one room in his tabernacle. But then the newly founded Oberlin College in Ohio invited him to establish a theology department. Guaranteed financial backing by the devoted Arthur Tappan, Finney left for Oberlin. He imposed only one condition: that music be established in the curriculum. He also insisted on retaining his pastorate in New York City, but after two years of dividing his ministry, his health suffered, and in 1837 he resigned his New York City charge.

For the next forty years, the second half of his vigorous life, Finney based himself at Oberlin, where he trained hundreds of ministers to carry his Christian crusade all over America and the British Isles. He preached himself during tours of England and Scotland in 1849–1850 and again in 1859–1860. Carrying on his evangelistic work part of each year, he also spread his views far and wide through the *Oberlin Evangelist,* the newspaper he founded in 1839 to disseminate his views on doctrine and practical matters. As he increasingly espoused perfectionism, holding that sin and holiness could not coexist in a person, he came under withering attack from Calvinists who had long held "Oberlin theology" in disrepute.

But Finney clung to an exalted idea of what a Christian should strive to attain. He insisted that churches should always be kept at revival pitch. He became the champion of an evangelical strain of American Christianity that opposed popular amusements that might hinder salvation and take time away from the reform agenda. His temperance campaign—he opposed not only alcohol consumption and the use of tobacco but even drinking coffee or tea—led in large part to the first prohibition movement that swept the North in the 1850s.

The visible fruits of Finney's brand of evangelism were phenomenal. The proportion of church members in America increased from one in fifteen in 1800 to one in seven in 1850. The college-founding movement, almost exclusively evangelical, increased the number of permanent Christian liberal arts colleges from 25 in 1799 to 182 in 1861. Finney went on writing until his death in 1875. Because of his work, thousands of voluntary associations were formed to promote reforms such as temperance, abolitionism, women's rights, coeducation of the sexes, health and prison reform, pacifism, and Sunday schools. Further, as historian William McLoughlin puts it, "both as motivation and as rationale" Finney's evangelical religion "lay behind the concept of rugged individualism in business enterprise, laissez faire in economic theory, constitutional democracy in political thought." It became "the Protestant ethic in morality and the millennial hope of white, Anglo-Saxon Protestant America to lead the world to its latter day glory."

JAMES FORTEN,
DISFRANCHISED
GENTLEMAN

NEVER WAS THE ANOMALY OF SLAVERY amid a struggle for freedom clearer than during the early days of the American Revolution. The British offered freedom to enslaved Americans who would fight against their masters. For many of the Founders, however, the freedom they fought for did not extend to blacks, who had no rights at all. But there were black Americans who had bought or inherited their freedom, and to them American freedom and independence were literal. Many blacks fought on each side, expecting their freedom and the full rights of citizenship at war's end. For James Forten and other free blacks, the prospect of full citizenship in a free and independent United States was worth the risk of being captured and sold into the slavery their forefathers had escaped once before. No group risked more in the American Revolution or had such grounds for disenchantment as slavery not only survived the struggle for liberty but rapidly grew in the early nineteenth century.

JAMES FORTEN was a marble-shooting boy of ten when the Revolutionary War came crushing down on his native Philadelphia in 1777. The young African-American, second generation of his family born free in America, marched off proudly as a drummer boy with militiamen who, like him, believed they were defending their homes and liberties against British invasion.

Both Forten's grandmother and grandfather had been born free in Africa and then kidnapped to America. Forten's grandfather had worked many hours beyond his required slave labors to buy first his own freedom, then his wife's. James's father, Thomas, had evidently been born in Philadelphia, where the first antislavery movement, planted by the Quakers, was taking root. Thomas Forten had a good job as a skilled sail maker in Robert Bridges's sail factory, and he owned his own home.

When James Forten was born in 1767, there were still slaves working plantations across the Delaware River in southern New Jersey, and serving in the households of prominent Philadelphians like Benjamin Franklin. But more and more moral pressure was being brought to bear by Quaker reformers. In 1750, Anthony Benezet, a Quaker schoolteacher of French Huguenot descent whose family had fled persecution in France, opened a free evening school for black children in his own home. Benezet's writings against slavery reached London, where his pamphlets profoundly influenced humanitarians such as William Wilberforce and Granville Sharp to roll up their sleeves and work to abolish slavery. By 1770, Quaker societies in England and Philadelphia had raised the money for a school building for free black children. James Forten enrolled at age eight in 1775, at the time of the Second Continental Congress.

In his only year of formal schooling, James learned to read, write, and do sums in his arithmetic book, *Dilworth's Assistant.* His schooling stopped abruptly in 1776 when his father fell into the Delaware River and drowned. Working first in a grocery store, James now had to help support his family. Militia service took him away briefly. Then a chance to make a lot more money came in July 1781: James, now fourteen years old and a robust six feet two, was recruited by the mate of the new Pennsylvania-built privateer, the twenty-two-gun *Royal Louis.* Its crew of two hundred was commanded by Stephen Decatur, Sr., a famous privateer who had already captured eight British ships on commerce-raiding voyages.

By this time, many free blacks were serving aboard American vessels. In all, about eight thousand blacks were fighting on the American side, with twice as many, at least sixteen thousand, enlisted on the British side. At first, slave-owning American leaders like George Washington had been reluctant to recruit black troops, but when the British proclaimed that any black American slave who ran away from his master to join the British army would be given his freedom and a grant of land in the American colonies, all but South Carolina and Georgia countered by accepting black recruits, in most states integrating blacks into white units.

On July 31, 1781, taking a chest of clothes, his Bible, and a bag of marbles, James Forten, along with nineteen other black recruits, climbed aboard the *Royal Louis*. His new job: powder boy. In battle it was his extremely hazardous job to carry canvas buckets of water, gunpowder, and cannonballs from the powder magazine below decks up a ladder to his gun crew and then race down for a fresh round under heavy (and explosive) enemy fire. Between engagements, he was a cabin boy, mostly helping the cook in the galley.

James got a first taste of war at sea almost at once. In Delaware Bay, the *Royal Louis* overtook the British brig *Active:* after a single deadly broadside at close range, the British ship surrendered. Sent back to Philadelphia to be auctioned off, the *Active* and its cargo became prizes of war, their value to be divided into shares. Even a lowly young powder boy would share in the booty. Life would become a little easier in the Forten household.

But James's luck did not hold. In her next engagement, the *Royal Louis* was surrounded by three British warships and forced to surrender. Now James Forten faced a fate far worse than he had ever known. Under the international rules of war, blacks captured on the high seas were treated not as prisoners of war but as part of their captors' booty; they were usually sold into slavery to work the rest of their lives on Caribbean sugar plantations, where heat, work, and disease often killed them in a year or two. Yet young Forten was again blessed with incredible good fortune, although he could not know it at first. On the *Amphyon,* where he was taken a prisoner, William, the young son of Captain John Beasly, spotted Forten's sack of marbles and asked him to play a game. The two boys became fast friends, and the British youth pleaded with his father to spare the black youth from being sold into slavery. Exercising his virtually total and arbitrary power as a British naval captain, Sir John gave James and the other black prisoners the choice of joining the Royal Navy or being held as prisoners until the war ended. Young Forten declined the first option: "I am here as a prisoner for the liberties of my country. I cannot prove a traitor to her interests."

Taken off the *Amphyon* and into New York harbor on another ship, James joined a thousand other prisoners confined below decks in a squalid, rotting prison ship, the dismasted hulk of the former warship *Jersey.* Moored in Wallabout Bay off Brooklyn, she became the tomb of eleven thousand Americans who died of disease, starvation, and maltreatment by British warders. More Americans died on the *Jersey* than in all the battles of the Revolution.

Locked below decks in total darkness in a foul, lice-infested, loathsome cell, roasting in summer and freezing in winter, James probably survived only because he found another ship's boy from the *Royal Louis:* Daniel Brewton, a white boy, who would remain a lifelong friend. Brewton's health was deteriorating, and when an American officer being exchanged for a British prisoner offered to slip Forten out hidden in his trunk, Forten asked him to take Brewton instead. After seven months on the *Jersey,* Forten too was released in a general prisoner exchange at war's end. In bare feet and rags, he walked across New Jersey to his home. More than half a century later, Daniel Brewton, steward of Philadelphia's free public hospital, told a black historian "with tears raining down his face" how his friend Forten had saved his life.

Forten must have been confused by the treatment of blacks after the Revolution. Many blacks found themselves returned to lives of servitude after the struggle for freedom as one state after another refused to affirm the civil rights of blacks. At least six thousand blacks who had fought with the British sailed for Caribbean islands. Yet in Pennsylvania, the first statewide abolition society had been founded during the Revolution and had put pressure on the Revolutionary government to end slavery. In November 1778, the state's ruling council requested the Pennsylvania Assembly to pass a law freeing infant blacks born to slaves. After a two-year procedural impasse, Pennsylvania became the first state to abolish slavery, "to extend a portion of that freedom to others which has been extended to us." Abolition was not outright: nobody then a slave in Pennsylvania was freed, but when the children of slaves reached twenty-eight years of age, they would become free. Just across the Delaware River, slavery would continue in New Jersey until 1847, long after James Forten died.

In 1784 Forten was a seventeen-year-old hero on the Philadelphia waterfront. When his sister Abigail's husband signed on the *Commerce,* he told Forten the ship was sailing in two weeks if she had a full crew. Forten enlisted as an able-bodied seaman and lugged aboard his Bible, his Shakespeare, and his warmest clothes. His destination was England, so recently the enemy but now America's largest shipping client. One wintry day in February 1784, the *Commerce* dropped down the Delaware. Four weeks later Forten landed in Liverpool, the center of the booming British slave trade. He found work as a stevedore on the Merseyside docks and took a room in a boardinghouse owned by a West Indian–born black man.

Forten soon introduced himself to local Quakers and attended his first antislavery meeting. He was pleased to learn that English Quakers had been stirred to action by the writings of his old Philadelphia teacher, Anthony Benezet. During the day he worked provisioning ships that he soon learned were preparing to take more human cargo from Africa to the Caribbean; at night he listened to the stirring words of Quaker disciples of Granville Sharp, a low-paid English civil servant who had put Benezet's words into action and had organized the fledgling English antislavery movement. Sharp's first victory had come as early as 1772, when all slaves in Britain had been declared free by the chief justice, Lord Mansfield. After a black man named Somerset, brought by his master from Virginia to England, had escaped, he had been recaptured and put on a ship bound for Jamaica to be resold. Sharp and his Quaker friends had hired a lawyer and briefed him with Sharp's own legal research. After a trial, Lord Mansfield decried the fact that slavery was still legal overseas.

> The state of slavery is of such a nature that it is incapable of being introduced on any reasons, moral or political, but only by positive law. . . . It is so odious that nothing can be suffered to support it but positive law. Whatever inconveniences, therefore, may follow from the decision, I cannot say this case is allowed or approved by the law of England; and therefore the black must be discharged.

Since no law had ever established slavery in Britain, slavery was illegal there. Fourteen thousand slaves were instantly freed.

The success of the abolitionists in Britain inspired James Forten. He left Liverpool, where more than 80 percent of all commerce still centered on the slave trade, and traveled to London to meet Granville Sharp in person. Using Quaker contacts, Forten wangled an invitation to a meeting where Sharp was to speak. There, he also saw for the first time products made in Africa by free Africans—ivory ornaments, dyes, beeswax, palm oil, fine cloth, leather goods, iron, gold. Stunned by the evidence of a higher black culture than he had seen in America, the eighteen-year-old black seaman slipped out of the meeting —too shy to introduce himself to Sharp, too moved ever to forget.

RETURNING TO PHILADELPHIA in 1786, James Forten signed articles of apprenticeship to Robert Bridges, sail maker, in whose sail loft his father had worked for so many years. Here, in a vast space above Thomas Willing's waterfront warehouse, the largest of eight in Philadelphia, Forten learned all the skills required to fit out the sails of ships built nearby. Within two years, he was promoted to foreman and had the new experience of supervising some forty workers, white and black. In the next ten years, as Forten learned how to manage the business, the elderly Robert Bridges turned it over to Forten's stewardship, finally offering to sell it to him in 1798. Forten was surprised when Thomas Willing, business partner of financier Robert Morris and one of the wealthiest men in America, bankrolled him on condition that he make the sails for his trading fleet. Forten promptly announced that he would not take orders for sails of ships in any way engaging in the slave trade.

Forten was well on his way to becoming wealthy himself. Much of his income would come from a new labor-saving device for hoisting sails that he invented, the hand-cranked winch. Its patent and his sail-making business helped him amass assets of $300,000 by the time he drew up a will in 1830. In modern terms, he was the first black American millionaire. But his importance went far beyond his wealth. He became one of a handful of influential blacks in pre–Civil War America.

In 1787, at the time the U.S. Constitution was being drawn up in Philadelphia (one that tabled all discussion of slavery by Congress for another twenty years), Forten joined two black clergymen, the Reverend Richard Allen and the Reverend Absalom Jones, in forming the Free African Society, a benevolent society organized to help free blacks in times of illness, unemployment, or other emergencies. It was the first society formed for black Philadelphians, who were even barred from membership in the Pennsylvania Abolition Society.

One of the society's early tasks, following an incident at Saint George's Methodist Church in 1791, was to form black churches in Philadelphia. As more and more blacks attended the Methodist Church, elders had a new gallery built and tried to compel black members to attend separate early morning services apart from white members. When the Reverend Allen, Forten, and other blacks insisted on sitting in the lower pews, elders tried to drag them from their knees. The blacks walked out in a group. Over the next three years, not one but two black churches were built, Mother Bethel African Methodist Episcopal (AME) Church, presided over by Richard Allen, and the African Episcopal Church of Saint Thomas, which James Forten helped to build and where he served as a vestryman for the rest of his life. While Allen's church would become the mother AME church that spread nationwide, Forten did not want to belong to a church that was only for blacks. He believed that in a black church within the larger Episcopal church, both whites and blacks would benefit. He had thus made his first integrationist decision.

After the nation's first Fugitive Slave Act was passed in 1793, encouraging the use of bounty hunters to track down slaves who had escaped to the North (sometimes resulting in free blacks being kidnapped and sold into slavery), Forten began to devote his money and his efforts to buying freedom for slaves and asserting himself politically to protect their rights. So widespread had the abductions become by 1800 that Forten helped to circulate a petition to Congress to end the slave trade as a first step toward emancipation. "We are happy and grateful to live in freedom under the American government," the petition began, asking Congress to relieve "the hard condition of our race," especially the "700,000 blacks in slavery." The Petition of the Free Blacks of Philadelphia, presented to Congress by Quaker Robert Waln, prompted an angry debate, during which John Rutledge of South Carolina insisted that some states would not have come into the Union if they had not been promised that Congress would never legislate on slavery. The debate raged for two days. Late the second day, proslavery members of Congress presented a counterresolution stating that the petition invited Congress to act illegally and had "a tendency to create disquiet and jealousy." Voting 85 to 1 in favor of this resolution, Congress deftly avoided ever taking up the petition.

At a meeting of dejected black leaders in Saint Thomas Church, Forten, now thirty-three, refused to be discouraged. "At least we have one steadfast friend in Congress [George Thacker of Massachusetts]. While one voice speaks for justice, there will be those who hear." He went home and wrote eloquently to Thacker:

> We, sir, Africans and descendants of that unhappy race, thank you for the philanthropic zeal with which you defended our cause. . . . Though our faces are black, yet we are man. . . . Judge what must be our feelings to find ourselves treated as a species of property. . . . A deep gloom now envelopes us. . . .

ONE BITTERLY COLD MORNING in January 1807, Forten the sail maker, nearing age forty, was standing on a wharf near his sail loft gazing out at the river before going on to the day's work. It was near this spot some thirty years earlier that his father had fallen into the fast current and drowned. Today, large chunks of ice were jostling in the gray water and a small boat was trying to pick its way through them to the dock. Suddenly the oarsman screamed and disappeared into the water. Forten plunged in after him, grabbed his hair as he began to go under, and hauled him back with one arm, swimming with the other. Wrapping him in his cloak, Forten carried the man up to his sail loft, laying him on a pile of canvas near a fire.

Over the years, James Forten by one count saved a dozen people from drowning. In 1821, one rescue prompted the Humane Society of Philadelphia to honor him at a ceremony for "rescuing, at imminent hazard of his life," so many drowning victims. Yet no one was keeping count of how many blacks Forten was rescuing as he became America's first civil rights leader, the voice and pen of freed blacks, escaped slaves, and the growing number in bondage. Sometimes he personally rescued many slaves by buying their freedom, but he was also emerging as the national spokesman for African-Americans. When the ban on congressional action on slavery imposed by the Constitutional Convention of 1787 expired in 1807, President Thomas Jefferson and his Democratic-Republican majority pushed a law through Congress prohibiting further importation of slaves after January 1, 1808. James Forten was among the black leaders who sent a resolution of thanks to Congress.

It was to be one of the last unanimous acts of the contemporary black leadership. In 1810, Granville Sharp's African Institution in London decided to launch a colony for freed blacks in Sierra Leone on the west coast of Africa. A close friend of Forten's from Newport, Rhode Island, the black ship's captain Paul Cuffe, also decided to launch a movement to transport freed blacks to Africa. His plan for "the redemption of Africa" was for "sober families of black people in America to settle among the Africans." On January 1, 1811, Cuffe sailed for Sierra Leone in his new ship *Traveller* with permission from British colonial authorities to plant a settlement there. But the War of 1812 soon broke out, interrupting the colonization movement and postponing the rift among black leaders.

During this war, James Forten emerged as the leader of the 7,400 free blacks who made up 10 percent of Philadelphia's population. In the Quaker city, blacks were admitted to free public hospitals and poorhouses. While they were barred from white schools, hundreds now attended Benezet's free school. But trouble arose as the city became a magnet for more and more blacks fleeing surrounding slave states. In January 1813, some white Philadelphians introduced a petition to the Pennsylvania legislature to require "all Negroes to register with the state" within twenty-four hours or be fined and jailed. The measure would have given the state the power "to sell for a term of years the services of those Negroes convicted of crimes" and would have levied a special tax on free blacks to support poor blacks. The bill's chief aim was to prevent further black immigration into the state.

The measure and the growing animosity behind it shocked Forten into writing *A Series of Letters by a Man of Color,* beginning with his anguished question, "Why are we not to be considered as men?"

> Has the God who made the white man and the black left any record declaring us a different species? Are we not sustained by the same power, supported by the same food, hurt by the same wounds, wounded by the same wrongs, pleased with the same delights and propagated by the same means? *And should we not then enjoy the same liberty and be protected by the same laws?*

The authors of Pennsylvania's constitution had not differentiated between white and black, he argued, "because they never supposed it would be made a question *whether we were men or not.*"

Forten marshaled evidence that black Pennsylvanians already paid more in property taxes than poor blacks cost the state. And he poured scorn on the proposal to make blacks register with police and carry identity papers: "The constable, whose antipathy generally against the black is very great, will take every opportunity of hurting his feelings." And he reserved his most eloquent plea until the end:

> Many of our ancestors were brought here more than 100 years ago: many of our fathers, many of ourselves, have fought and bled for the independence of our country. Do not expose us to sale. Let not the spirit of the father behold the son robbed of that liberty which he died to establish.

With his own money, James Forten published his letters to the legislature and bombarded its members with them. After reading his powerful appeal, Pennsylvania's lawmakers defeated the Registration Bill of 1813. In that year, the peak of the War of 1812, nearly 20 percent of all American naval crews were black. Scarcely more than a year later, when the British attacked Baltimore and Washington, Forten recruited 2,500 blacks to defend Philadelphia. The all-black battalion marched to Gray's Ferry and fortified the city's western approaches. But the attack never

came. The black citizens of New Orleans had helped Andrew
Jackson to repel the last British invasion on U.S. soil.

The struggle that pitted black against black in America
now began. Southern white leaders formed the American
Colonization Society to relocate freed blacks (and blacks they
chose to free) to a new African colony fifty miles north of
Sierra Leone. To be named Liberia, the colony was to be
purchased with private American funds. Blacks were to be
transported free on American warships lent to the society,
which had the warm support of President James Monroe, a
Virginia slave owner; indeed, the society, presided over by
Judge Bushrod Washington, nephew of George Washington,
named the capital of the new American colony Monrovia in
his honor.

At first, when Paul Cuffe asked for support, Forten called a
meeting of Philadelphia blacks to present his proposal. But
when some three thousand anxious blacks crowded into tiny
Mother Bethel Church, Forten wrote Cuffe of their fears and his
that the society's plan was actually a scheme to deport freed
blacks and remove the incentive of Southern slaves to revolt or
escape to the North. Moreover, Forten was not convinced that
all American slaves would be freed to go to Africa. Only free
people of color had been mentioned in the proposal. The plan
might also mask the slave owners' intention to "free" troublesome blacks and deport them to Africa.

On January 25, 1817, Forten wrote Cuffe,

Esteemed friend,

. . . The whole continent seems to be agitated concerning
the colonization of the People of Color. . . . Indeed the People of Color here was very much frightened at first. They
were afraid that all the free people would be compelled to
go, particularly in the Southern states. We had a large
meeting of males at the Rev. Richard Allen's Church. . . .
Three thousand at least attended and there was not one
soul that was in favor of going to Africa.

Forten, who had been asked by Reverend Allen to chair the mass meeting, spared Cuffe an exact description of the hysterical meeting at Mother Bethel as the city's freedmen looked to him for help. "They think the slaveholders want to get rid of them so as to make their property more secure," he added, noting that he was able to calm the meeting enough to win support for a petition drive against the colonization society's plan "to exile us from the land of our nativity."

Forten had come prepared to the meeting. Now, he read in his strong, clear voice,

> Whereas our ancestors (not of choice) were the first successful cultivators of the wilds of America, we, their descendants, feel ourselves entitled to participate in the blessings of her luxuriant soil, which their blood and sweat manured . . . any [measure] having a tendency to banish us from her bosom would not only be cruel but in direct violation of those principles which have been the boast of this republic.

Forten's resolutions, unanimously adopted by the crowd, condemned the "unmerited stigma" cast by Southern whites on the reputation of hardworking, law-abiding free blacks, reminding the nation how recently they had enlisted in the war during America's "hour of danger." They further vowed, "we will never separate ourselves voluntarily from the slave population in this country."

The protest meeting at Mother Bethel Church did not deter the colonizers from going ahead with their plan. The organization opened an office in Philadelphia and asked Forten to swing over his support in exchange for being appointed the chief justice of Liberia. Outraged, Forten refused. More and more, Forten feared that the influential colonizers would persuade Congress to pass a law to deport all freed blacks to Africa. After the colonization society set up its Philadelphia auxiliary, thousands of free blacks crowded into a schoolhouse on August 10, 1817.

Forten, drafted to chair this first avowedly anticolonization protest meeting, read to the quiet assemblage his "Address to the Humane and Benevolent Inhabitants" of Philadelphia, which he had written in collaboration with other black leaders.

Condemning colonization on behalf of both freed and enslaved blacks who could not speak for themselves, Forten called the African colonies a constant danger. Any black who showed a tendency to stand up to whites would be deported, and only submissive blacks would remain in America in ever-worsening bondage:

> Parents will be torn from their children—husbands from their wives—brothers from brothers—and all the heartrending agonies which were endured by our forefathers when they were dragged into bondage from Africa will be again renewed, and with increased anguish. . . . Let not a purpose be assisted which will stay the cause of the entire abolition of slavery in the United States and which may defeat it altogether.

SOON AFTERWARD, Paul Cuffe, the mainspring of the black colonization movement, died. In the first seven years of the Liberia colony, only 225 freed black Americans emigrated. Of these, only 140 remained alive there; 40 died, and the rest went to Sierra Leone or returned to the United States. Forten's lonely stand had slowed the colonization movement long enough for most blacks and whites to take a second look.

Yet many whites still feared the presence and increasing number of free blacks. In 1813, there had been an estimated fourteen thousand blacks in Philadelphia; by 1830, there were forty thousand, 10 percent of the population. White hostility toward blacks deepened after the bitter congressional debates over the Missouri Compromise of 1820 and after a series of slave uprisings in the 1820s and 1830s. The 1822 uprising in Charleston, South Carolina, led by a free black from San Domingo named Denmark Vesey, evoked all the horror among slave owners of the mass killings of whites by blacks a generation earlier. A harsh legislative reaction also set in. In 1824, Virginia passed a law imposing a year in prison on anyone, black or white, who assisted a slave's escape. It was already illegal in the state to teach slaves to read and write; Virginia now made it a crime to teach *free* blacks to read and write. James Forten, who recognized the political importance of black literacy, made it one of his most urgent demands. He insisted on literacy as a political right for blacks, believing that if they could read and write, they could learn to speak out for themselves against slavery. And everywhere, the slave catchers grew bolder.

Virginia's laws tried to suppress a movement already too forceful to be reversed. By the late 1820s, a new antislavery movement based on education and literacy arose even as race relations deteriorated. In 1827, John B. Russworn, the first black college graduate (of Bowdoin College in Maine), launched *Freedom's Journal.* An initial subscriber, James Forten agreed with its call for education and job training. For the forty years since he had returned from England, Forten had given free classes, first in his home and then in Saint Thomas's Church, teaching black children to read, write, and do arithmetic. When Pennsylvania opened free public schools in 1818 and black children were excluded, he brought pressure that resulted in the donation of a building by the Pennsylvania Abolition Society and state funds to supply teachers. He also helped to launch the Infant School for Colored Children, forerunner of the modern Head Start Program, in 1828. In an unsigned article he no doubt wrote in *Freedom's Journal,* Forten warned that black children needed to be prepared for school for two years.

Yet Forten continued to worry about the colonization scheme. When Russworn continually endorsed it in his pages, Forten withdrew his support, shifting it soon afterward to a new and far more radical paper, *The Liberator,* edited in Boston by William Lloyd Garrison, who had served two years in prison for libeling a slave trader. On December 15, 1830, Forten wrote to Garrison, sending along the money from twenty-seven badly needed subscriptions he had personally sold and adding his wish that *"The Liberator* be the means of exposing more and more the odious system of slavery. . . . May America awake from the apathy in which she has long slumbered." By 1830, Forten was ready to endorse Garrison's breathtaking call not for a gradual end to slavery but for immediate total abolition. After one of many visits to Forten in the 1830s, Garrison wrote, "There are colored men and women, young men and young ladies, who have few superiors in refinement, in moral worth and in all that makes the human character worthy of admiration and praise." He expressed his shame at being part of a race which "has done you so much harm."

The very next year, 1831, Forten launched a series of annual black conventions in Philadelphia and invited Garrison to address the free black American leaders he had summoned from seven Northern states. Forten had already won the endorsement of other Philadelphia black leaders for this new white champion of abolition. Eventually, Forten led other blacks to provide 80 percent of *The Liberator's* subscriptions and became Garrison's number two financial backer. Forten's generosity was outdone only by that of Arthur Tappan, a nephew of Benjamin Franklin.*

Now the leading black in Philadelphia, Forten urged the Pioneer Black Convention of 1831 to launch a black college at New Haven, Connecticut. But the plan was presented just before the news broke of a massive slave insurrection in Southhampton County, Virginia, led by Nat Turner, in which seventy slaves killed sixty white men, women, and children. In the ensuing wave of panic, militant statements about emancipation and moderate calls for black education were drowned out by demands for harsher laws to control both slaves and free blacks. In New Haven, Forten's plan for a college was voted down 700 to 4 by a town meeting. In Pennsylvania, the state legislature passed two repressive resolutions. The first called for a law to protect whites from "the evils arising from the emigration of

* Tappan also bankrolled Charles Grandison Finney.

free blacks from other states"; the state also called for a state fugitive slave law harsher than the existing federal law.

In January 1832, Forten, now sixty-five, called a mass meeting to launch a statewide petition drive. Free blacks had long depended on Pennsylvania to provide protections denied by the federal and slave state governments: why this harsh new code now?

> Why are her borders to be surrounded by a wall of iron against freemen whose complexions fall below the wavering and uncertain shades of white. . . . ? It is [no longer] to be asked, is he brave, is he honest, is he just, is he free from stain of crime, but, is he black, is he brown, is he yellow, is he other than white?

Once again, Forten's powerful reasoning and rhetoric and his ability to mobilize thousands of reputable, tax-paying blacks repulsed repressive laws. The statewide petition drive he launched deluged the state legislature with such strong protest that the white politicians were obliged to rescind their repressive resolutions. But now, in addition to the fear of black rebellion, increasing unemployment among a rising tide of unskilled white immigrants arriving in Northern cities from Ireland and Germany created a perception that blacks were competing for unskilled as well as skilled jobs.

The new surfeit of white labor deprived blacks of construction work, mechanical jobs, carpentry, sail-making, and other skills. The prosperity that had drawn Europeans to the mills and farms was fading as excessive speculation in western lands and Jacksonian banking practices led to the terrible depression and bank failures of the late 1830s. These troubles especially hurt Philadelphia, then the capital of the national banking system. Soon there was widespread unemployment and fierce competition for even the menial jobs so long held by freed blacks. Blacks began to clash with the newly arrived and equally impoverished Irish in the fetid slums along the Schuylkill River. Unlike any of the earlier waves of immigrants, the Irish were determined to stay in the cities—and not head west to farm-lands on the prairies. Indeed, they were encouraged by their religious hierarchy *not* to disperse across the land but instead to remain a cohesive political and economic force. As in Boston, the Philadelphia Irish actively opposed the abolitionists. At the same time, the abolition movement made Philadelphia the cen-ter of its national organizing efforts. In 1833 Garrison formed the American Anti-Slavery Society there while he boarded with the family of a black dentist and barber. The stage was set for ten years of the bloodiest confrontation in Philadelphia history.

What began as a scuffle between gangs at a carousel in August 1834 flared into widespread riots by the next night. That summer, in Boston and New York, club-wielding crowds broke up antislavery rallies. In New York City, the homes of leading abolitionists were targeted, while the homes and churches of blacks were burned as hundreds fled the city. In Philadelphia, large numbers of white boys and young men as-sembled. Armed with sticks and clubs, they marched downtown to a vacant lot on the edge of Society Hill, then a black neigh-borhood.* From here they moved through alleys, smashing win-dows, breaking down doors, throwing furniture into the street, and mercilessly beating any blacks they caught.

The neighborhood watch (there was still no central city police force) was helpless. After several hours of unchecked riot-ing, the mayor of Philadelphia, John Swift, the city constables, and a large body of the city's watchmen arrived and charged the rioters, taking twenty prisoners and dispersing the mob. On the evening of August 9, when one of Forten's sons was on his way home from doing an errand for his father, he was attacked "by a gang of fifty or sixty young men in blue jackets and trousers and low-crowned straw hats." The boy was able to escape in time to warn his family. Three nights later, one of the most conspicuous targets of the Philadelphia mob was the large brick townhouse of James Forten at 92 Lombard Street. According to the 1830

* Before the Revolution, this area was home to such wealthy white families as that of Margaret Shippen Arnold.

census, he there lived with twenty-one relatives, guests, and servants, who helped him to fight off the rioters.

Undeterred, Forten helped to organize another national black convention the next year. In December 1833, sixty-two delegates, both black and white, came to Philadelphia from ten Northern states to attend the first National Anti-Slavery Convention, openly supported and organized by Forten and his Philadelphia friends and publicized in Garrison's *Liberator.* One of the delegates, twenty-six-year-old poet John Greenleaf Whittier, described most of his fellow delegates as "little known, strong only in their convictions and faith in the justice of their cause." To accommodate future abolitionist meetings, Forten raised funds for a lecture hall for visiting activists called Pennsylvania Hall.

When abolitionists gathered there almost five years later in May 1838 for a three-day convention featuring speeches by Garrison and the Grimké sisters from Charleston, the mayor refused them police protection and asked them to disband their meeting. On May 16, as Angelina Grimké rose to speak, a white mob crowded into the hall, hissed her, and then stoned members of the audience as their supporters outside smashed the windows. The frightened women cut short the meeting. Appeals to the mayor failed to produce a constable's guard for the third and final night's meeting. By 10 P.M. a mob of three thousand had gathered, extinguished the street lights, battered down the doors, broken the blinds, turned on the gas, and set fires that quickly engulfed the building. Across the street, James Forten watched the destruction of the hall he had built as he stood by helplessly with John and Lucretia Mott. Philadelphia, so long called the City of Brotherly Love, he said, had become the city of mobs. When the volunteer fire companies arrived, they confined their efforts to hosing down surrounding buildings. The mob did not deter these efforts, moving on instead to burn the Quaker-run Shelter for Colored Orphans.

Racially motivated riots were not confined to Philadelphia. Each summer they grew in intensity. The entire free black quarter of Cincinnati burned, and some two thousand black Ohioans were forced to flee to Ontario province, where Forten helped resettle them. In 1835 alone, *The Liberator* recounted more than one hundred mob attacks on abolitionist speakers such as Garrison, who was twice mobbed in his native Boston. Between 1830 and 1860, *The Liberator* counted 209 race riots in the United States; historian Richard Maxwell Brown has counted some thirty-five major race riots in Philadelphia, Baltimore, New York, and Boston during that time. So frequent and disquieting had the violence become that a young Illinois lawmaker, Abraham Lincoln, wrote in 1838:

> There is even now something of an ill omen amongst us. . . . Accounts of outrages committed by mobs form the everyday news of the times. They have pervaded the country from New England to Louisiana; they are neither peculiar to the eternal snows of the former nor the burning suns of the latter; they are not the creatures of climate, neither are they confined to the slaveholding nor the non-slaveholding states. . . . Whatever their causes be, it is common to the whole country.

A further setback came in October 1838, when the Pennsylvania legislature amended its constitution to strip blacks of the voting rights they had enjoyed since 1780, ignoring Forten's final public plea, his passionate *Appeal of Forty Thousand Citizens*. No black voted again in his beloved state until 1873. By this time, James Forten had decided to use much of his fortune to help his final cause, the Vigilant Committee of Philadelphia, founded in 1839 to guide and finance slaves escaping to Canada along what became known as the Underground Railroad. Early committee records in Forten's handwriting show that he had in old age relented somewhat on the subject of black emigration. Case 31, for instance, shows "woman from Virginia, emancipated on condition of going to Liberia." Case 40 included "eight persons from Virginia. A very interesting family. Sent to Canada."

James Forten never recovered from being stripped, along

with forty thousand free black citizens, of his coveted state citizenship. He worked so hard now to give away his money to help blacks and white abolitionists that his fortune dwindled by 80 percent in his last ten years. As the elder statesman of black America, he also supported a moral reform movement, and in 1835 was elected president of the American Moral Reform Society, one of whose chief aims was to seek equal rights for women as well as blacks and to support the growing temperance movement. In February 1842, at age seventy-five, Forten went to bed one day quietly reading his Bible and from time to time reciting his favorite poems to his five-year-old granddaughter, Charlotte, daughter of his son, Robert Bridges Forten. On February 24, he summoned his wife, Charlotte, and all of his eight children. His last words were to extend his love not only to his family but to all his abolitionist friends, "especially to Garrison."

He was buried in the graveyard of Saint Thomas's Church. The Philadelphia *North American* noted the passing of "the leading sailmaker" of the city under the headline "Death of an Excellent Man," but did not mention that he was America's first civil rights leader. Some five thousand people marched behind his coffin, "white and colored, male and female, about one-half white," noted the amazed *Philadelphia Public Ledger.* "Among the white portion were seen some of our wealthiest merchants and shippers, and captains of vessels." In recent years it had become dangerous for whites and blacks to walk together through the streets of Philadelphia. James Forten's funeral, wrote Lucretia Mott, was "a real amalgamation." Then James Forten, the last of its original members to die, was buried beside the first black church in America.

ANNIE TURNER WITTENMYER, FRONTIER REFORMER

*T*HE EXPANDING BORDERS OF THE UNITED States in the nineteenth century changed the demographic profile of Americans. The center of the country moved far to the west, to places not settled by English seekers of religious freedom. The frontier, which had been the edge of colonial America for the first two centuries of settlement, came more and more to represent American life. For women, life on the frontier presented physical hardship but, just as difficult, the prospect of isolation, loneliness, and in most cases a permanent separation from family members. This was especially hard on those who moved from eastern cities with more refined culture —by American standards. But those same deprivations prepared women for the added trial of losing the help of husbands and sons later on when the Civil War took so many men away from home to fight. Annie Turner Wittenmyer became an early woman executive and reform organizer, an extraordinary example of a woman from the frontier who invented ways of distinguishing herself to help others.

Annie Turner belonged to an old Louisville family and claimed descent through her mother from John Smith of Virginia, the famed explorer. Her family later moved to Adams

County, Ohio, where she was born on August 26, 1827. Because of the advanced thinking of both her parents, she was better educated than was typical for women at the time. They saw to it that her studies continued through the completion of training at an Ohio seminary for women. Even as a young girl she showed a literary side, publishing her first poem at age twelve; as an adult she made her name as the author of hymns.

At age twenty she married William Wittenmyer, considerably older than she was, with whom she moved to Iowa. Their new home, the "Gate City" of Keokuk, thrived because of its location as a Mississippi River port, as it grew commercially important for the transport of supplies to the west and the arrival point for new settlers. Before Chicago had established itself as the center of commerce and transport, Mississippi River ports like Keokuk let men get rich selling supplies to the arriving hordes who needed everything before they set out to cross the plains. Married to a prosperous businessman, the young Mrs. Wittenmyer found ways of applying her wealth to make social changes without being asked. In Keokuk she saw school-aged children who roamed the streets, a commonplace sight when education was neither free nor compulsory. She started a school for excluded children, a private school in her own home. Over time this school expanded and moved to a larger building, a warehouse, where its enrollment grew to two hundred students. Her interest in children remained a lifelong focus in her charitable work—a poignant fact, since of her own four children, only one lived beyond infancy.

A combination of talent and circumstances allowed Annie Turner Wittenmyer to distinguish herself when the great test of the Civil War began. A natural leader whom other women instinctively asked for help, she spoke effectively and persuasively in public, and this ability allowed her to raise money for a local group of women who intended to help Iowa's soldiers. She also wrote so well that she could persuade political and, later, military leaders to take her seriously. People living in and near Keokuk understood the effects of the war in human terms: new recruits were shipped out from there on their way to fight, and barges of wounded men returned to the same port after battles. When her elderly husband died, Wittenmyer found herself a well-off widow with only one small child. Annie Wittenmyer's fortune could have given her a comfortable and tranquil life, yet her education, sense of duty, and athletic energy inclined her to a life of effort against huge resistance. Because her mother and sister were willing to care for the child, at the war's outbreak she was free to travel, to go to field hospitals and see the wounded. In addition to this experience, her good analytical mind let her see problems clearly and imagine practical solutions. Fresh eggs, for example, could not easily be transported to soldiers, because cornmeal, the usual packing material, heated up and ruined the eggs. Oats, Mrs. Wittenmyer directed, would work.

In 1861, when the Soldiers' Aid Society of Keokuk held its first meeting, everyone could see the need for help. Men at the front needed material support of the kind that women back home could provide: bandages; blankets; and, as the women soon learned, pillows, sheets, and lightweight clothing to replace heavy army uniforms. What Annie Wittenmyer understood from her first visit to a field hospital as the first executive secretary of the group was the equally acute need on all sides for up-to-date information. (Once she went to Saint Joseph, Missouri, to help the wounded of the Second Iowa Infantry, for example, only to learn that they were no longer there and that she would have to follow them to Saint Louis.) People at home needed to know exactly what the men lacked and where they were; the army needed to know which groups were able and ready to provide which kinds of help. Reports had come back of excess food going unused in one hospital while men nearby went hungry, of clothing being abandoned because no one was there to wash it. And charitable organizations needed to know about the work of other, similar groups. The general public wanted to help, but needed to know exactly how and where to send donations. Frontier settlers had developed a way of life built around not having much information of the kind that changed quickly. The whole concept of publicity, in their world, remained primitive. At least one large event, a sanitary fair, was organized for which no one made posters. A Keokuk newspaper, appealing to local women for aid, added: "Papers throughout the State please copy."

Frontier life had not given Iowa women experience in organizing themselves in any way, a lack which could have been disastrous. Annie Wittenmyer began regular visits to field hospitals to see what was needed most acutely. On one hospital visit she found that her own ailing sixteen-year-old brother, Davis C. Turner, had just refused the unhealthy breakfast being served all wounded men: one piece of bacon floating in its own grease, a slab of bread, and a cup of black coffee. By speaking with the men and questioning officers, she learned that wounded men were fed exactly the same diet as men in combat. Rather than find a way to improve food at that one hospital, Annie Wittenmyer organized a system to see that Iowa men everywhere received adequate food. She understood that a wounded man's chances of recovery could be improved if he ate well, an idea that the army nevertheless could not "sell" to Congress. Early in 1863 the Senate considered a proposed law that would provide each army unit with a professional cook, grant $10 per month for matrons in hospitals, and change the ration by adding tobacco, sold to the men at cost. In its debate of the bill, the Senate spent most of its time discussing the moral aspect of promoting the use of tobacco. Even after it passed the Senate, the bill never left the House, proof that the health of the army did not greatly concern political leaders.

Problems in the field did not stop with diet. Field hospitals were not antiseptic because the concept of sepsis was not yet understood. While the notion of public health had begun to make inroads since the Mexican War of 1846–1847, young and progressive physicians who accepted modern beliefs were not in the field at the beginning of the Civil War. Only later, after huge loss of life from disease and infection, did the new thinkers come to positions of influence. Men as young as Wittenmyer's brother often fell ill from exposure to childhood diseases such as mumps and measles, which presented an acute problem because men from the sparsely populated frontier had not developed immunities to these sicknesses, and they therefore spread rapidly when army men lived crammed together in camps. Mrs. Wittenmyer may not have known just how vulnerable her brother was: the rate of death from disease was 43 percent higher among Union soldiers from places west of the Appalachians than among easterners. Yet everyone understood that being in a hospital put a man's life in danger. As the war went on, she became more active in writing letters to have ailing and wounded men sent home on furlough, where they were more likely to recover, than in a military hospital. In a later report, Annie Wittenmyer described the strain she experienced as an observer, not only seeing but also hearing wounded men. To their groans was added "the drip, drip, drip of leaking vessels," a result of the improvised technique of placing pans over the heads of the worst wounded so that falling drops of water would keep the bandages cool.

The same lack of organization that made Wittenmyer's efforts necessary in the first place also caused them to be unappreciated or misunderstood. Funding, like other aspects of war relief work, had no systematic organization to begin with. No umbrella organization existed to direct smaller, local efforts. As early as April 1861, Mrs. Wittenmyer was writing to a woman in Iowa to report on her visit to Iowa regiments, a visit she had undertaken without prompting. To get herself to such sites, Annie Wittenmyer used her own money rather than wait until funds could be approved, a process that would surely not have gone smoothly or quickly. Later, she was reimbursed for part of her expenses, but rumors eventually started that she had financed her activities by buying supplies and then selling them, making a profit for herself.

In fact, early in the war, she did purchase vegetables to distribute because Governor Kirkwood of Iowa directed her to do so. He did not know that the men could not buy anything because they had not been paid. Understandably, Mrs. Wittenmyer gave away what she had paid for, yet found herself accused of cheating. She denied all such charges, explaining that at times she had bought supplies with her own money and then sold them to surgeons in charge of hospitals, but she had no "proceeds" from such sales because there were none.

The Iowa General Assembly passed a law in special session requiring the governor to appoint two or more state sanitary agents, one of whom, the law specified, should be Mrs. Annie Wittenmyer. Still, she met resistance from the army. In the beginning, there was conflict among the Iowa State Sanitary Commission (her group), the Iowa Sanitary Commission (a group unfriendly to her), the United States Sanitary Commission, and the Army Sanitary Commission. Worse, corruption complicated the divided territory. After she created a rigorous protocol of systematic written reports from her aides (weekly, observing detailed guidelines), Wittenmyer found out that at one hospital the surgeon in charge insisted on the odd practice of saving used coffee grounds and drying them out. By investigating further, she learned that the dried grounds were brewed with "log wood" (bark and wood) to restore a coffeelike color. This dubious drink was reserved for wounded men so that the surgeon could sell for his own profit the coffee that they should have been given. When Wittenmyer learned the name of the surgeon, she reported him to General R. C. Wood in Louisville and insisted that he be dismissed and, if she had her way, "be hung higher than Haman." General Wood began a military investigation of the charges, but the surgeon resigned before its conclusion.

Because of her experience in organizing groups and in managing information, Wittenmyer understood publicity better than some officers she confronted. In August 1861, for example, a visit to Helena, Arkansas, made her threaten to expose how more than two thousand men lay wounded in the sweltering heat of late summer. Because they were camped near a swamp, insects pestered the men and carried disease, adding malaria to their ailments. The only available drinking water came from the sun-warmed Mississippi and stood growing warmer in sun-drenched barrels, while a barge carrying ice was moored at the river's edge. In the line of army authority, no one present had the right to order the ice distributed. But Annie Wittenmyer had money to buy it, which meant that she could and did have it put in the drinking water. When she finally reached the general in charge—he was absent because of illness—she left him little leeway in deciding what to do. Four steamers, she told him, should be brought as soon as possible to remove the wounded men from "that death trap." Even the general's agreement did not satisfy her. "I want the order issued before I leave this office." Not entirely convinced that she could count on prompt cooperation, she reminded the general of how she might follow through. "Remember. I have no other appeal but the newspapers and the great, generous people of the North who sustain them, if you fail."

Whether or not they liked her methods, officers as well as soldiers appreciated Wittenmyer's efficient help at the front, something they knew the army could not always deliver. Political complications, which Wittenmyer and some of her aides ignored, often slowed down the good intentions of army leaders. Near the foot of Lookout Mountain in Tennessee, for example, men were freezing to death for lack of fuel at a large field hospital, where the wounded slept in tents with no floors. A nurse, not a general, acted decisively. Mary Bickerdyke ordered men helping her to remove logs from a nearby Confederate fort that had surrendered. The surgeon present reminded her that she had acted illegally, in effect stealing government property, because she had received no order to help herself to the wood. The nurse, knowing that men would die before any order could be arranged, was willing to risk defending her decision later, something the surgeon did not dare to do.

The army in the 1860s faced structural problems in assuring medical care. First of all, it could not easily recruit the best surgeons because there could be no promise of promotion or advancement. The horrible experience of the Crimean War in Russia (1854–1856) had shown how disastrous were the attempts of medical men to give orders to officers who refused to obey anyone of lower rank. In the Civil War, politicians persisted in holding a low opinion of surgeons. A project for better training of army surgeons, for example, got nowhere. When he heard the proposal that surgeons be enabled to upgrade their skills by attending evening classes, Secretary of War Edwin M. Stanton refused to sanction the idea because he was sure that the young students would skip off to attend the theater rather than go to class. The result was that army surgeons improved their skills on the battlefield.

Her willingness to travel sometimes exposed Mrs. Wittenmyer to danger equal to that of the army surgeons she helped. At Vicksburg, as she talked to a surgeon inside a tent, she could not understand why she saw grass outside moving and bending, an odd sight on a hot and still June day. As she tells the story in her book *Under the Guns,* the surgeon let her know she was seeing movement caused by bullets. Only a few days later an officer would sit in the same chair where she had been and be killed by such bullets. Because a Union hospital had been set up under the guns of both sides during the siege of Vicksburg, Annie Wittenmyer sent supplies to it. The surgeon who received these believed that a visit from her would do the men more good than the food and supplies alone. He offered a horse if she would accept. She rode on a cavalry saddle, even crossing a canal on horseback, as mortar shells from both sides exploded. When she reached the men she experienced not relief but outrage, for the wounded were being kept near constant noise. The following morning she presented herself to General Grant and told him what she had seen. Instantly, the general issued an order to move the men that night to a hospital twenty-five miles away. Wittenmyer served with remarkable physical stamina at Shiloh, where she worked tirelessly without even stopping to eat for over twenty-four hours.

Thanks to her talents and persistence, Wittenmyer succeeded in creating as many as one hundred diet kitchens in military hospitals. She sent two women to be in charge of each kitchen with very explicit written instructions on their duties and comportment in seeing to the dietary needs of wounded men, always following the directions of the surgeon in charge, always giving comfort to the wounded. This last recommendation brought some of her aides into conflict with surgeons who saw the women merely as cooks—that is, servants who belonged in the kitchen. In some cases, therefore, the aides' written instructions from Mrs. Wittenmyer went against the directions of the officer to whom they were assigned. A related unforeseen problem arose from Wittenmyer's choice of women. While another energetic worker in the war relief effort, Dorothea Dix, enlisted the help of "homely" women, making sure to avoid the presence of attractive women among soldiers, Annie Wittenmyer saw no reason for such a superficial criterion. She advised her workers to dress plainly and always to comport themselves in a "Christian" manner, but she never refused the help of a woman on the basis of physical appearance. Conflicts of this order continued to distract but not impede her efforts.

While carrying on her field work and letter-writing and fund-raising efforts, Wittenmyer continued her prewar efforts to help children. The direction of this work now changed slightly. She appealed to the state and the army to take responsibility for the care of "war orphans." By this she did not mean children who had lost both parents in the war but children without fathers. Wittenmyer understood that only in the rarest cases could a woman with small children and without a husband provide for their well-being. In a farm state the hardship of keeping a family going burdened widows excessively.

At the end of the war, Wittenmyer continued to protect the interests of the people who had helped her. Some of the women who had given their services for the entire war found themselves in need, yet excluded from any kind of war pension because of a bureaucratic technicality: they had not formally enlisted. Through a campaign of letter writing and personal advice and intervention, Wittenmyer made sure that her helpers received the twelve dollars per month that was designated for army nurses. Her own pension, in the amount of twenty-five dollars per month, never reached her until 1898, decades after the war.

Many American women thought that the trials of the Civil War entitled them to compensation after the war in the form of

acknowledgment for their work. The reaction that they encountered left them disappointed, however. The abolitionists, in particular, let it be known that the end of the war brought, as
Frederick Douglass put it, "the Negro's hour." In other words,
the women would have to wait. One effect of this refusal was to
keep alive the spirit of solidarity that women had experienced
as helpers in hospitals. Keeping their habits of communication
intact, women recognized a new problem, one directly related
to the war. Of the men who survived the horrible battles and
returned from the conflict, many had learned to drink heavily in
their years away from home. Drunken husbands did not give
the relief and help that their wives and families counted on
with the war's end. The wives' reaction was forceful and better
organized than the earlier efforts by women to create sanitary
commissions. No one expressed surprise that the Women's
Christian Temperance League, an antidrinking organization,
elected Annie Turner Wittenmyer as its first president when it
met in Cleveland on November 18, 1874. She was reelected
without opposition in 1875 and 1876.

Wittenmyer wrote persuasively about the problem of alcohol, which she had the courage to say was not an exclusively
male vice. A far worse problem, in her eyes, came from the
growing numbers of women who drank, creating an even more
destabilizing social threat, since alcohol made mothers unable
to care for their own children. Wittenmyer recognized that the
nature of women's drinking went unnoticed because of a social
difference. Women bought their alcohol less openly, turning not
to whiskey but to patent medicines marketed primarily to
women. These elixirs and "tonics" first exposed, then addicted,
many mothers to alcohol. Such remedies often contained only
spirits and sweeteners but produced the same result as hard
liquor.

As a temperance leader, Wittenmyer continued lecturing
energetically, sometimes giving six public talks in one week.
Her wartime habit of travel in the name of a cause continued,
except that she could now travel much more freely—both

because the war had ended and because the railroad joined both coasts. Her travels covered the continent, from Maine to California.

Not content with writing letters to officers and senators, Wittenmyer worked systematically as she started two papers: *The Christian Woman,* which continued for eleven years, and later *The Christian Child.* In her late sixties she wrote her own memoir of the Civil War, *Under the Guns* (1894), recounting her battlefield experiences and demonstrating her role, on unofficial assignments, as America's first woman war correspondent. The widow of General U. S. Grant wrote an introduction to this remarkable book. Writing at a time when the country was disinclined to pensions, Wittenmyer intended the book, probably in part at least, to clear her own name from the malicious and unproven accusations made by her enemies during the war years. At her seventieth birthday in 1897 she was honored by congratulations and gifts from all over the country. Indefatigable to the end, she died on February 2, 1900, at her home in Sanatoga, Pennsylvania, after giving a lecture in nearby Pottstown earlier in the day.

THE
CIVIL WAR
MISSION OF
CHARLOTTE FORTEN

OUTSTRIPPING THE SIZE OF GREAT BRITain, its mother country, the United States soon had enough territory to show strong regional characteristics as different areas imitated different strains of British culture. The North, with more concentrated population centers, had an economy increasingly based on trade and manufacturing and higher literacy. It resembled the Britain of the Industrial Revolution and emulated just as closely the reformist spirit that sprang up in Britain to defend humanitarian values. The same outlook that inspired campaigns for improved conditions in British factories and mines found expression in the abolitionist journalism of the North.

Another strand of British consciousness turned away from grimy factory towns and consumptive children to contemplate the tranquility of a romantic past, made newly and immensely popular by the novels of Sir Walter Scott. In the United States, Southerners esteemed these novels as ennobling and as upholding the legitimacy of the rural, agricultural way of life.

In the small territory of the British Isles, partisans of the two views had to make accommodations and find a way for their philosophies to coexist. The luxury of abundant space in North America for decades allowed each side to claim its own considerable turf, but Northerners of the reformist frame of mind saw a new enemy on this side of the Atlantic. Northern abolitionists in particular, the most zealous human rights activists up to the civil rights movement of the 1960s, saw fellow Americans who owned slaves as the enemy. Southerners saw abolitionists as trouble-making meddlers. The conflict became bitter beyond the possibility of compromise because it opposed two positions based first of all on belief, but then reinforced by people's experience, by an economy, and by a way of life. Black Americans, excluded from participating in most civic activities, found themselves largely excluded from the debates and discussions of their treatment and of their future. But there were notable exceptions.

A PRECOCIOUS YOUNG WOMAN with an aptitude for literary studies, the shy Charlotte Forten energetically attended public talks and literary gatherings organized in Salem, Massachusetts, and even in Boston in the 1850s. Born to a well-to-do family on August 17, 1837, she met people only under close supervision, as was the custom for young ladies being prepared to be New England leaders. But she must have stood out every time because, unlike most proper young Massachusetts women, Charlotte Forten was black. A modest and valuable witness to the atmosphere of women's education in New England, Charlotte Forten recorded in her diary the inner life of a person she saw with disturbing objectivity, as if she were outside herself at times. Not for one minute, it seems, did she forget that people pointed to her as evidence that black Americans could be made literate.

While she received an excellent education in Salem, her family stayed in Philadelphia, where they were well known and respected both for their considerable wealth and because of their active and generous participation in civic causes.* The Fortens

---

* Charlotte's grandfather, James Forten, had made a fortune from an invention to ease the handling of sails on ships.

worked to end slavery but also to win equal treatment for women at a time when those causes were still linked. Her famous grandfather had been asked to serve as first president of the American Moral Reform Society, an organization that saw women and blacks as worthy of greater social and political justice.

Although he could have afforded to send his daughter to a private school in Philadelphia, Robert Bridges Forten chose not to use that easy way around a legalized injustice: no public school in Philadelphia would admit a black child. When Charlotte Forten was born, Philadelphia saw tension over race explode in race riots and the vindictive burning of Pennsylvania Hall, built through her grandfather's efforts as a forum for abolitionist speakers. After her mother died in 1840 when Charlotte was three, her father arranged to educate her at home by engaging private tutors. Through his strong association with New England antislavery groups, however, Robert Forten learned about the good integrated public schools in Salem, Massachusetts, away from the resentment that black children would learn from whites in Philadelphia. When he sent his daughter off to Higginson Grammar School in Salem, Robert Forten did not know, perhaps, that she would keep a diary of what she experienced, and he could not have known that because of her diary her reputation would endure.

Charlotte Forten's journal begins in 1854, shortly after the sixteen-year-old moved to Salem, to a radically different climate and culture, far from her family. Yet New England in the mid-nineteenth century could not have been a better place for a young woman of her temperament and interests. A serious commitment to the abolition of slavery impassioned many leaders in Massachusetts. From her own home in Philadelphia, a home to which black leaders had always been welcomed, Charlotte saw only people like her educated family members intent on opposing the South, but in Massachusetts antislavery feelings permeated the entire society. What the South had viewed as a necessary economic solution to the problem of running plantations was becoming, in the eyes of Northerners, a morally outrageous arrangement and a reason to despise its practitioners and upholders.

The rhetoric of antislavery publications at the time, including *The Liberator,* equated the South with a rising tide of despotism. To end what they saw as the evil and unequal treatment of "Negro Americans," the abolitionists intended to destroy the South by taking away its moral ground, by exposing slavery as absolutely indefensible. Their cause did not stop in North America. When Great Britain passed antislavery legislation in 1833, abolitionists everywhere felt heartened. When the World Anti-Slavery Convention met in London in 1840, among the most impressive speakers was Robert Purvis, who married an aunt of Charlotte Forten. At that same meeting her Salem host, Charles Lenox Redmond, rejected the seating plan, which segregated no one by race but put women in the gallery upstairs. Redmond gave up his place on the main floor to sit with women in protest.

Abolitionism in Massachusetts was so not much a point of view as it was a way of life. In her diary, Charlotte Forten notes the numerous lectures she attended that abolitionists sponsored, sometimes a series or "course" of lectures sponsored through the Salem Female Anti-Slavery League, which she officially joined in 1856. Besides the public lectures, there were fund-raising society benefits such as the annual Anti-Slavery Bazaar in Salem, and another in Boston. The abolitionists lived by their own calendar, which honored such dates as the twentieth anniversary of the end of slavery in all British colonies and the anniversary of the day when a crowd chased William Lloyd Garrison, editor of *The Liberator,* through the streets of Boston with a noose on his neck.

Women played a central role in this network and understood that they must draw audiences of both sexes. Such intelligent and imaginative women as Mary Shephard, principal of the Higginson Grammar School, understood that to draw a large crowd they needed speakers who were not just competent but also famous. Ralph Waldo Emerson accepted their invitations to speak, as did the "Poet Laureate of Abolition," John Greenleaf

Whittier. Charlotte Forten sometimes attended such talks, enhancing her knowledge of politics and of Boston society. People must have known who she was by sight, but her diary gives no hint of how people reacted to a cultivated, well-brought-up black woman who lived at the Salem home of Charles Lenox Redmond. Her writing reflects her intellectual maturity, the result of the considerable self-discipline she developed through study and also through separation from her family. But when the diary begins, Charlotte was just sixteen, an age at which few young people can bear to describe themselves, let alone describe how people react to them.

Circumstances suggest that this motherless, isolated girl must have suffered from loneliness. But more than any self-indulgent sentiment, a sense of duty compelled her, according to what she wrote. She saw herself as owing her race a great deal. Because she had the good fortune to study at a fine school, she felt obliged to *prove* that a black student was as capable as a white of "self-improvement." We know that in the student body of two hundred she was the only black, but she herself never says so. In fact, when she mentions people, in Salem or in Philadelphia, she does not identify them by race. Even when she felt contempt for a group, she did not use racial words to characterize them. She viewed "the military" with great contempt after she saw soldiers guarding an escaped slave, a fugitive caught on the streets of Salem, "as if he were a criminal." In rage, in her one outburst, she referred to the soldiers as "doughfaces," the one nearly explicit antiwhite term she used.

In Charlotte Forten's record of her energetic pace in the name of education—so many public talks, discussions, poetry readings, regular contact with the Female Anti-Slavery Society —we read between the lines that no young women or men were making efforts to befriend her. Older people recognized her exceptionally stalwart personality—her principal became a lifelong friend, and the poet Whittier took pains to help her—but few bonds linked her to other adolescents. Forten talked about her studies as "my best friends" while at school, as the diary hinted at how hard she worked. One manuscript of the diary contains a list of the books she read in one year, a list that ran to one hundred titles.

If anyone in Salem had not noticed Charlotte Forten when she started to attend Higginson, no one could ignore her at graduation. All the students were invited beforehand to submit hymns, one of which would be chosen for the students to sing at the ceremony. On that day, Miss Forten hesitated to acknowledge to the public that the poem chosen was hers.

The record of her work habits shows how greatly it mattered to Charlotte Forten not only to pass in school but to excel. Studying harder than any student needed to, strictly speaking, she worked to teach herself German after she had learned French and Latin at school. On her own she produced a translation of a French novel, which she eventually published. Obviously, her efforts were not part of a plan to win credentials and start a career. Far beyond practical aims, she believed that her academic success would help remove the question of whether a black person could stand up to the rigors of scholastic work and thereby improve herself. The need to prove that fact to herself in part explains the existence of the diary. Early in her diary she writes that she intends to record her thoughts over a long enough period of time to enable her to see improvement in her way of reasoning. Knowing that aim, readers may find it odd that her way of expressing herself does not change markedly from 1854 to 1864, not because she did not develop but because she was such a skilled writer and clear thinker to begin with.

After graduating from Higginson Grammar School in 1855, Charlotte Forten enrolled in the Salem Normal School, the next step for women hoping to teach. Young women usually studied for three terms before being allowed to teach young children. In exchange for free tuition, graduates promised to teach in Massachusetts public schools. In their year of advanced study they took one course on methods of teaching, but the accent fell on proper language. The typical curriculum included arithmetic, algebra, geometry, geography, spelling, reading, etymology, critical study of English authors, history of English literature,

English grammar, art of reasoning, rhetoric and composition, Latin, and theory and practice of teaching.

Not long after graduating from Salem Normal School, Forten found a good position in town at the Eps Grammar School. Before her, no black person had ever been a teacher in Salem, a fact that Forten's diary omits to mention. Poor health forced her to leave in 1857. She returned to Philadelphia and then went back to Salem, always trying to stay in touch with the community where she had come of age. While she was back in Salem, John Greenleaf Whittier suggested that she look into a new kind of teaching in which he thought she would excel. The outbreak of the Civil War offered Charlotte an unusual opportunity. As part of a "social experiment," teachers were going south to Port Royal, a settlement off the coast of South Carolina captured by Union soldiers in 1861. The experiment meant testing the hypothesis, still not widely accepted, that former slaves could be educated. Teachers went down from Northern cities to work at teaching this population to read and write. Most of those teachers, it goes without saying, were white.

When she applied from Boston, Charlotte Forten was turned down, supposedly because she was a woman, even though other women were being sent. After this initial refusal, Forten went home to Philadelphia to reapply from a different city. The Philadelphia Board accepted her and she went to the island of Saint Helena in late 1862. The record shows that of the teachers who arrived from the North with her she was the only black, though again her diary does not refer to the racial makeup of her group. Charlotte Forten arrived full of goodwill, but she soon experienced culture shock. She found it quite difficult to understand the free slaves' speech. Her diary records her embarrassment when she could not decode the words of the songs they sang. From her practice of writing down the sound of slave speech in 1862, we can guess that she had rarely heard such an accent, even if she had read such speech in *Uncle Tom's Cabin*. Because she had spent so much time in Salem, Charlotte Forten had acquired the sensibilities of an educated New England woman.

She describes the costumes at slave weddings that took place—sometimes as many as six at a time—as comical.

Probably the most moving entry in the entire diary was written on January 1, 1863, while Charlotte Forten was still in the South. Without explanation she begins by calling it "The most glorious day this nation has yet seen, I think." Before Charlotte Forten had left for the South, President Lincoln had announced in late September that on January 1 the Emancipation Proclamation would take effect. Forten reported on the ceremony at Camp Saxton and told how everyone present felt touched when a group of freed slaves started to sing spontaneously, "My Country 'Tis of Thee." She remained at Port Royal until 1864, not long after the death of her father, when her old respiratory ailment ("lung fever" in the language of the times) bothered her.

When Charlotte returned North, an old friend bowled her over with a proposition. The well-respected and well-connected poet John Greenleaf Whittier asked her to write up her experiences at Port Royal for the *Atlantic Monthly,* already a prestigious journal of the New England literary establishment. When he forwarded her work to the editor, he added a brief note, which appeared in the magazine following the title of the article, "Life on the Sea Islands." The note said:

> The following graceful and picturesque description of the new condition of things on the Sea Islands of South Carolina, originally written for private perusal, seems to me worthy of a place in the "Atlantic." Its young author—herself akin to the long-suffering race whose Exodus she so pleasantly describes—is still engaged in her labor of love on St. Helena Island.—J.G.W.

In her article, which ran in two issues, May and June 1864, Forten described in slightly expanded form her arrival and work in South Carolina. White readers could respect the emotion she mentioned on her way to work among the "freed people," as she repeatedly called the former slaves: "We thought how easy it would be for a band of guerrillas, had they chanced that way, to seize and hang us; but we were in that excited, jubilant state of mind, which makes fear impossible. . . ." Her readers also understood, even if Forten did not make it explicit, that if a band of Confederate guerrillas had found her and the other black teachers on their way to the settlement, the teachers might have been enslaved and never heard from again.

When Forten's article described the great day of emancipation, as her diary noted, she treated it as a fact well known in the South. *Atlantic* readers of May 1864 may have believed her, but in fact Abraham Lincoln, at that time, anxiously pondered what he saw as the failure of his Emancipation Proclamation. Lincoln feared for slaves more than ever, because he saw how weak his chances of reelection had become. Without him the proclamation would be withdrawn and slavery would continue. In any case, Lincoln knew that slaves were not making a mass exodus out of Confederate territory, which his proclamation said they had to do in order to be liberated.

To try to understand why this exodus was not happening, President Lincoln spoke with his respected adviser on all questions related to slavery, Frederick Douglass. The black man saw an explanation that Lincoln had not counted on in the deceitful behavior of slave owners. Probably a great many slaves had never even heard of the Emancipation Proclamation, Douglass reasoned, because their "masters" had made sure that they did not find out that anything had changed. Together, Lincoln and Douglass worked out a plan for sending undercover agents to the South to spread the news, a plan that never had to be used because the Union Army started winning battles and helping Lincoln's chances for reelection.

In many ways, Forten's article could not have been more timely. Racism, not just slavery, divided voters in that election year. Lincoln spelled out for voters that to be against emancipation meant being against a victory for the North, in other words, being against the Union. At the time of the election, it helped

Lincoln's Republicans tremendously to see that, after a campaign to get soldiers to "vote as they shot," three-quarters of the absentee votes of soldiers were on their side.

In her article Forten spoke about her tremendous admiration for Colonel Robert Shaw and his soldiers. *Atlantic* readers did not need a note from the editor to explain why the schoolteacher should talk in such an admiring and moving way about that officer in particular. Shaw had led a brigade that had already become famous, the Fifty-fourth Massachusetts Infantry. Shaw, a white officer, led the black brigade in July 1863 in its attack against Fort Wagner, the Confederate defense at the entrance to Charleston harbor. The famous black regiment led by Shaw, who came from an important abolitionist family, fought ahead of others in the capture of the fort. Almost half of the regiment died in that assault, among them Shaw himself, who was found shot through the heart. Some Massachusetts readers no doubt knew that when his family had asked for the return of their son's body, a Confederate officer was said to have answered, "We have buried him with his niggers." The attack on Fort Wagner quickly became for black Americans the equivalent of Bunker Hill for patriotic families of Massachusetts, a day with which descendants proudly claimed a connection.

Other readers would have known that at the very same time as the fighting was taking place at Fort Wagner, New York City had witnessed draft riots because so many white Americans, recent immigrants from Ireland in particular, refused to join up and risk their lives for slaves, blacks whom Charlotte Forten knew had already been Americans for generations.

Forten's excellent diary stops in 1864, so that our knowledge of her subjective experience does not continue past her teaching days. After emancipation Forten worked in Boston for the New England branch of the Freedmen's Union Commission. From 1865 to 1871 she served as the link between teachers of freed slaves in the South and the teachers and other Northerners who wanted to help them. After teaching in Washington, D.C., for a short time, she worked as a "first-class clerk" at the Treasury Department.

Charlotte Forten kept her federal job until 1878, when at age forty-one, she married Francis Grimké, a student at Princeton Theological Seminary thirteen years her junior. Her husband's upbringing showed none of the same wealth and privilege of his wife's distinguished family. Although Francis was the nephew of the well-known abolitionist Angelina Grimké, for many years Charlotte did not know they were related. In fact, Francis Grimké had been a slave partly through the treachery of his white half-brother, who sold him. Great physical courage and intellectual stamina distinguished Francis Grimké, however. He escaped, eventually graduated from Lincoln College in Pennsylvania (as class valedictorian), and studied law at Howard University before turning to theology at Princeton.

At age forty-three Charlotte Forten had her only child, who died as an infant. Although she did not enjoy strong health for much of her life, she lived to the age of seventy-six. For the last year of her life, Charlotte Forten was an invalid, always cared for devotedly by her husband. They worked together to provide every kind of support to former slaves. She died in Washington on July 22, 1914.

SITTING BULL
AND THE
CLOSING
FRONTIER

CULTURE, FOR NINETEENTH-CENTURY Americans, came from the East and could be carried by pioneers who headed past the western edge of civilization, which by the mid-1800s had spread all the way to Minnesota. When easterners loaded volumes of Shakespeare into the wagon along with cooking pots, they thought they guaranteed the transmission of culture. Europeans who sailed up the Mississippi and disembarked at Keokuk for points west brought their Goethe for the same reason. But these Americans could not think of the native population as having anything like a culture, because they had no written culture. White and black Americans, even those who had risked their lives or lost family members in a war to end slavery, moved west in the hope of clearing the land of these "savages." Like the buffalo, in white eyes the native tribes stood no hope against progress, the proof of culture.

⚜

THE NAME of Tatanka Iyotanka ("Sitting Bull"), like every other significant part of his culture, referred to buffalo. The image of a bull buffalo on its haunches, having resolved not to budge from the fight, depicts with uncanny accuracy the man who won that name for himself at age fourteen. The child born in 1831 (by the most recently accepted estimate) to the elder Sitting Bull and Her-Holy-Door belonged to the people who called themselves Lakota; their particular tribe was the Hunkpapas. In the East, their kinfolk, related by language and culture, designated themselves as Dakotas. Both groups taken together were called "enemy" by the Chippewa in a word that ended up as "Sioux" when outsiders tried to say it. As fighters and hunters, the Sioux followed the buffalo herd in a nomadic way of life that sustained them successfully even in the severe winters of the northern Plains. They counted on the buffalo not only for meat but also for hides to make their tepees, clothing, shirts and leggings, moccasins, and even shields. Ponies, their transport and also their sign and measure of wealth, let them go where the herds led, in a region covering six western states.

No one could have predicted to a Plains boy born in 1831 that before he was fifty the buffalo would be practically extinct. The Sioux would be destroyed by the same changes that diminished the herds: whites looking for gold after it was discovered in the Black Hills in 1874; the Northern Pacific railroad that set out to link Saint Paul and Seattle; and white forts penetrating ever more deeply into hunting grounds. In 1831, when the boy who would become Sitting Bull was born near the Grand River, the nearest whites were five hundred miles to the southeast. The world he knew depended on hunting, a dangerous and essential undertaking that sometimes required making war on neighboring enemy tribes to preserve or win hunting ground. The winner stayed and hunted, the defeated side had to leave. That code organized the society of the Lakota and their neighbors, such as the enemy Crow tribe.

"Jumping Badger," the name given at birth to the elder Sitting Bull's son, did not suit the solemn boy. His father quickly renamed him Hunkesni ("Slow"). To succeed in a culture that depended on hunting as well as fighting to win, a child needed to be trained and encouraged in the direction of physical courage, or taking chances. To put your safety at risk proved bravery. Soldiers who would later berate the Sioux as "wild Indians" did not recognize the rules that warriors observed as they attacked. Nor did the soldiers know the consequences of their performance in battle for these warriors. In fighting bravely, Lakota men won respect within their tribe and, more important, merit in the spirit world. But their spirit world did not mean "heaven" or any such unearthly remote place as Christian soldiers believed in. For the Lakotas, as for other tribes, the spirits belonged to their daily world, inhabiting every aspect of nature: rain, the earth, the buffalo, and all the rest.

At age fourteen, Slow became Sitting Bull when he won a first "hit," or "coup," against an enemy. By Lakota protocols, any claim to have gotten the honor of the first (or any up to the fourth) strike touching the enemy with a special stick had to be confirmed by witnesses from the tribe. In a code that upheld valor above mere survival, to kill, that is, simply to eliminate an opponent, did not automatically confer glory. For example, to kill a man from far away never made a story, and did not enhance a warrior's reputation for bravery. Sometimes the Lakota mutilated bodies after bitter fighting—a final revenge because a body that was disfigured could not easily pass to the spirit world.

Making war in the correct way assured the continuation of the tribe's way of life. Warriors learned to tell when they had fought enough. They stopped at that point and went back, either to dance and sing of their victory in celebration, or to remain silent in shame if they had not won or had not had victorious moments. Lakotas did not fight to wipe out another tribe. They thought about fighting in the same way as the other tribes of the Plains whom they fought, such as the Crow. But the white soldiers, especially veterans of the Civil War, had seen carnage on a scale so immense that it brutalized them. In tribal terms, they did not fight bravely and did not know when to stop. They made no sense.

From his earliest fights, Sitting Bull showed outstanding courage and strength. He fought well because he had developed the strength and skills that Lakotas respected: an unusually good rider, he could stay on his pony and "disappear" by hugging the mount from one side, and holding its mane. Like other Lakotas, he rode without a saddle. He had won that distinction of first coup, marked by an eagle feather, by arriving on the scene ahead of the other warriors. Most eagle feathers went to braves who had gone out ahead and had fought away from their comrades, in other words without protection. Extraordinary risks of that order won respect in the style of fighting that Sitting Bull understood.

From boyhood games, Sitting Bull had become an excellent shot with a bow and arrow. At age ten, he killed his first buffalo. Everyone recognized that he would continue to distinguish himself by fighting. In Lakota culture, those accomplishments meant that he would be acknowledged as a leader, one chief among others in the tribe. The tribe's social order, developed without reference to white ways, put men of ability in positions of respect, but no single person held unique or absolute authority. Leaders worked to achieve not dominance but agreement, so that the tribe could act in unity.

Inevitably, people who chose to expose themselves to danger got hurt. Early in his fighting career, Sitting Bull was hit in the foot, a wound that changed the way he walked for the rest of his life. But that injury, because it did not change his way of riding, did not detract from his distinction as a fighter. Because he distinguished himself so precociously and advanced so easily along the path to a position of authority, it did not violate the normal course of tribal life when he later chose to add another domain to his achievements.

In addition to respecting its warriors, the tribe also looked up to men with spiritual gifts such as the ability to foresee important events or to cure physically or spiritually troubled members of the community. Thus, the young Sitting Bull turned in the direction of becoming a medicine man. Part of the initiation to that special circle involved rites intended to tame the flesh by testing physical endurance. The Sun Dance, a grueling ceremony that has been shown in modern films, required men to stick pieces of buffalo bone through their flesh, on the chest and on the back. Long strips of stretched hide were attached to these pegs on one end with the other end lashed to the top of a pole. After fasting and remaining suspended by their own skin in this dramatic way, would-be medicine men had to "dance" and pull against their own flesh in hope of seeing some great spiritual truth in a vision. Men sometimes hung and waited for the vision for days, eventually tearing their flesh. Sitting Bull voluntarily went through this test more than once and had scars front and back to prove it. His endurance of this gruesome trial makes mere racist prejudice of early biographical accounts suggesting that he was cowardly or somehow deficient in choosing to become a medicine man. Some accounts wrongly indicate that he lacked the courage to go on as a warrior, when in fact he continued to fight.

The scant contact between the Lakota and whites explains the ignorance with which each side regarded the other. Because he seldom saw whites in his youth, Sitting Bull knew almost no English for most of his life and later, as a matter of principle, he did not want to talk to the foreigners he had learned to distrust. But that reticent stance resulted in inconvenience and, later, exploitation. Even without English (or French), Sitting Bull could deal with traders. These rough and colorful characters, often the offspring of French trappers and Indian wives, learned what merchants have always known, that commerce transcends language. In exchanges that could be as full of ritual as hunting or war, the traders met with Lakotas in tepees set up for the purpose of exchange. Sitting Bull or other Lakotas would give buffalo hides and receive rifles and ammunition. By Lakota logic, the exchange made sense: weapons that they could not make given for hides they could not use. In the days of plentiful herds, trade extended the ways in which the buffalo hides motivated the economy of village life.

Very quickly, this reasoning and the natural rhythm of Lakota life were ripped apart when technology came screaming out of the East. Railroad locomotives brought, first of all, noise louder than anything ever heard on the Plains, noise powerful enough to frighten off and scatter buffalo herds. Before long, the trains also brought a new kind of white. Not traders but tourists now came west and expected to kill a bison from wherever they got off the train. Fashion had created another force in the East totally beyond the imagination of the practical Lakotas, an increased demand for buffalo hides. Before long, trains were bringing commercial hunters, who could kill as many as one hundred buffalo in an hour. Between 1872 and 1874 estimates put the number of buffalo killed at nine million. The buffalo's paths of migration also had to change with the advance of the railroad, one more force that transformed the opening West. And anything that radically altered the habits of buffalo dictated a corresponding major change for the Lakotas.

Even before technology wrecked the ecosystem that governed the Lakota way of life, political events in the East changed how Washington viewed the tribes of the Great Plains. The end of the Mexican War in 1847 guaranteed the United States more territory, just as the Webster-Ashburton Treaty of 1842 with Great Britain had opened up Oregon. By the summer of 1848, one thousand covered wagons carrying whites were heading west along the Oregon Trail every week. When Lakotas and other tribes saw settlers in wagons driving game off their hunting grounds, they attacked, as they would have fought off any encroaching enemy tribe. The U.S. government, wanting to protect its citizens, looked for a treaty to end the attacks.

The first important treaty in Sitting Bull's lifetime, the Fort Laramie Treaty of 1851, attempted to make all the Plains tribes peaceful. Not only did the treaty require the people of the Plains to stop attacking settlers, miners, and other whites headed west, it added the naïve provision that the tribes stop fighting each other. In all likelihood the tribal leaders who signed it—who did not even include Sitting Bull—did not understand that in doing so they were accepting an unthinkable condition: to stop fighting their enemies. To add to the confusion, the U.S. Senate came up with changes to the treaty limiting the term of government payments, which were then "signed" by still another set of chiefs. The Sioux had begun to accept limits on their territory —on paper.

Back East, where distinctions between tribes were not recognized, newspaper reports changed what Americans in general believed about the native inhabitants of the Plains. The Santee Sioux had seen their territory reduced to a strip ten miles wide that ran along the Minnesota River for about 150 miles. Fear distorted the reports that journalists sent from that frontier on the way to Washington. In 1862 word reached the capital that war had broken out between the Sioux and white settlers. Unfortunately for the Sioux, the U.S. Army was already fighting the Civil War. The commanding officer sent to Minnesota had lost the second Battle of Bull Run, where he saw sixteen thousand Union soldiers killed or wounded in two days. General John Pope looked for armed conflict of a kind the Sioux did not practice: "It is my purpose utterly to exterminate the Sioux," he said. His instructions to his men made clear that he knew everything he wanted to about the enemy: "They are to be treated as maniacs or wild beasts and by no means as people with whom treaties and compromises can be made." His forces, led by Colonel Henry Sibley, did capture 1,800 Sioux warriors. Pope wanted a mass execution of 303 Indians. Abraham Lincoln intervened and insisted on seeing the records of the courtsmartial that had condemned them. In the largest public execution ever held in the United States, President Lincoln consented to the public hanging of thirty-eight Sioux. The public showed a strong and indignant reaction: why so few?

Only two years later, in 1864, Colorado militia massacred four hundred southern Cheyenne at Sand Creek in Colorado. The band had felt secure because they had been promised safety by the commander of a nearby fort. Their leader, Black Kettle, flew an American flag in front of his tepee—a flag that Abraham Lincoln had given him with assurances of peace during his visit to Washington. Even the medicine of that flag could not protect the Cheyenne from Colonel John Chivington's command to "kill and scalp all, big and little." The civilizations of the Plains were changing the way white soldiers fought.

A small number of generals understood that a tribe fought only in reaction to unfair treatment. Generals George Crook and

Oliver O. Howard tried to explain to politicians that treaties should offer some advantage to both sides, that promises had to be honored. Arguments by experienced generals could not reduce the gulf between two alien ways of thinking. In the East, geography had provided a specious solution: send the Indians west. But unfortunately for the Indians, this traditional white method of dealing with them would no longer work in the West. The continent was running out of "rug" under which they could be swept. By white reasoning, progress had to be acknowledged as irresistible. The Indians could not be allowed to continue living as they used to and wanted to continue to do. They would have to turn themselves in at Indian agencies, accept white education, and *become* white.

Sitting Bull never expected a treaty to do what it promised. If anyone had asked him, he knew exactly what he wanted for his people. Nothing could be simpler: whites should stop scaring the game away and interrupting the paths of buffalo herds. Whites should stop coming. If they did not, he would attack. They should remain as traders if they wanted, but not go any further than they had gone. How arrogantly they behaved, and what senseless demands they made! Some of the land they asked for the Lakotas had only recently won from the Crow. Now, without a fight, the "walking soldiers" expected them to hand it over. Senseless. To a chief who had known the respect of his people his whole life, the idea of compromise, of giving up a little land, spelled the beginning of dishonor. In the eyes of many of his people, he behaved with enormous integrity. True to his name, he had made up his mind and did not budge. To the United States he was labeled a "hostile," the name for Indians who were not willing to accept white civilization. Indians who cooperated were called "progressives."

In June 1868, a distinguished and courageous visitor arrived in Sitting Bull's Hunkpapa village on a peace mission that succeeded, according to some official accounts. Father Pierre-Jean de Smet, a Jesuit missionary known as Black Robe to many Indians of the Plains, brought a request for representatives to accompany him to a peace conference. He spent three nights staying with Sitting Bull, who received him as an honored guest. Politeness required all the hosts to listen with respectful attention. After the formal greetings and requests were presented, even after his own formal talk, Sitting Bull said what many of his tribe thought. The Lakotas wanted their land left alone. Whites should go back where they came from or expect to be attacked. When de Smet prepared to leave, he asked for some representatives of the tribe to accompany him to Fort Rice. Sitting Bull, because of his own reluctance to make any agreement, sent chiefs less important than himself. These Lakotas, including his friend Gall, did not grasp that what they told de Smet, and later the soldiers, bore no relation at all to the paper they then signed.

That document, which had originally been prepared as part of the Fort Laramie Treaty of 1851, contained a blueprint for the fate of the Sioux. Words they could not have comprehended, words like "reservation" and "annuity," described a way of life they could not imagine. Schools would be built, training would convert the Sioux from hunters into farmers. For the next thirty years the government would give them food rations, and clothing of the kind white people wore. Sitting Bull could not have understood these concepts either, but he knew that he had signed nothing. As a man of his word, he had a clean conscience. No one, he thought, could expect to hold him to agreements signed by less important chiefs.

Sitting Bull continued to start fights with whites, as he had told Black Robe he would. When the Lakotas around him saw that settlers did not stop coming, they made a structural change in their tribal confederation in order to allow, for the first time, authority that surpassed one tribe. Four Horns, an uncle of Sitting Bull, wanted all the Lakota tribes and even some neighboring ones to acknowledge a supreme commander, one leader who would speak for many tribes on the question of when to make war. The tribes chose Sitting Bull as that commander.

According to estimates by Robert M. Utley, Sitting Bull's biographer, one-third of the Lakota followed Sitting Bull's leadership and beliefs. By fighting, they would keep whites away and guarantee the continuation of the way of life they knew. Because their attachment to the land rationalized that life, any loss of land, even by treaty, spelled humiliation in their terms. On his side, Sitting Bull had enormous credibility because he had fought so valiantly so many times and had already refused any compromise. In practical terms, he knew how to win, an art that depended on knowing when to make war. After 1870, Sitting Bull stopped carrying out attacks on settlers passing through any tribe's land and concentrated more on defending the land that his people already claimed. That policy let Sitting Bull satisfy his followers until everything changed, when a man ambitious for a reputation trespassed on a place that already had one.

Lieutenant Colonel George Armstrong Custer, identified by the Sioux as Long Hair, came west with the Seventh Cavalry in 1872. When he started an expedition into Paha Sapa (the Black Hills) in 1874, he violated a taboo. The Sioux did not go there much, and seldom camped in the region that some feared and some spoke of as holy. Every Sioux understood that something made those hills unique. Leaders like Sitting Bull knew that even when game grew scarce in other places, the hills could be counted on for food and for tall, straight trees suited for the frames of tepees. Custer was not hunting when he went there, at least not for food. Besides soldiers, Custer had miners and equipment with him. He wanted to be the man credited with confirming rumors of gold in the Black Hills. The special status of Paha Sapa obliged Sitting Bull and the Lakotas to threaten to attack. But the Sioux did not fight Custer there in 1874. Instead, when a fort was built as a federal agency for the Crow, the traditional enemy of the Lakotas, Sitting Bull attacked it, adding to his reputation as a "hostile."

The Sioux' most famous victory, when they killed Custer near the Little Bighorn River in June 1876, did not deceive Sitting Bull. As medicine man, he had predicted Custer's defeat, and had participated in it by making medicine, not by fighting. When the battle ended, he also knew that the whites would be ready for revenge and would be able to send enough soldiers to guarantee their success. Because Custer had hoped to be a candidate for president, news of his death appeared on the front pages of newspapers back east. That story shared the front page with a less dramatic historical event, the hundredth anniversary of the United States.

Rather than stay and be forced into a fight that he ultimately could not win, Sitting Bull sought safety in flight rather than risk being taken to a reservation. With around two thousand followers, Sitting Bull crossed the border to Canada in May 1877, expecting the protection of Queen Victoria—"Grandmother," as he referred to her.

Besides peace, Sitting Bull also hoped to find food when he took his people to the new hunting ground north of the border, but the hunters stayed hungry, unable to find enough game. Canadian winters strained the Sioux capacity for misery and caused some to desert their leader. News of their hardship reached army forts to the south. In reply to an invitation from the government of the United States in July 1881, Sitting Bull appeared at Fort Buford, Montana, where he used to go to trade, and turned himself in along with his people. As a chief, he made the hard decision for the well-being of those he governed, people who had become desperately hungry and demoralized in Canada. From what he knew of treaties and the worthlessness of their promises, Sitting Bull may have been less than surprised when he was taken prisoner even after he was promised a pardon. From Fort Buford he was taken to Fort Randall, South Dakota.

Because of his national reputation, Sitting Bull was given special permission to leave the reservation to go on a national tour. As he became more widely known, fantastic rumors about him spread. According to some, he was a West Point graduate. Others held that he could write in Latin. A new kind of reputation, unrelated to Lakota bravery, drew curious crowds who wanted to see the chief who did not fear the U.S. Army. When he headed east, he knew that he would not be paid for the tour but that he would be allowed to sell his autograph. As he traveled, Sitting Bull made speeches in theaters to audiences who did not understand anything he said, just as he did not understand the translator who followed him. In Philadelphia, the audience included an English-speaking Sioux boy who recognized an unfaithful translation. In his speech, Sitting Bull announced he would see the "Grandfather," or president of the United States in Washington, D.C. (He never did.) He said he was glad to know his children would be educated when he saw so many white people. "There is no use fighting any longer," he went on. "The buffalo are all gone, as well as the rest of the game." The translator then explained to the audience that they had been listening to a gory description of what happened at the Little Bighorn from a chief who boasted that he had personally killed Custer. The people who heard those false claims from the translator also saw the tired-looking warrior as he gave away money to hungry and filthy white children.

When he returned to the West to live on the Standing Rock Reservation (in present-day South Dakota), Sitting Bull had to deal with new deceptions. In the new style of trading, the Sioux faced government commissioners who offered money for land. Sitting Bull, predictably, did not want to give up even one Sioux acre, not until he could believe in promises from older agreements. Not wanting to come across as simply belligerent, Sitting Bull tried to explain the bond between the Sioux and their land. In frustration, he saw that the bored-looking commissioners were indifferent to his being a chief: to them, he was just one more Indian. In turn he lived at the Grand River Camp on the reservation, far from white authorities.

One white man understood Sitting Bull's authority at the Standing Rock Reservation so well that he vowed not to defer to it. James McLaughlin, an Indian agent married to a Dakota woman, zealously set out to bring Sitting Bull to his knees, to persuade him that he could not hold out against progress. In an odd rivalry with his famous captive, McLaughlin exerted his authority in the hope of diminishing that of Sitting Bull. He had an opportunity to display his importance when William (Buffalo Bill) Cody wanted Sitting Bull to make a second tour, this time as part of his Wild West Show. Cody and Sitting Bull had become good friends during the chief's first tour, a friendship sealed by Cody's gift of a trick pony. The new proposition came to involve McLaughlin because, as a reservation Indian, the Sioux chief could not leave without his permission. Seeing a chance to display his own importance, McLaughlin refused outright, maybe because he understood that by coming back with stories of his travels, Sitting Bull would enhance his standing on the reservation.

Another unforeseen outside force elevated Sitting Bull and bedeviled McLaughlin. Far more significant than Buffalo Bill's glamour, a religious movement with an urgent spirit of revival now come from the West, started by a Paiute native of Nevada who had a mystical experience in which he saw salvation for all the Indians. Whites would leave, the forest would be full of game again because the Messiah was about to come, he predicted. According to the vision, the redemption would take place in the spring of 1891, the following year.

As an aspect of American Indian religion, that vision in itself did not necessarily have to threaten whites, but the medium that passed the news terrified them. In this ancient culture, the powerful message could not be forcefully transmitted if it were simply told. Words conveyed very little; dance was necessary to demonstrate a truth of such magnitude for the community. The fervor attached to the news inspired a new dance, a revolutionary dance with messianic overtones, a spiritual craze that left dancers on the ground, some transported beyond their bodies into a mystical dimension in which they heard more recent news of the Messiah, whom the Indians pledged to treat decently—not as the whites had done. To outsiders, these spiritual rites looked like hysteria, partly because the Indians had just invented it, proof that they were lying about becoming white and were in fact very dangerous. Dancers started talking about new medicine related to the "Ghost Dance," about a shirt that protected its wearer from bullets and other white weapons.

When settlers got word of this cult, they asked the government in Washington for help against the wild fanatics whom they saw as ready to start a war of religion. Washington did not doubt the power of new medicine in North and South Dakota. The Senate voted to give each of those states guns and ammunition for citizens and citizen armies to protect themselves. The secretary of war would authorize that federal help, but first he had to convince the secretary of the interior, who argued that the government should send food to the Indians, not guns to the whites. Food already promised by treaties had never been sent. Even if Indians could not read, they could see that their rations were being cut down, that their children were getting sick. Shortages did not occur by accident. Officials in Washington believed that hungry Indians could be counted on to cooperate. Meanwhile, the Ghost Dance spread.

James McLaughlin knew about the Ghost Dance and the magic shirt. Hoping to substitute a stabilizing fad for a disruptive one, McLaughlin had already offered the reservation Sioux a shirt that gave worldly rather than mystical status. Blue army uniforms with shiny buttons transformed Sioux into Indian police, a force that helped McLaughlin spy on Sitting Bull and follow his movements. But against the Ghost Dance fervor, McLaughlin knew he was as helpless as the government. After all that they had given up, the Indians would not put up with white meddling in their religion. How could Washington hope to make a dance illegal? But McLaughlin considered that if he could take Sitting Bull out of the picture, the Sioux would lose interest in the dance, because they would lose all hope—including hope of a Messiah.

Word had reached Sitting Bull that the Messiah would appear even sooner than predicted, in December 1890, at the Pine Ridge camp of Red Cloud, who was a longtime friend of Sitting Bull. To visit that camp to the east of Standing Rock, near the border of Nebraska, Sitting Bull needed permission from McLaughlin. He sent his written request to McLaughlin, who wanted Sitting Bull to stay put. On December 14, 1890, the night before Sitting Bull expected to leave for Red Cloud's camp, McLaughlin sent, but did not accompany, forty-three Indian police to arrest the chief. By daybreak, the police reached Sitting Bull's cabin and told him he was under arrest, provoking anger and confusion that have never been completely untangled. One of the chief's loyal friends may have fired the first shot on the Indian police. Minutes later, Sitting Bull lay dead and mutilated, shot in the chest. The fighting did not stop. As planned, soldiers from a nearby fort arrived with an automatic weapon, a Hotchkiss gun, which they fired into the camp. Outside, the pony given to Sitting Bull by Buffalo Bill did what he had done so many times when he heard shots in the Wild West Show: he started his routine of stunts.

In February 1891, not even two months after the death of Sitting Bull, Senator Lyman Casey of North Dakota wrote from Washington asking the Indian Office to take steps to negotiate with Sitting Bull's widow for the dead chief's belongings. Obliging the senator, the office did give the state title to the cabin in which Sitting Bull had died. It appeared as part of the 1893 Columbian Exposition in Chicago in the exhibit from North Dakota, in commemoration of the four-hundredth anniversary of the arrival of Columbus in the New World.

MYRA COLBY
BRADWELL, ESQ.

*A*FTER THE CIVIL WAR ITS VETERANS RE-
turned to a country much altered from the one they
had left. In their long absences from home, many men had been
hardened through brutal fighting and whiskey, the battlefield
anesthetic and cure-all. Back at home, women had shown themselves that they could keep family farms and businesses going.
Advances in weapons technology had made fighting more dangerous, but Northern factories had also produced lightweight
farm machinery that women could operate. In this new style of
agriculture, women found that stamina could be worth as much
as brawn. That same spirit inspired urban women, who expected
to hold on to at least some of the liberty—and cash—they had
earned and were learning to enjoy. In the North, where factories
relied on machines, women now made up one-third of the work-
force. When husbands returned home, therefore, many women
had already become emancipated from their prewar emotional
and economic dependence.

Myra Colby Bradwell, the first woman licensed to practice
law in the United States, fought for years to change laws and
institutions in ways that would correct the official inequality of
men and women in so many domains. Brilliantly successful at

business, proud of her husband and family, she withheld her endorsement and financial backing from Susan B. Anthony's suffrage forces. For that difference, Bradwell lost the approval of the author of the *History of Woman Suffrage,* who hoped that diminishing Bradwell's status would also diminish her importance.

❈

MYRA COLBY WAS TAUGHT as a girl that when extreme demands tested members of the Colby family, they became heroes every time in order to prove the family tradition. Colbys in America knew that they had ancestors who had died at Bunker Hill. But when Myra Colby was born near Manchester, Vermont, on February 12, 1831, her parents had already made plans to leave New England. By the time she was two, her abolitionist parents had moved the family to western New York state and, after that, to Illinois. Another hero whose praises Myra heard her parents sing was Elijah Parish Lovejoy, an abolitionist journalist and friend of the Colbys. He was killed by a mob in Illinois as he tried to protect his newest press. The imprint of those stories heard in girlhood would reappear in the linking of journalism and idealism that influenced the brave path Colby later pioneered.

Like many other daughters of educated middle-class parents, as a young woman Myra Colby received her education at a women's seminary. For three years, typically, young women studied geography, history, English literature, and sometimes languages. Seminary training—in her case in Elgin, Illinois— did not direct young women toward life in a religious community. Yet it carried a strong moral stamp, an emphasis that helped to reinforce a view of women that most men and many women of the nineteenth century would not think to question: in terms of their morality, women stood superior to men. In the restricted and controlled sphere in which they lived their lives, women were expected to be considerate of others, kind, thoughtful, modest and pious to a degree impossible for "the rougher sex."

Because women did not go after and earn money, they remained untainted by greed and ambition; because their sensual desires did not go beyond the wish to reproduce, they functioned above lust. Like children, they needed the protection of men. And as with children, not much was demanded of women, nor were they taken seriously.

This concept of virtuous womanhood describes the cultural milieu of the early 1860s, a continuation of what Americans had believed for generations. The only ripple on that tranquil surface came from the unusual women who preached temperance, who condemned the demon rum, and who sometimes organized meetings. For women in general, the lasting importance of the temperance movement would turn out to be that it taught women to gather in large meetings that concentrated on a shared idea. But during the Civil War, women's behavior had to change in the absence of their husbands' protection, a period of trial that would eventually force a hard look at old attitudes. Myra Colby, reared on prewar beliefs, did not come into her own either until after the war, after the relations of men and women in society changed, but before people recognized the contradictions between what they believed and what they saw around them.

Myra Colby started to mystify and displease her family when she married James Bradwell. The Colbys had thought so well of their pretty, intelligent daughter's prospects that they would have chosen a more promising young man for her, that is, if she had asked. The Bradwell family, unlike the Colbys, had not fought at Bunker Hill. They had not even left England until 1830, when James was two years old, and had next to nothing to show for it. No one knows if Myra was deliberately looking for a husband who did not belong to the respectable class, who did not accept the same beliefs about women that a more "suitable" young man would have held. Whatever attracted their daughter so passionately and defiantly to young Bradwell remained an enigma to the Colbys long after 1852, when Myra and James eloped.

From the beginning of her marriage, Myra Colby Bradwell knew two things: she wanted to use her education and she wanted to work alongside her husband. Throughout her life, especially when women began to insist on the freedom to follow any career they chose, she repeated her conviction that the most satisfying arrangement for a marriage allowed a husband and wife to work side by side. That belief shaped, but did not ultimately limit, her career plans and decisions.

The newly married Bradwells moved to Memphis in 1853 and started a private school where Myra taught, working with James at what turned into a successful effort.* The school quickly attracted more and more students and held promise of continuing to grow. Showing the kind of courage that had enabled her parents to leave New England, Myra and James left the thriving school in Memphis to move to Illinois. James, with three years of college but no degree, turned out to have a drive for hard work that the Colbys had not noticed. In 1854 the couple moved to Chicago after the birth of their first child, a girl also called Myra. While the Bradwells were in Chicago, James studied law and in 1855 passed the bar, a career choice that would not necessarily have won over his in-laws, given the generally low estimation in which lawyers were held. During those same years, Myra had three more children: Thomas in 1856, Bessie in 1858, and James in 1864.

When the Civil War interrupted all normal routines, Myra Bradwell put aside her lively intellectual interests and worked with local women as president of their Soldiers' Aid Society, helping organize sanitary fairs, contributing all her free time to the support and relief effort that claimed the energy of other educated women. Meanwhile, her husband had set up a practice with Myra's brother, who had finally gotten over his early prejudice against James Bradwell. The partnership grew, and in 1861

---

* At about the same time Annie Turner Wittenmeyer was starting a school in Keokuk, Iowa.

James Bradwell became county and probate judge for Cook County.

After the war, when her children were no longer babies—James had died in infancy in 1864 and her daughter Myra in 1861 at age seven—Mrs. Bradwell let her husband help in her new undertaking. With his guidance, she wanted to read law and then take the Illinois state bar exam. Bradwell saw herself as having the mental capacity for study and the advantage of a husband who found her plan sensible and possible, even if no other woman in Illinois had ever attempted what she now had in mind. In fact, nowhere else in the United States was there a woman attorney practicing the law.

Before long, everyone associated with the law in Illinois—whether lawyer, judge, or law student—and many businesspeople knew the name of Myra Bradwell, because in 1868 she started a weekly legal newspaper called the *Chicago Legal News*. At the outset she claimed that it would appear weekly on Saturday and would be four pages long. In her own words on the first page of the first collected volume, it was "A Journal of Legal Intelligence containing cases decided in the various United States courts; the Supreme Court of Illinois, and other states; head-notes to important cases, in advance of their publication in the reports of the state courts; the public laws of Illinois, passed in 1869; recent English cases; legal information and general news."

Bradwell's judgment about the need for such a paper had been so astute that she regularly failed to keep it to four pages and soon had to increase its length to print all the advertising space that her paper sold. The news pages of the *Chicago Legal News* show the unusual cast of Myra Bradwell's mind, while the advertisements show the direction of growth in Chicago. Many notices appeared with the names of lawyers, announcing their practices to the public. Alongside these are legal notices of the kind that still appear in newspapers, as well as new areas of business such as insurance companies from Connecticut and real estate brokers. Legal publishers claimed important space in the early issues and seem to have inspired Myra Bradwell to begin her own legal publishing, printing, and binding company, the Chicago Legal News Company, a short time after starting the paper. Only by a special charter from the state was she allowed to be president of both the newspaper and the publishing company. State law dictated, however, that as a married woman she lacked the legal status to own a company.

Bradwell's practical nature recognized needs that were not being satisfied, a category that included the publication not only of new laws passed by the state legislature but also of standardized legal forms. Lawyers counted on her newspaper to publish new laws and on her printing company to provide them with the stationery they used. Bradwell regularly went to the state capitol at Springfield to get the text of laws passed by the legislature in order to print them before anyone else. Without that effort of hers, the public sometimes had to wait several months to read the new legislation. In the pages of the *Chicago Legal News,* only one name is credited for the writing, the editorials, and the choice of material—Myra Bradwell.

The language of the *Chicago Legal News* conveys the energy of its author as well as attesting to the vitality of her interest in the law. If its pages are read closely, the choice of subjects implies a coherent point of view that is then reinforced more subtly in the arrangement of stories on the page. From the earliest issues, its columns assert, "Now that there is so much talk in regard to the law relating to woman and her right to vote. . . ." Whether or not that was true among the community of readers of the paper, when they read that the subject interested people, the claim became true. In other words, the paper set the agenda for discussion among its readers, who included judges and legislators. When the paper started, James Bradwell himself was still a judge, but soon resigned in 1869. Through their relations with the judge, many of the paper's readers certainly had met the Myra Bradwell whose words they read and came to discuss.

In 1869, after Myra Bradwell had studied the law for several years, she passed her bar examination in a way that was called "most creditable." But the Supreme Court of Illinois denied her application, explaining that they had no choice but to say no because she was married, a state that constituted a "disability" for a woman in legal terms. (In Iowa, Arabella Babb Mansfield passed the state bar exam that same year, but never attempted to put her credential to use.) Readers of the *Chicago Legal News* may have remembered its story concerning English common law according to which, when a woman married, her identity had no further independent existence apart from that of her husband. A married woman, for example, could not enter into a contract, could not own property, could not act legally without the consent of her husband. In America, those prohibitions were accepted and made even more explicit. So unequal were husband and wife that in cases that required a woman to sign along with her husband, as in the transfer of real property, the wife had to be taken aside and asked to confirm under oath, out of the hearing of her husband, that she had not been forced into signing.

Myra Bradwell refused to let the court base its decision on the grounds that she was married, because she wanted to force the judges to say what they really meant. She wrote a brief that destroyed their arguments concerning marital "disability" and succeeded in requiring them to say more. The next time they wrote a refusal to Myra Bradwell, the justices said what she believed they should have stated originally: that she could not practice law in Illinois because she was a woman. In reply, Myra Bradwell prepared a petition to the U.S. Supreme Court. No answer at all came back for several years.

The reasoning behind the Illinois decision reveals and artic-ulates beliefs about women that were widely held, although they were less easy to defend now that the Civil War had changed the social environment governing relations between men and women. To a great extent, the practice of the law appeared too rough a profession for women. No one on the court said that Myra Bradwell or women in general lacked intelligence, nor did anyone argue that the mental ability to study the law and master its subtleties lay beyond their potential (although many people, women included, believed that because women had smaller skulls than men, they were less suited for cerebral work).

The resistance to the idea of a woman lawyer also had to do with public speaking and with the adversarial atmosphere of a courtroom. On the one hand, women did not speak in public, or should not, according to many men. To do so would mean a loss of feminine qualities such as passivity. People had begun to use the phrase "strong-minded woman"—not a compliment— to describe what some saw as a new kind of woman, one not satisfied with the stay-at-home role that had been seen as normal. In addition, imagining women in the courtroom as their opponents, many lawyers saw themselves at a great disadvantage against an adversary who could charm a judge or a jury. Such an inequality would put justice at risk, the reasoning ran.

After the second refusal, Myra Bradwell never again asked to be admitted to the Illinois bar, a silence that expressed a definite choice, especially since in 1872 Illinois passed a law that allowed people to pursue whatever career they chose. But while she awaited a U.S. Supreme Court decision, the question Bradwell had raised invited talk and speculation precisely because it hung for so long without an answer. When the Supreme Court finally ruled in 1873, it upheld the decision of the Illinois court and suggested that the crux of the matter was states' rights.

Meanwhile, in the pages of the *Chicago Legal News,* a story appeared about a Mrs. Ada H. Kepley who had applied to the bar of Illinois after having passed her exam successfully. The point of the story, however, concerned another candidate who applied at the same time was accepted, a Mr. Richard A. Dawson, who was black. The headline made its point plainly, "The Negro Ahead of the Woman," as did its first witty sentence: "The woman, in the race to obtain the legal right to practice law in Illinois, has been distanced by a negro."

The *Chicago Legal News* helped spread the name of its "editress," as some people called her (the paper listed her as "Editor"). It circulated stories of what would be called today her "special interest" in the way that the law as an institution treated women. Because Myra Bradwell oversaw the composition of the paper, she could arrange stories in ways that conveyed messages on the overall page that were not expressed in any individual story. On one occasion, for example, she grouped a story about the status of women's citizenship alongside a story titled "The Custody of a Child," thus linking the status of women and children. In another number, she put an item titled "Woman's Right to Vote" next to a story on "Bankruptcy," a problem for many women because of the property laws they could not change without the vote. In another, she printed a story, "The Constitutional Convention," which argued that if women could be counted in calculations to decide the number of political representatives, they should be allowed to vote. Immediately after it, a title set off a story on the results of an election, "Cook County Officers." That is, in the layout of the page Bradwell invited readers to consider that different candidates might have won had women voted. (Her readers no doubt included candidates for state offices.) Because she started the *Chicago Legal News* right after the Civil War, Myra Bradwell recorded the subjects that spawned the most confusion and controversy in that period of massive national reorganization. In much of the United States, inside and outside the South, Americans had to work out how to deal with a large population of newly liberated people, many of them homeless, many in need of training to develop new skills, especially if they attempted to leave the agricultural economy of the rural South. But at the end of the war, American women, who had not been legally emancipated, expected some compensation for the new roles they had taken during the war years. Myra Bradwell's desire to practice law fit into the huge social mosaic that Americans were attempting to reorder and rationalize in a new design. When she printed "The Negro Ahead of the Woman," she spelled out what puzzled and distressed many Americans. White women especially saw themselves in a contest with black Americans, black American men in particular.

East of Chicago, especially in New York state, women in

favor of what was called "woman suffrage" worked to ensure for women the right to register to vote. Susan B. Anthony, not the earliest but today the best known of these women, worked hard to address groups of women at large public meetings in the hope of changing their thinking. For many women, as well as men, resisted the idea of women voting. Even if women were allowed to vote, many argued, they would not. Less hypothetical and more honest in a way, many men argued that if the law gave women the right to vote and thereby permission to oppose their husbands, then harmony within the family would be disrupted forever. The most superficial and least convincing of the arguments pointed out that polls were rough places that women did well to avoid. Had women thought what it would be like to have cigar smoke blown in their faces?

To Myra Bradwell's way of thinking, which was the thinking of a lawyer, the question of woman suffrage had to be considered and analyzed carefully as a legal question. While she brought out her paper every week with indefatigable energy, all the while upholding the obligation of the law to treat women justly in every domain of their experience, she kept her distance from the more strident feminists, with whom she differed on fundamental points. The unmarried Susan B. Anthony, for example, used passionate language to rouse rallies of women, encouraging them to see men as "tyrants." Myra Bradwell, on the other hand, liked to point out that she was herself a wife and mother, and extremely fond of her family. Bradwell's commitment to equality of men and women helps explain her views: men did not have to choose between professional life and family life. Why should women be expected to take only one over the other? Bradwell consistently pointed out other women like herself who had families and still expected to use their minds.

Myra Bradwell insisted on fairness, even when it stung. She took her professional commitment so seriously that she even printed articles critical of badly argued positions on the subject of woman suffrage. She worked with men and wrote for men, and she ran her business so skillfully that she succeeded better than most men. Myra Bradwell the newspaperwoman and publisher got rich. Leaders of the woman suffrage movement, recognizing her success, wanted both to associate themselves with it and claim a part in it to help their cause. Susan B. Anthony recognized that women needed examples of other women who had helped in improving the position of women. Anthony believed that only by winning the right to vote could women change their status as the morally superior but otherwise weaker sex. Men could not be counted on to vote for legislative changes to help women, according to Anthony. Only by voting could women choose their political leaders and influence legislation in their interest.

While Myra Bradwell did not question suffrage as essential to women's needs under the law, she did see many avenues to achieving the prize of the vote. She worked in shaping political debate by keeping the issue of women's legal rights in the faces of judges who read her *Chicago Legal News.* She also worked to influence legislation in such areas as the property rights of married women. She worked for legislative changes to allow women to be elected to school boards in Illinois, then to other offices, then to be notary publics. But her general commitment remained to the law and to its application to guarantee equality.

Myra Bradwell and Susan B. Anthony could not agree on the most fruitful way to help women most in their race with blacks. After the passage of the Fourteenth Amendment, Susan B. Anthony made plain to her followers her indignant reaction at being expected to uphold the right of blacks to vote when women could not. Other women who had been allies of Anthony split with her at this point and issued a summons to form a new and different organization. Calling themselves the American Woman Suffrage Association, distinct from Anthony's National Woman Suffrage Association, the newly organized group met in Cleveland in November 1869.

After many years of working on the cause she considered her own, Susan B. Anthony edited the *History of Woman Suffrage* with two of her colleagues. That first volume reprints the entire text of the Supreme Court decision that refused Myra Bradwell the right to practice law and shows a portrait of Myra Bradwell, but mentions nothing about who Bradwell was nor gives any hint of her accomplishments as a publisher, an advocate for women, and a skilled businesswoman. The reason Anthony over-looked such an important woman—one who had, after all, helped organize the first suffrage convention in the Midwest—appears at the end of the volume. There Anthony lists every single contributor to her project, from the tiny number who gave the lavish sum of one hundred dollars, to the lengthy list of one-dollar contributors, all the way down to fifty, twenty-five, and even ten cents. The famous and well-off Myra Bradwell chose not to be part of that effort.

Politically, the question of whether to allow women to vote erupted in the years immediately after the Civil War when lawmakers finally acknowledged that times were changing. The Fourteenth Amendment, passed in 1869, said that Americans had to be allowed to vote despite "previous condition of servi-tude," the language that changed the life of men who were former slaves. Then in 1873 the Fifteenth Amendment changed the basis of political representation. Women who saw blacks being given political rights wanted to have that same opportu-nity, whether or not they found it fitting that blacks should vote. Myra Bradwell, because of her conviction about equality and the need for the law to make equality real, wanted no part of proponents of woman suffrage who, like Anthony, refused to work for "Sambo." Unlike Susan B., as she was known, Myra Bradwell wanted legislation to usher in broader changes that would alter the political context and, indirectly perhaps, thus make woman suffrage inevitable.

In the pages of her extremely popular *Chicago Legal News,* Myra Bradwell wrote in favor of specific legislative changes, some of which she drafted herself, and lobbied as well, often with the collaboration of her husband. Her efforts and writing carried the day to change the law concerning the property of married women. She wrote the sad and true account of a woman who worked because she had to, cleaning houses to support her children, whose alcoholic father contributed nothing to his family. But that same husband ran such a high tab at a bar that the tavern owner came after the couple for satisfaction of the debt, and was paid because a court ruled that any earnings of the wife belonged first of all to her husband.

As a mother, Myra Bradwell crusaded for the rights of the children who legally endured inhuman conditions at the Chicago Reform School. When a superintendent of the school wrote an irate letter to the *Chicago Legal News* denying her report, Bradwell printed his letter in full along with her own answer, saying that she stood by what she had written and dared the official to sue her for libel. Eventually, the Chicago Reform School was abolished.

As the strong editor of a leading legal publication, Myra Bradwell fought for the right of women to sit on school boards, then to vote for limited offices in limited cases. Her tactical success in achieving those ends was inspired because it changed the nature of political debate; readers could not but notice the inconsistency of allowing women to hold office while still not allowing them to vote.

Because Myra Bradwell stayed at the center of legal questions by making herself a source of fact—courts allowed her newspaper to be used as evidence—the whole issue of not allowing her to practice law became a technicality. Maybe Bradwell did not stand before judges or plead cases on retainer from individual clients, but every week her writing put her reasoning and her agenda before judges, the entire legal establishment of Illinois, and legal leaders in many other states.

Myra Bradwell's resilience and business sense were put to an extreme test in 1871, when the Chicago fire destroyed a strip one mile wide and seven miles long in the heart of the city. The *Chicago Legal News* figured on the list of lost businesses. By happenstance, Myra's thirteen-year-old daughter managed to save the notebook containing the newspaper's list of subscribers. Rather than use the disaster as an excuse to interrupt the publication schedule for even one week, Bradwell got on a train and went to Milwaukee, where she wrote that week's paper and had it printed. At that juncture, which could have been viewed as hopeless, Bradwell recognized a great opportunity for her enterprise. She reported to her readers that every lawyer in Chicago had lost his law library and would need to replace it. Since those lawyers were her readers, she also helped boost her own revenues when she encouraged publishers of legal books to advertise in her pages to help inform and guide lawyers who needed whole shelves of new books.

Although not a conventional lawyer, Myra Bradwell showed her powers of persuasion in her most celebrated crusade against a man she saw using the law to treat a woman unfairly. The man was Robert Lincoln, Abraham Lincoln's only surviving child, a man apparently motivated by greed in his extreme cruelty to his mother. Mary Todd Lincoln, Abraham Lincoln's widow, was Myra Bradwell's friend. As far as anyone can tell now, in a case in which the documents have all been destroyed—as recently as the 1940s as a result of directions in wills—the conflict had to do with money.

Everyone who knew Mrs. Lincoln saw that the violent death of her husband traumatized her, especially because the death of two other sons had left her in a state that people then called melancholy. One manifestation of her unhappiness was what people now call compulsive behavior, in particular compulsive shopping. Because her tastes had always been luxurious, Mrs. Lincoln's shopping ventures cost her family, that is, her husband's estate, a great deal. Her son Robert thought he had a good, if extreme, solution when in May 1875 he decided to have his fifty-seven-year-old mother put in an insane asylum to make her stop shopping.

To no one's surprise, life in the asylum in Batavia, Illinois, only made Mrs. Lincoln more melancholy. Through a vigorous campaign of writing letters—always that same belief in the power of rational argument—Myra Bradwell prevailed on the hospital director, Dr. Patterson, to release Mrs. Lincoln after five months. It did not hurt that the Chicago newspapers became involved, publishing what amounted to a debate. Bradwell even arranged to have a newspaper reporter interview Mrs. Lincoln without the consent of either Robert or the doctor. But the tactic worked. "She is no more insane than I am," argued Myra

Bradwell, whose name was synonymous with clear-headed thinking.

Myra Bradwell's activities look like a catalog of every important issue in the history of the United States in the late nineteenth century. She worked hard on the committee that planned the rebuilding of Chicago after the fire, pioneering the concept of zoning laws to control urban land use. She proposed ways to upgrade the standards of the legal profession, trying to make it harder to qualify without attending law school. She worked to encourage states to establish bar associations, to raise the level of argument, and to increase professional awareness among lawyers. She worked to make the retirement of judges at age sixty-five compulsory. Her energy and efforts, including a trip to Washington to talk to congressmen, resulted in the choice of Chicago as the site of the 1893 Columbian Exposition.*

Why did Bradwell never resubmit her application to be allowed to practice law? She may have seen it as pointless to invite the same justices to turn her down again. Or she may have seen that the extent of her influence through the *Chicago Legal News* achieved far more reform than she might have realized as a courtroom lawyer. Then, without a request from her, the Illinois Supreme Court admitted Bradwell to the state bar in 1890, twenty-one years after her request. The language of the decision said that it was made "nunc pro tunc," Latin for "now for then," in effect a retroactive decision. Never before in the history of Illinois—and probably not since—had anyone been granted a license on the court's motion.

Myra Bradwell continued to work on the *Chicago Legal News* until 1894, when she was suffering from the cancer that claimed her life. Her daughter, also a lawyer, of whom Myra Bradwell loved to tell people she was extremely proud, took over the *Chicago Legal News,* the most important legal newspaper west of the Alleghenies, which was exactly what Myra Bradwell had wanted it to be.

* At this fair the cabin in which Sitting Bull died was put on display.

LOUIS
SOCKALEXIS,
THE ORIGINAL
CLEVELAND INDIAN

URING THE FINAL DECADE OF THE
nineteenth century, as Andrew Carnegie, John D.
Rockefeller, and Thomas Edison struggled to impose order and
system on industry and the workplace, sports, too, became organized, coming more and more to resemble other aspects of an
emerging corporate America. "Baseball," wrote Mark Twain, "is
the very symbol, the outward and visible expression of the drive
and push and struggle of the raging, tearing, booming nineteenth century." Professional baseball had much in common
with the new American landscape. It was urban, its seasonal
labor took place between planting and harvesting time, its intri-
cate schedules depended on cheap, predictable transportation
over great distances, and above all it was increasingly driven by
the need to yield higher profits for its owners and investors.

Although baseball's green playing fields and timeless games
retained traces of country life, these were merely symbolic: Eb-
bets Field was built over a Brooklyn landfill; Cleveland's League
Park was completely surrounded by rail yards, smoky foundries,
and locomotive works. But most of all, team managers were like
shop foremen enforcing the wishes of a management that bound
players to a harsh regimen for the good of the team. As sports

reinforced teamwork, Pinkerton detectives, if not teammates, were used to enforce vestigial Victorian values, such as sobriety, punctuality, and hard work six days a week for low pay. League Park was filled with white-collar workers, local shopkeepers, farmers, and easterners who had moved west—hardly the place one would expect to find a full-blooded Indian only six years after Sitting Bull's murder.

⊰⧉⊱

By 1870 the professional sport of baseball had already come of age. Making use of the just completed transcontinental railroad for the first time, the Cincinnati Red Stockings made a coast-to-coast tour in 1869. Playing other professional teams from New York City to San Francisco, they won fifty-seven games, losing none and tying only once. More than 200,000 spectators paid (and nobody knows how many didn't) to see the triumphant Cincinnati team. Cigar-chomping President Ulysses S. Grant watched them in Washington, D.C., and some 23,000 fans in New York City attended games during a single six-day week (Sunday baseball was forbidden). The Red Stockings' tour dramatized not only the possibility of a professional national baseball league but also its potential for profit: here was a game that could earn millions if only it could be harnessed and controlled.

Louis Francis Sockalexis was born on October 24, 1871, on Indian Island in the Penobscot River off Old Town, Maine. By 1876, as Sitting Bull and Red Cloud sent their warriors to facilitate Custer's last stand on the Little Bighorn, and Thomas Edison threw a light switch at the Philadelphia Centennial Exposition, the boy was learning to skip a stone over the Penobscot. Meanwhile, also in 1876, William A. Hulbert and several farsighted business associates were forming the National League, which was organized not around free-spirited athletic players but around owners and club franchises in a system that encouraged monopolies. In each designated city, competition was eliminated—not only competition for profit, but for players who were sold for cash by owners, had no right to refuse transfers, and in fact had nothing at all to say about their purchase or sale.

By the time Louis Sockalexis was finishing his studies at the French-Canadian Roman Catholic mission grammar school on the shores of the Penobscot, baseball had become incontestably "the national pastime." The *New York Mercury* seems to have coined this phrase in its December 5, 1856, edition: by this time there were fifty baseball clubs in Manhattan alone. According to legend, the game had been founded by Abner Doubleday when he laid out the first diamond-shaped field at Cooperstown, New York, in 1839, near the site of today's Baseball Hall of Fame. Historians dispute this notion and point out the resemblance to rounders, an ancient English game that was transported to America before the Revolution. Still others equally hotly insist that if any one person "invented" baseball, it was Alexander Joy Cartwright, Jr., a New York City stationer who wrote the first baseball rulebook in 1845. The game really began to flourish during the Civil War, when players North and South, even in prisoner-of-war camps, distracted themselves between battles with bats and balls. By 1865, baseball had followed Cartwright and his rulebook all the way to Honolulu, Hawaii, where he still had the original baseball he had thrown in New York.

Somehow, baseball was as much made for a young Penobscot Abenaki Indian as he was for it: the game took great vitality, an accurate hurling arm, a sharp eye, and an ability to thrive in a group of equally able men. Moreover, Penobscots were peculiarly suited to pursuing a new path to integrate themselves into what had already become an all-white sport. Of all the native tribes in the Northeast, historically the Penobscot branch of the Abenakis had attempted more than any to integrate with their white neighbors. Fishermen, hunters, expert woodsmen, they had volunteered to fight in the American Revolution on the side of the Revolutionaries, only to have their original offer rebuffed by George Washington. When Benedict Arnold led an expedition through Maine to attack Canada in 1775, Penobscots shadowed the starving Continentals, killing game and placing it with other food in the path of the soldiers. When Arnold's troops became hopelessly lost in the swamps, the Abenakis appeared in their camp, led them to safety, and then fought alongside them in the attack on Quebec. One Abenaki woman even eloped with Arnold's aide, Aaron Burr, only to be killed by a sniper's bullet as she fetched water for him.

Throughout the nineteenth century, Penobscots from Indian Island, including Louis's father, Chief Sockalexis, acted as skilled Maine guides for wealthy summer vacationers on hunting and fishing trips. They then went into the woods every winter to earn money hunting game for loggers. The life of a boy on Indian Island changed only slowly over the years. Every boy had his own gun, his dog, and his birch bark canoe. He learned to construct his canoe with great care, forming the thin struts of wood and then covering them with birch bark sewn with the roots of spruce trees. The canoe could carry four people but was light enough for the young Indian to carry alone. Louis learned that, in a downpour, he could take shelter under it. He also learned to make snowshoes of birchwood and elk gut and to smear himself all over with deer or beaver fat to ward off black flies and mosquitoes. He was taught to survive on the juice of spruce or sugar maple or birch trees. Long ago converted to Catholicism, the Penobscots had their children educated by French-speaking priests and nuns.

By the time Louis was thirteen and able to throw a baseball across the Penobscot, he was already fascinated by the game sweeping every New England town. For a short while, there was no color line in baseball, at least not in the North. The first African-American professional baseball player was hired by a major league club: Moses Walker, son of an Ohio clergyman and an Oberlin College graduate, joined Toledo as a catcher in 1884. He immediately encountered cries from a teammate to "get that nigger off the field." When Toledo traveled to Richmond, Virginia, Walker received a death threat from "seventy-five determined men" who threatened to mob him if he stepped onto the field. His contract sold to Newark, New Jersey, in the International League, Walker was long a favorite with the fans, even though a sportswriter for a rival city called him "the coon catcher." One player confessed to a reporter for the *Sporting News* that "about half the pitchers try their best to hit these colored players." Southern-born ballplayers in particular had trouble with the idea of playing with blacks. Two Syracuse Stars teammates of black pitcher Robert Higgins refused to sit for a team picture with him. One told a reporter, "I am a Southerner by birth and I tell you I would rather have my heart cut out before I would consent to have my picture in the group."

By 1887, there was organized resistance to black ballplayers in the majors. A majority of players for the Saint Louis Browns refused to play even an exhibition game against a black club and sent this petition to management: "We the undersigned members of the Saint Louis Baseball Club do not agree to play against negroes tomorrow." No player was more adamant than Cap Anson, veteran manager of the Chicago White Stockings, who made it clear neither he nor any of his players would consent to go on a field with a black player. By 1887, major league owners made a "gentleman's agreement" to hire no more blacks, despite the objections of fans and the press. Mourned the *Newark Call:*

> If anywhere in this world the social barriers are broken down it is on the ball field. There, many men of low birth and poor breeding are the idols of the rich and cultured; the best man is he who plays best. Even men of churlish disposition and coarse habits are tolerated on the field. In view of these facts the objection to colored men is ridiculous. If social distinctions are to be made, half the players in the country will be shut out. Better make character and personal habits the test.

There were sporadic attempts to reintroduce blacks to the majors as the nineteenth century ended. John McGraw tried to introduce a black second baseman, Charlie Grant, to the roster by calling him a Cherokee and renaming him Charlie Tokahoma. "If he really keeps this Indian," snarled Charles Comiskey, president of the Chicago White Stockings, "I will get a China-man of my acquaintance and put him on third."

Louis Sockalexis learned to hunt and fish along the Penob-scot, which abounded with salmon, from his father. The Abe-naki chief was an expert outdoorsman who also excelled at sports. Their hunting forays into the forests yielded bear, moose, and deer that provided food and clothing—shirts, shoes, leg-gings, fur-lined coats and hats. Undoubtedly a good shot, Louis learned to run with the deer that his father taught him to track and kill. But he also felt the tug of the white culture all around his poverty-stricken island village, especially in the summers, when wealthy New Yorkers and Bostonians came down east to their "camps," as their elaborate summer houses were called. And eastern Maine was certainly not devoid of victims of the baseball fever that was spreading in the 1890s: Bangor, then the logging capital of the world, was only twelve miles away, and Louis could get himself there to watch the muscular loggers and shipbuilders take on challengers from all of New England. All over Maine, college boys came to play baseball. It was probably at one of these games that Louis made his college "debut."

As he traveled around Knox County playing ball for what-ever money they would pay him (the going rate was $10 a game), Louis caught the eye of Maine journalist Gilbert Patten. After putting the Camden newspaper to bed at night, Patten banged out short stories and "dime" novels that he would mail off to New York City. Patten liked to play baseball, even if he had never made the first string of anything. His publisher was looking for a fictional hero for a series of dime novels, until then based on western gunslingers, but this time to be about a para-gon of Victorian virtue and robust good health. Rejecting a purely Anglo-Saxon schoolboy model, Patten, who had seen Sockalexis play, came up with a new character he named Frank Merriwell. "The name was symbolic of the chief characteristics I desired my hero to have—*Frank* for frankness, *merry* for a happy disposition, *well* for health and abounding vitality," Pat-ten wrote in his memoirs. The first of 648 Merriwell paperbacks would appear in 1896; in all, 500 million copies of his dime novels would make their clean-cut, polite, athletic hero the model for three generations of American boys, outselling any other American book series ever published.

A catcher for Holy Cross college, Michael "Doc" Powers (who later joined the Philadelphia Athletics), came to play ball in Maine in the summer of 1895. He was impressed by Louis Sockalexis's great accuracy in throwing a ball with his right hand, his great speed in the outfield, and his powerful left-handed hitting. That autumn, Powers took his friend Louis aboard the steamboat from Bangor to Boston, then west by rail to Worcester to try out for a scholarship at Holy Cross. Louis was impressive: almost six feet tall, he could run a hundred yards in ten seconds in his spiked shoes. The Holy Cross coach, Jesse Burkett (who played third base for the Cleveland Spiders during the professional season), signed him up. At twenty-five, Louis became a college student and a collegiate baseball star. The Crusaders became one of the best teams in the East the next two seasons. Louis played the outfield and pitched three no-hitters. He batted .436 and .444. In a game against Harvard, Louis made a lightning throw to the catcher to prevent a runner from scoring. Two Harvard professors measured the distance and announced that Sockalexis had set a world record of 138 yards. Coach Burkett was offered a better job as the Notre Dame coach in South Bend, Indiana—just so long as he brought his star outfielder with him.

In the summer of 1896, Louis traveled to New York with the Notre Dame team to play an exhibition match against the New York Giants at the Polo Grounds. Louis hit an inside-the-park home run, streaking around the bases before the Giants could make the play on him. The Giants' manager, John Ward, immediately wrote to Patsy Tabeau, the player-manager of the Cleveland Spiders. Tabeau offered Louis a job as soon as he finished college. In the fall of 1896, Louis and his coach boarded a train west, all his belongings stuffed into a cardboard suitcase.

At Notre Dame, Louis became one of the most talked-about players. Tall for those days (5'11") and stocky (185 pounds), the fast outfielder had another fabulous season. By April 1897, Louis had become one of the most talked-about players in college baseball. The talk wasn't always friendly. In a savage new kind of journalism, sportswriters attacked the reputation of a rival player to build up the home team. By the time Louis left South Bend, the pundits were writing that he and a teammate had been expelled from Notre Dame for breaking up a brothel in a drunken binge. The two key elements of scandal that would be hurled at him again and again had been unloosed. Fortunately, there are record books that prove quite the opposite, that Sockalexis quickly became Notre Dame's best athlete with no hint of misbehavior marring his outstanding record at the college.

After the 1897 collegiate season, Louis borrowed money from Coach Burkett to take the train to Cleveland, where he had been offered a major league tryout. Manager Patsy Tabeau offered him a place on the roster of the Cleveland Spiders, always a pennant contender in the National League and runner-up the year before. Louis's eyes must have grown big as he ran out onto the field at League Park in his new blue and white professional uniform for the first time on April 22, 1897. The first Native American professional athlete (and for many years the only non-white in the majors), he made such an impression that *Sporting Life,* the national weekly sports magazine, ran a two-column line drawing of him in the 1897's season's first edition, introducing him in an essay-length caption:

SOCKALEXIS,
THE INDIAN BALL PLAYER NOW
PLAYING WITH THE CLEVELAND CLUB.

Sockalexis is not a well-greased Greek, notwithstanding the Hellenic hint his name conveys. He is a well-educated Indian. Furthermore, he is a professional baseball player, and during this season he will travel through the country playing right field. . . . Of course, the "rooters" will have no end of fun with his name . . . as he merrily chases the ball over the field or legs it for bases. Captain Tabeau of the Cleveland nine counts himself a fortunate man in having him on his team. . . .

◆◆

THE ELONGATED CAPTION went on to describe Louis's background, pointing out that "his origin shows clearly enough in his dark complexion, straight black hair" and in his "somewhat modified but still noticeable high cheekbones. . . . He is over six feet tall, of powerful physique and noted as a hard, reliable and safe hitter. . . . He is nimble and fleet-footed in the field . . . he throws as straight as a rifle shot." The long-winded description ended with an aside, that Sockalexis was also a formidable handball player who had even beaten Captain Tebeau, "a remarkably alert player."

Louis Sockalexis left no record of his impressions of his teammates or of the city of Cleveland, so far from the Maine woods, but few places in North America could have been more antithetical to his Old Town. In 1897 Cleveland's population was already nearing 400,000, having tripled in only twenty-five years as it became the great, sooty, grimy center of oil refining in the United States and a crossroads for shiploads and rail cars of iron ore bound from Lake Superior to the city's iron foundries and the steel mills of Pittsburgh. The sky was a perpetual yellowish-gray from the burning of soft bituminous coal, yet pollution was the hallmark of employment for the thousands of Hungarian, Lithuanian, Polish, and Russian immigrants arriving to seek jobs every year.

There were few outlets for relaxation for the workers in the few hours they had to unwind from the urban drudgery of their jobs. Louis could not know that he had walked into a crossfire of controversy over which fans were to be allowed into League Field to see the pennant-contending Spiders play. The city of Cleveland had a strict ban on Sunday baseball. In the era before electrified night games became possible, this all but shut out the workers, who toiled every day but Sunday. As a further disincentive, the National League ticket price was 50 cents a game at a time when only skilled workers earned 90 cents to $1 a day. There were a few 25-cent seats, but as one sportswriter put it, they were in Erie (about one hundred miles away). On average, only about eight hundred fans attended a Cleveland home game, a small percentage of the league average. Attendance rarely hit five thousand even for a Saturday game, when middle- or upper-class gentlemen could come.

The game was rough in those days. Umpires could expect to be crippled by the spikes of disapproving ballplayers, and to be pelted with trash, garbage, and sometimes stones. Player-managers were selected more for their lung power and their ability to hurl verbal abuse than for any managerial skill. Yet Louis Sockalexis could hardly have been luckier than in having third baseman Patsy Tabeau for his player-manager. The two became not only handball partners but close friends. He also was fortunate in having a tall farm boy, Denton Tecumseh "Cy" Young, the leading pitcher in baseball, as his teammate and friend. Young had joined the team so poor, one sports historian notes, that "his sleeves failed to cover his wrists and his trousers appeared sawed off at the ankles." The manager had to buy him "a complete new outfit" so he "would not be ridiculed."

Quiet, smiling, determined, Louis Sockalexis came to the plate of his first major league game batting third in the lineup. Fans let out war whoops, a sound he would hear over and over that season. Until he swung. Time after time, his wooden bat connected solidly in those opening weeks, usually for a double, a triple, a home run. The unfortunately named Spiders surged ahead into the league lead, winning eight of their first ten games. Like his fictional counterpart Frank Merriwell, Louis became famous for game-winning, ninth-inning homers with a man on base. Four times in nine games in late May, he made such dramatic finishes.

There was, as a sportswriter covering Cleveland for *Sporting Life* saw clearly, enormous pressure on Sockalexis. After he made his first error two weeks into the season, Elmer E. Bates, author of the regular weekly column *Cleveland Chatter,* observed:

All eyes are on the Indian in every game. He is expected not only to play right field like a veteran but to do a little more batting than anyone else. Columns of silly poetry are written about him; hideous looking cartoons adorn the sporting pages of nearly every paper. He is hooted and howled at by the thimble-brained brigade on the bleachers. Despite all this handicap, the red man has played good, steady ball.

When Cleveland made its first grueling month-long railroad trip east, playing from Pittsburgh to Washington, D.C., to Boston, sportswriters were waiting for him, their poisoned pens ready. The New York *Tribune* predicted that the Giants' fireball king, Amos Rusie, would strike Louis out in his first trip to the plate at the Polo Grounds. As the fans warwhooped and yelled "Ki-yi's," Louis quietly demolished Rusie by sending the first fast-breaking curve ball flying over the centerfield fence for a home run. Nearly half a century later, Giants manager John J. McGraw, there that day, still ranked Sockalexis the number one ballplayer of all time. After feeding Louis several such pitches that year, Philadelphia pitcher Andy Coakley echoed McGraw's accolade. "He had a gorgeous left-hand swing, hit the ball almost as far as Babe Ruth," recalled Coakley, who coached baseball at Columbia University for many years. In four consecutive games before July 4, Louis hit 11 times out of 21 at-bats. "He was faster than Ty Cobb and as good a base runner. He had the outfielding skill of Tris Speaker. He threw like Bob Meusel, which means that no one could throw a ball farther or more accurately."

The years of hurling a baseball across the Penobscot from the island to the mainland were paying off. Players and fans were astonished at Louis's speed and his accurate throwing. Few baserunners dared run on him. His batting average rose to .386 by May 17, then to .413 by July 31. Handsome, "with a perfect Indian profile," and his long black hair streaming after him as he ran, Louis Sockalexis became the baseball sensation of the

1897 season. Today he would be paid millions; at the time, the top player's salary was $2,000 and he did not even make that. He gloried in the adulation of the fans, though, and he clipped all the newspaper articles and carried them with him. One sportswriter wrote a poem in Hiawatha-like meter about "Sockalexis, Chief of Sockem." However, the barbs of rival writers cut deeply, and the hard life of cheap boardinghouses and endless train trips began to take a toll.

After an all-night Fourth of July party with his teammates, Louis slipped out of his hotel room window to drink bourbon with friends. He had never had anything stronger than milk before leaving Old Town. After the July 4 binge, Louis could not play for two days. (Modern medical science has proven that many Native Americans have particular difficulty resisting addiction to alcohol.)

When Sockalexis returned to the lineup, he made only two hits in each of the next three games. Then he began to stagger and make errors in the outfield. In mid-July, Coach Tabeau assigned another player to room with him to make sure he did not keep going out at night. One night, as Louis tried to elude his warders, he climbed out his second-floor hotel window and jumped or fell to the ground, severely injuring an ankle. He played one game a few weeks later, was suspended for drunkenness, benched for another month, then made two errors in the final game of the season. He ended the season with a .331 average for 66 games.

The newspaper pundits showed no mercy. Some insisted that he had hurt himself while jumping out of a brothel window; others, that the injury followed "a tryst with a pale-faced maiden" as well as a "dalliance with grape." *Sporting Life* came to his defense: its Cleveland correspondent wrote that

much of the stuff written about his dalliance with grape juice and his trysts with pale-faced maidens is pure speculation. . . . Too much popularity has ruined Sockalexis. . . . It is no longer a secret that the Cleveland management can no longer control Sockalexis.

Louis's friend, Captain Tabeau, did not give up on him. He told *Sporting Life* that Louis would be back the next season at the top of the lineup. He had an X ray taken (belatedly) of Louis's injured foot and announced to the press that it wasn't broken, only badly inflamed. But Louis was lame.

Other factors were at work over the winter that neither player nor manager could understand. Cleveland's owner, trolley-car magnate Frank DeHaas Robinson, had been waging a legal battle all season to open up League Park for Sunday games, a move that he predicted would quadruple attendance—and his profits. Robinson was a visionary businessman who had resuscitated the team after it had failed in the 1880s; and now he wanted to make money. When the city fathers fought him to a legal stalemate on Sunday games, he won league approval to change the rule forbidding interlocking boards of directors and bought another team, the Saint Louis Browns, the worst team in baseball.

When the 1898 season began, Louis Sockalexis returned from Maine to find that all of the best players, including Cy Young and his close friend, Patsy Tabeau, had been shipped to Saint Louis and the Saint Louis lineup and manager shuttled to Cleveland. Further, owner Robinson put the Cleveland team on the road far more that season; he could make more money in other cities, where he divided a larger gate. The home fans deserted League Park and gave the Spiders new nicknames, such as the Cleveland Misfits, the Exiles, the Wanderers. The hapless new manager, Lave Cross, confronted owner Robinson and begged for help. "I need about five players to have a pretty good team, Mr. Robinson. A couple of pitchers and a shortstop would help." Robinson stared at the man and answered, "I'm not interested in winning games here." The Spiders were headed for the worst season record in the history of baseball, winning only 20 games, losing 134.

Louis, increasingly lame, could no longer race across the outfield and was used only as a pinchhitter. In 1897, he had batted 278 times in 66 games; in 1898, only 67 times in 21 games. Instead of 94 hits, he connected only 15 times for a .224

batting average. Lonely and dejected, he began to drink more. But there was less and less press interest in an alcoholic ball-player. There was all the excitement of the outbreak of the Spanish-American War. Few people other than the astute *Sporting Life* correspondent wrote about Louis Sockalexis or his "fall from grace," as Elmer Bates put it. Lave Cross was not allowed to transfer Louis to Saint Louis to rejoin his friends. And when Sockalexis returned to Cleveland for his third and last season in 1899, the stands were virtually empty. There were no war whoops as he posted his worst record, producing only six hits in the seven games in which he was allowed to play. His major league career was over with the nineteenth century. In all, in his three-year major league career, Sockalexis had chalked up 115 hits (including three homers), stolen 16 bases, and played in 94 games, with a solid .313 career batting average.

For the next three years, Louis played minor league ball in New England, drifting down to Hartford, then to Lowell, but his alcoholism led one manager after another to drop him. Sick from his addiction, and once again as poor as all his neighbors, he rarely left Indian Island after 1903 except to pull the ferry across the Penobscot, and, when the river froze over, to go deep into the winter woods, as his forebears had done, to hunt and trap on snowshoes. In the summers he taught young Indians on the island how to play baseball as his father had done, teaching them that they must learn to excel at the white man's game. As the snow piled up in the winter of 1913, Louis went into the winter woods one last time. He died on Christmas Eve at the age of forty-two, clutching the press clippings that he always carried tucked inside his shirt. He was buried beside the other tribal chiefs on the shore of the Penobscot.

Two years later, the Cleveland fans were asked to choose a permanent name for their team, which now played to tens of thousands of fans on Sundays. Remembering Chief Louis Socka-lexis's meteoric career, they named it the Cleveland Indians in honor of his memory.

BIBLIOGRAPHY

ADAMS, GEORGE WORTHINGTON. *Doctors in Blue: The Medical History of the Union Army in the Civil War.* New York: Henry Schuman, 1952.

ALEXANDER, CHARLES C. *Our Game: An American Baseball History.* New York: Holt, 1991.

ANDRIST, RALPH K. *The Long Death: The Last Days of the Plains Indians.* New York: Macmillan, 1964.

BAILYN, BERNARD. *Ideological Origins of the American Revolution.* Cambridge, Mass.: Harvard Univ. Press, 1967.

BAKER, JEAN H. *Mary Todd Lincoln: A Biography.* New York: Norton, 1987.

BATTIS, EMERY. *Saints and Sectaries: Anne Hutchinson and the Antinomian Controversy.* Chapel Hill, N.C.: Institute of Early American History and Culture, 1962.

BILLINGTON, RAY ALLEN, AND RIDGE, MARTIN. *Westward Expansion: A History of the American Frontier.* 5th ed. New York: Macmillan, 1982.

BILLINGTON, RAY ALLEN, ED. *The Journal of Charlotte Forten: A Free Negro in the Slave Era.* New York: Norton, 1953.

BONOMI, PATRICIA V. *Under the Cape of Heaven: Religion, Society and Politics in Colonial America.* New York: Oxford Univ. Press, 1986.

BOORSTIN, DANIEL J. *The Americans*. 3 vols. New York: Random House, 1958–73.

———. *Lost World of Thomas Jefferson*. New York: Holt, 1948.

BOYD, JULIAN P., ED. *Indian Treaties Printed by Benjamin Franklin, 1736–1762*. Philadelphia: Historical Society of Pennsylvania, 1938.

BRADFORD, WILLIAM. *Of Plymouth Plantation*. Boston: Wright & Potter, 1898.

BRINTON, D. G., ED. *The Lenape and Their Legends*. New York: AMS Press, 1969.

BUSHMAN, RICHARD L. *From Puritan to Yankee*. Cambridge, Mass.: Harvard Univ. Press, 1967.

CALHOUN, ROBERT M. *The Loyalists in Revolutionary America, 1760–1781*. New York: Harcourt, Brace, 1973.

CALLOWAY, COLIN G. *The American Revolution in Indian Country: Crisis and Diversity in Native American Communities*. Cambridge, U.K.: Cambridge Univ. Press, 1995.

CAMPBELL, STANLEY W. *The Slave Catchers: Enforcement of the Fugitive Slave Law, 1850–1860*. Chapel Hill: Univ. of North Carolina Press, 1970.

CAPPON, LESTER J., ED. *The Adams-Jefferson Letters*. Chapel Hill: Univ. of North Carolina Press, 1988.

CARWARDINE, RICHARD J. *Evangelicals and Politics in Antebellum America*. New Haven, Conn.: Yale Univ. Press, 1993.

CLARK, DENNIS. *The Irish in Philadelphia*. Philadelphia: Temple Univ. Press, 1973.

CLINTON, CATHERINE. *The Other Civil War: American Women in the Nineteenth Century*. New York: Hill & Wang, 1984.

CONNELLY, THOMAS L. *The Marble Man: Robert E. Lee*. New York: Knopf, 1977.

CORNISH, DUDLEY T. *The Sable Arm: Negro Troops in the Union Army*. 2d ed. New York: Longmans, Green, 1956.

CRAWFORD, DEBORAH. *Four Women in a Violent Time*. New York: Crown, 1970.

CREMIN, LAWRENCE. *American Education: Metropolitan Experience, 1783–1876*. New York: Harper & Row, 1980.

CRONON, WILLIAM. *Changes in the Land*. New York: Hill & Wang, 1983.

CROSS, WHITNEY. *The Burned-Over District*. New York: Harper & Row, 1950.

CUNNINGHAM, NOBLE E., JR. *In Pursuit of Reason: The Life of Thomas Jefferson.* New York: Ballantine, 1987.

CURRY, LEONARD P. *The Free Black in Urban America, 1800–1850.* Chicago: Univ. of Chicago Press, 1981.

DABNEY, VIRGINIUS. *The Jefferson Scandals: A Rebuttal.* New York: Dodd, Mead, 1980.

DAVIS, ALLEN F., AND MARK H. HALLER, EDS. *The Peoples of Philadelphia: A History of Ethnic Groups and Lower-Class Life, 1790–1940.* Philadelphia: Temple Univ. Press, 1973.

DAVIS, BURKE. *Black Heroes of the American Revolution.* New York: Odyssey/Harcourt Brace Jovanovich, 1976.

DAVIS, DAVID BRION. *Ante-Bellum Reform.* New York: Harper & Row, 1967.

———. *The Problem of Slavery in Western Culture.* Ithaca, N.Y.: Cornell Univ. Press, 1966.

DEMOS, JOHN. *Entertaining Satan: Witchcraft and the Culture of Early New England.* New York: Oxford Univ. Press, 1982.

DOUTY, ESTHER M. *Forten the Sailmaker.* Chicago: Rand McNally, 1968.

DOWNES, RANDOLPH C. *Council Fires on the Upper Ohio.* Pittsburgh: Univ. of Pittsburgh Press, 1940.

DUBOIS, W. E. B. *The Philadelphia Negro.* Philadelphia, 1899. Repr. New York: Arns, 1967.

EAST, ROBERT A., AND JACOB JUBB, EDS. *The Loyalist Americans: A Focus on Greater New York.* Tarrytown, N.Y.: Sleepy Hollow Press, 1975.

EDMUNDS, R. DAVID. *The Shawnee Prophet.* Lincoln: Univ. of Nebraska Press, 1983.

———. *Tecumseh and the Quest for Indian Leadership.* Boston: Little, Brown, 1984.

ENGLE, PAUL. *Revolutionary Women.* Chicago: Follett, 1976.

EVANS, SARA M. *Born for Liberty: A History of Women in America.* New York: Free Press, 1989.

FELDBERG, MICHAEL. *The Turbulent Era: Riot and Disorder in Jacksonian America.* New York: Oxford Univ. Press, 1980.

———. *Philadelphia Riots of 1844.* Westport, Conn.: Greenwood, 1975.

FENNELLY, CATHERINE. "William Franklin of New Jersey." *William and Mary Quarterly,* 3d ser. (1949): 362–382.

FINNEY, CHARLES GRANDISON. *Memoirs: The Complete Restored Text.*

Richard·A. G. Dupuis and Garth M. Rosell, eds. Grand Rapids: Academic Books, 1989.

FLEXNER, ELEANOR. *Century of Struggle: The Women's Rights Movement in the United States.* Rev. ed. Cambridge, Mass.: Belknap Press at Harvard, 1975.

FLICK, ALEXANDER C. "The Sullivan-Clinton Campaign of 1779." *New York Historical Association Proceedings,* 15 (1934), 185–216.

FONER, ERIC. *Free Soil, Free Labor, Free Men.* New York: Oxford Univ. Press, 1970.

FOOTE, SHELBY. *The Civil War.* 3 vols. New York: Random House, 1958–1974.

FORTEN, CHARLOTTE. "Life on the Sea Islands." *Atlantic Monthly,* May 1864, 587–596; June 1864, 666–676.

FRANKLIN, BENJAMIN. *Papers.* 28 vols. to date. Leonard W. Labaree et al., eds. New Haven: Yale University Press, 1959–   .

FREEHLING, WILLIAM W. *The Road to Disunion.* New York: Oxford Univ. Press, 1990.

FRIEDENBERG, DANIEL M. *Life, Liberty and the Pursuit of Land: The Plunders of America.* Buffalo, N.Y.: Prometheus Press, 1992.

FRIEDMAN, JANE. *America's First Woman Lawyer: The Biography of Myra Bradwell.* Buffalo, N.Y.: Prometheus Press, 1993.

FULLBROOK, EARL S. "Relief Work in Iowa During the Civil War." *Iowa Journal of History and Politics,* vol. XVI, April 1918, 155–274.

GALE, GEORGE W. "Myra Bradwell: The First Woman Lawyer." *American Bar Association Journal,* vol. 39, Dec. 1953, 1080ff.

GALLAHER, RUTH. "Annie Turner Wittenmyer." *Iowa Journal of History and Politics,* vol. 29, no. 4, Oct. 1931, 518–569.

———. "The Wittenmyer Diet Kitchens." *The Palimpsest,* vol. XII, no. 9, Sept. 1931.

GINZBERG, LORI D. *Women and the Work of Benevolence.* New Haven, Conn.: Yale Univ. Press, 1990.

HALL, DAVID D. *The Antinomian Crisis, 1636–1638: A Documentary History.* 2d ed. Durham, N.C.: Duke Univ. Press, 1990.

HAMILTON, JAMES E. "Finney: An Appreciation." *Christianity Today.* 19 (no. 22, 1975), 13–16.

HARDESTY, NANCY A. *Women Called to Witness: Evangelical Feminism in the Nineteenth Century.* Nashville: Abingdon, 1984.

HARDMAN, KEITH L. *Charles Grandison Finney, 1792–1875: Revivalist to Reformer.* Syracuse, N.Y.: Syracuse Univ. Press, 1987.

HARLING, FREDERICK, AND MARTIN KAUFMAN. *The Ethnic Contribution to the American Revolution.* Westfield, Mass.: Historical Journal of Western Massachusetts, 1976.

HATCH, NATHAN O. *Democratization of American Christianity.* New Haven, Conn.: Yale Univ. Press, 1989.

HAWKE, DAVID FREEMAN. *Everyday Life in Early America.* New York: Harper & Row, 1988.

HEDRICK, JOAN D. *Harriet Beecher Stowe, A Life.* New York: Oxford Univ. Press, 1993.

HOFFMAN, RONALD, AND PETER J. ALBERT, EDS. *Women in the Age of the American Revolution.* Charlottesville: Univ. of Virginia Press, 1989.

HOFSTADTER, RICHARD. *America at 1750.* New York: Knopf, 1971.

———. *The Idea of a Party System: The Rise of Legitimate Opposition in the U.S.* Berkeley: Univ. of California Press, 1969.

HOLWAY, JOHN B. *Voices from the Great Black Baseball Leagues.* New York: Dodd, Mead, 1975.

JEFFERSON, THOMAS. *Papers.* 28 vols. to date. Julian Boyd et al., eds. Princeton, N.J.: Princeton Univ. Press, 1950–

JENNINGS, FRANCIS. *The Ambiguous Iroquois Empire.* New York: Norton, 1983.

———. *Empire of Fortune: Crowns, Colonies, and Tribes in the Seven Years' War in America.* New York: Norton, 1988.

———. *The Invasion of America.* Chapel Hill: Univ. of North Carolina Press, 1975.

JOHNSON, CURTIS D. *Islands of Holiness: Rural Religion in Upstate New York, 1790–1860.* Ithaca, N.Y.: Cornell Univ. Press, 1989.

JOHNSON, DOROTHY M. *Warrior for a Lost Nation: A Biography of Sitting Bull.* Philadelphia: Westminster Press, 1969.

JOHNSON, PAUL E. *A Shopkeeper's Millennium: Society and Revivals in Rochester, New York, 1815–1837.* New York: Hill & Wang, 1978.

JORDAN, WINTHROP D. *White over Black: American Attitudes Toward the Negro, 1550–1812.* Chapel Hill: Univ. of North Carolina Press, 1968.

JOSEPHY, ALVIN M., JR. "Tecumseh, the Greatest Indian," in Josephy, *The Patriot Chiefs: A Chronicle of American Indian Leadership.* New York: Viking, 1961.

————. *500 Nations: An Illustrated History of North American Indians.* New York: Knopf, 1994.

KLEIN, HERBERT S. *The Middle Passage.* Princeton, N.J.: Princeton Univ. Press, 1978.

KLEIN, RANDOLPH S. "The Shippens of Pennsylvania: A Generational Study in Colonial and Revolutionary Pennsylvania." Unpub. Ph.D. dissertation. Rutgers University, 1972.

KOLCHIN, PETER. *American Slavery, 1619–1877.* New York: Hill & Wang, 1993.

KUNHARDT, PHILIP B., JR., PHILIP B. KUNHARDT, III, AND PETER W. KUNHARDT. *Lincoln: An Illustrated Biography.* New York: Knopf, 1992.

LANG, AMY SCRAGER. *Prophetic Women: Anne Hutchinson and the Problem of Dissent in the Literature of New England.* Berkeley: Univ. of California Press, 1987.

LARKIN, JACK. *The Reshaping of Everyday Life, 1790–1840.* New York: Harper & Row, 1988.

LERNER, GERDA. *The Grimké Sisters from South Carolina.* Boston: Houghton Mifflin, 1967.

————. *The Majority Finds Its Past: Placing Women in History.* New York: Oxford Univ. Press, 1979.

LITWACK, LEON F. *North of Slavery: The Negro in the Free States, 1790–1860.* Chicago: Univ. of Chicago Press, 1961.

LOPEZ, CLAUDE-ANNE AND EUGENIA W. HERBERT. *The Private Franklin.* New York: Norton, 1975.

MADISON, JAMES. *Papers.* 17 vols. to date. Chicago: Univ. of Chicago Press, 1962– .

MAIER, PAULINE. *From Resistance to Revolution.* New York: Knopf, 1972.

————. *The Old Revolutionaries.* New York: Knopf, 1980.

MAIN, JACKSON T. *Political Parties Before the Constitution.* Chapel Hill: Univ. of North Carolina Press, 1973.

MALONE, DUMAS. *Thomas Jefferson and His Times.* 6 vols. Boston: Little, Brown, 1948–81.

MARCHIONE, MARGHERITA. *Philip Mazzei and the Constitutional Society of 1784.* Rutherford, N.J.: Fairleigh Dickinson Univ. Press, 1984.

MARSDEN, GEORGE M. *Religion and American Culture.* New York: Oxford Univ. Press, 1990.

MASSEY, MARY E. *Bonnet Brigades: Women and the Civil War.* New York: Knopf, 1966.

McCORMICK, RICHARD P. *Experiment in Independence: New Jersey in the Critical Period.* New Brunswick, N.J.: Rutgers Univ. Press, 1950.

————. *The Second American Party System.* Chapel Hill: Univ. of North Carolina Press, 1966.

McLAUGHLIN, JACK. *Jefferson and Monticello.* New York: Holt, 1988.

McLOUGHLIN, WILLIAM G. *Modern Revivalism: Charles Grandison Finney to Billy Graham.* New York: Ronald Press, 1959.

McLOUGHLIN, WILLIAM G., ED. *Religion in America.* Boston: Houghton Mifflin, 1968.

McPHERSON, JAMES M. *Battle Cry of Freedom: The Civil War Era.* New York: Ballantine, 1988.

————. *Ordeal by Fire: The Civil War and Reconstruction.* New York: Knopf, 1982.

MIDDLEKAUF, ROBERT. *The Glorious Cause.* New York: Oxford Univ. Press, 1982.

MILLER, PERRY. *The Life of the Mind in America from the Revolution to the Civil War.* Ithaca, N.Y.: Cornell Univ. Press, 1965.

————. *The New England Mind: The Seventeenth Century.* Cambridge, Mass.: Belknap, 1959.

MILNER, CLYDE A., ET AL. *The Oxford History of the American West.* New York: Oxford Univ. Press, 1994.

MINTZ, STEVEN. *Moralists and Modernizers: America's Pre–Civil War Reformers.* Baltimore: Johns Hopkins Univ. Press, 1995.

MORGAN, EDMUND S. *American Slavery, American Freedom.* New York: Norton, 1975.

————. *The Puritan Dilemma: The Story of John Winthrop.* Boston: Little, Brown, 1958.

MORGAN, EDMUND S. AND HELEN M. *The Stamp Act Crisis.* Chapel Hill: Univ. of North Carolina Press, 1953.

NASH, GARY B. *Quakers and Politics.* Princeton, N.J.: Princeton Univ. Press, 1968.

————. *Forging Freedom: The Formation of Philadelphia's Black Community.* Cambridge, Mass.: Harvard Univ. Press, 1988.

NEELY, MARK E., JR., AND R. GERALD McMURTY. *The Insanity File: The Case of Mary Todd Lincoln.* Carbondale, Ill: Southern Illinois Univ. Press, 1986.

NELSON, WILLIAM H. *The American Tory.* Boston: Little, Brown, 1961.

NEWCOMB, WELLINGTON. "Anne Hutchinson Versus Massachusetts." *American Heritage,* June 1974, 12–15, 78–81.

OATES, STEPHEN B. *To Purge This Land with Blood: A Biography of John Brown.* New York: Harper & Row, 1970.

———. *With Malice Toward None: The Life of Abraham Lincoln.* New York: Harper & Row, 1977.

———. *A Woman of Valor: Clara Barton and the Civil War.* New York: Free Press, 1994.

PARKMAN, FRANCIS. *Pioneers of France in the New World.* 20th ed. Boston: Little, Brown, 1883.

PASCOSOLIDO, CARL, AND PAMELA GLEASON. *The Proud Italians.* Seabrook, N.H.: Latium, 1991.

PECKHAM, HOWARD H. *The Colonial Wars, 1689–1762.* Chicago: Univ. of Chicago Press, 1964.

PERRY, LEWIS, AND MICHAEL FALLMAN, EDS. *Anti-Slavery Reconsidered.* Baton Rouge: Louisiana State Univ. Press, 1979.

———. *Intellectual Life in America.* New York: F. Watts, 1984.

PETERSON, MERRILL. *Thomas Jefferson and the New Nation.* New York: Oxford Univ. Press, 1970.

PETTIT, NORMAN. *The Heart Prepared.* New Haven, Conn.: Yale Univ. Press, 1966.

POTTER, DAVID M. *The Impending Crisis, 1848–1861.* New York: Harper & Row, 1976.

QUARLES, BENJAMIN. *Black Abolitionists.* New York: Oxford Univ. Press, 1969.

———. *The Negro in the American Revolution.* Chapel Hill, N.C.: Institute of Early American History and Culture, 1961.

RADER, BENJAMIN G. *Baseball: A History of America's Game.* Urbana: Univ. of Illinois, 1992.

RAKOVE, JACK N. *The Beginnings of National Politics.* New York: Knopf, 1975.

RANDALL, JAMES G. *Lincoln the Liberal Statesman.* New York: Dodd, Mead, 1947.

RANDALL, WILLARD STERNE. *Benedict Arnold: Patriot and Traitor.* New York: William Morrow, 1990.

———. *A Little Revenge: Benjamin Franklin and His Son.* Boston: Little, Brown, 1984.

———. *Thomas Jefferson: A Life.* New York: Holt, 1993.

————. *The Proprietary House at Amboy.* Trenton, N.J.: Whitechapel, 1975.

RANDALL, WILLARD STERNE, AND DAVID R. BOLDT, EDS. *The Founding City.* Philadelphia: Chilton/Inquirer Books, 1976.

RANDALL, WILLARD STERNE, AND NANCY NAHRA. *American Lives.* 2 vols. New York: Longman, 1997.

REICHEL, WILLIAM C., ED. *Memorials of the Moravian Church.* Philadelphia: Lippincott, 1870.

RICHARDS, LEONARD L. *Gentlemen of Property and Standing.* New York: Oxford Univ. Press, 1970.

RIESS, STEVEN A. *Touching Base: Professional Baseball and American Culture in the Progressive Era.* Westport, Conn.: Greenwood, 1980.

RILEY, GLENDA. *Frontierswomen: The Iowa Experience.* Ames: Iowa State Univ. Press, 1981.

RIMMER, ROBERT H. *The Resurrection of Anne Hutchinson.* Buffalo, N.Y.: Prometheus Books, 1987.

ROSE, WILLIE LEE. *Rehearsal for Reconstruction: The Port Royal Experiment.* Indianapolis, Ind.: Bobbs, Merrill, 1964.

RUTMAN, DARRETT B. *Winthrop's Boston.* Chapel Hill: Univ. of North Carolina Press, 1965.

SAMMARTINO, PETER, ED. *Seven Italians Involved in the Creation of America.* Washington, D.C.: National Italian American Foundation, 1984.

SATZ, R. N. *American Indian Policy in the Jacksonian Era.* Lincoln: Univ. of Nebraska Press, 1975.

SCHLESINGER, ARTHUR M., JR. *The Age of Jackson.* Boston: Little, Brown, 1945.

SEYMOUR, HAROLD. *Baseball: The Early Years.* New York: Oxford Univ. Press, 1960.

SMITH, JAMES MORTON. *The Republic of Letters: Correspondence Between Thomas Jefferson and James Madison, 1776–1826.* 3 vols. New York: Norton, 1995.

SMITH, PAUL H. *Loyalists and Redcoats.* Chapel Hill, N.C.: Institute of Early American History and Culture, 1964.

SMITH, ROBERT M. *Baseball.* New York: Simon & Schuster, 1970.

SMITH-ROSENBERG, CARROLL. *Disorderly Conduct: Visions of Gender in Victorian America.* New York: Knopf, 1985.

SOSIN, JACK M. *Whitehall and the Wilderness.* Lincoln: Univ. of Nebraska Press, 1961.

STANLEY, GEORGE F. "The Six Nations and the American Revolution." *Ontario History,* 56 (1964), 217–232.

STAUDENRAUS, P. J. *The African Colonization Movement.* New York: Columbia Univ. Press, 1961.

STEELE, IAN K. *Warpaths: Invasions of North America.* New York: Oxford Univ. Press, 1994.

STERLING, DOROTHY, ED. *We Are Your Sisters: Black Women in the Nineteenth Century.* New York: Norton, 1984.

STEVENSON, BRENDA, ED. *The Journals of Charlotte Forten Grimké.* New York: Oxford Univ. Press, 1988.

SULLIVAN, JAMES, ED. *Papers of Sir William Johnson.* 9 vols. Albany, N.Y.: Univ. of State of New York, 1921–1939.

SUSAN B. ANTHONY, ED. *History of Woman Suffrage.* Rochester, N.Y.: Charles Mann, 1881.

TAYLOR, PHILIP. *The Distant Magnet: European Emigration to the U.S.A.* London: Eyre & Spottiswoode, 1971.

TAYLOR, WILLIAM R. *Cavalier and Yankee.* New York: G. Braziller, 1961.

THOMAS, EMORY M. *The Confederate Nation, 1861–1865.* New York: Harper & Row, 1979.

THOMAS, JOHN L. *The Liberator: William Lloyd Garrison.* Boston: Little, Brown, 1963.

TURNER, C. FRANK. *Across the Medicine Line.* Toronto: McClelland, 1973.

TUSHNET, MARK. *The American Law of Slavery, 1810–1860.* Princeton, N.J.: Princeton Univ. Press, 1981.

TYLER, ALICE FELT. *Freedom's Ferment: Phases of American Social History to 1860.* New York: Harper & Row, 1962.

ULRICH, L. T. *Good Wives: Image and Reality in the Lives of Women in Northern New England.* New York: Knopf, 1982.

UTLEY, ROBERT M. *The Lance and the Shield: The Life and Times of Sitting Bull.* New York: Holt, 1993.

VAN DOREN, CARL C. *Benjamin Franklin.* New York: Doubleday, 1938.

———. *Secret History of the American Revolution.* New York: Viking, 1941.

VAUGHAN, ALDEN T. *New England Frontier.* Boston: Little, Brown, 1965.

VESTAL, STANLEY. *Sitting Bull, Champion of the Sioux.* Norman: Univ. of Oklahoma Press, 1957.

WALLACE, ANTHONY F. C. *Teedyuscung: King of the Delawares.* Philadelphia: Univ. of Pennsylvania Press, 1949.

WALLACE, PAUL A. W. *Conrad Weiser: Friend of Colonist and Mohawk.* Philadelphia: Univ. of Pennsylvania Press, 1945.

WALTERS, RONALD G. *American Reformers, 1815–1860.* New York: Hill & Wang, 1978.

WARD, GEOFFREY C., AND KEN BURNS. *Baseball: An Illustrated History.* New York: Knopf, 1994.

WARNER, SAM BASS, JR. *The Private City: Philadelphia in Three Periods of Its Growth.* Philadelphia: Univ. of Pennsylvania Press, 1968.

WASHBURN, WILCOMB E. *The Indian in America.* New York: Harper & Row, 1975.

———. *Red Man's Land/White Man's Law.* Norman: Univ. of Oklahoma Press, 1995.

WESLAGER, C. A. *The Delaware Indians.* New Brunswick, N.J.: Rutgers Univ. Press, 1972.

WILLIAMS, SELMA R. *Divine Rebel: The Life of Anne Marbury Hutchinson.* New York: Holt, 1981.

WINCH, JULIE. *Philadelphia's Black Elite: Activism, Accommodation and the Struggle for Autonomy.* Philadelphia: Temple Univ. Press, 1988.

WOODWARD, C. VANN, ED. *Mary Chesnut's Civil War.* New Haven, Conn.: Yale Univ. Press, 1981.

WRIGHT, ESMOND. *Franklin of Philadelphia.* Cambridge, Mass.: Belknap, 1985.

WYATT-BROWN, BERTRAM. *Lewis Tappan and the Evangelical War Against Slavery.* Cleveland: Case Western Reserve Press, 1969.

ZAREFSKY, DAVID. *Lincoln, Douglas and Slavery.* Chicago: Univ. of Chicago Press, 1990.

ZILVERSMIT, ARTHUR. *The First Emancipation. The Abolition of Slavery in the North.* Chicago: Univ. of Chicago Press, 1967.

After a successful career in journalism, WILLARD STERNE RAN-
DALL switched paths to pursue advanced studies in history at
Princeton University. He has become one of the country's most
respected popular historians, a contributing editor to *MHQ: The
Quarterly Journal of Military History,* and Visiting Professor of
American History at John Cabot University in Rome. As an
investigative journalist, Randall was the recipient of the Sidney
Hillman Prize and the Gerald Loeb Award, as well as the Na-
tional Magazine Award for Public Service from the Columbia
Graduate School of Journalism. Randall's writing on the birth
of the republic has won awards from the American Revolution
Round Table, the Sons of the American Revolution, and the
Colonial Dames of America.

NANCY NAHRA is Visiting Professor of Humanities at John
Cabot University in Rome, where she teaches courses on Greek
and Latin literature and civilization as well as modern poetry.
Her own poetry has won national distinction with the John
Masefield Award for Narrative Poetry from the Poetry Society of
America and her selection as a semifinalist in the National Po-
etry Series Open Competition for her book-length manuscript
Strong Dreams. She has published three volumes of poetry, as well
as scholarly articles in history journals. Nahra is a Phi Beta
Kappa graduate of Colby College in Maine, and has a master's
degree from Stanford and a doctorate from Princeton University.

Randall and Nahra live with their daughter, Lucy, in Burlington, Vermont.

INDEX